Other books by Jean Gould

YOUNG MARINER MELVILLE

THAT DUNBAR BOY

I have fought a good fight,
I have finished my course,
I have kept the faith.
                              —II Timothy, iv, 7

I'm an old campaigner, and I love a good fight!
                              —F.D.R.

THE STORY OF
F.D.R.'S CONQUEST OF POLIO

A GOOD FIGHT

by

JEAN GOULD

DODD, MEAD & COMPANY

NEW YORK · 1960

Library of Congress Catalog Card Number: 60-12336

Printed in the United States of America
by The Cornwall Press, Inc., Cornwall, N. Y.

To
E. H. D., Jr.
who gave me this book to write

ACKNOWLEDGMENTS

The narrative of F.D.R.'s victory over polio could not have been written without valuable aid from a number of sources. Particular thanks go to a friend of long standing, Dr. A. L. VanHorn, Medical Director, Kate Macy Ladd Convalescent Home, who checked the medical data in the manuscript; to Dr. Robert L. Bennett, Medical Director of the Georgia Warm Springs Foundation; and to Dr. Salo Rosenbaum, M.D., who helped me to overcome the hardest handicap of all—the one that didn't exist.

I wish also to express my appreciation to Mrs. Eleanor Roosevelt, who was so gracious and helpful in granting interviews; to James Roosevelt; and to Miss Margaret Suckley, cousin of F.D.R., who recalled details of his convalescence at Hyde Park. To her, and to the rest of the staff at the Roosevelt Library, I am most grateful; Dr. Herman Kahn, Director of the library, and Robert Jacoby, research librarian, gave extensive cooperation in furnishing files of material in my field and related subjects.

Mr. Basil O'Connor, President of the National Foundation, gave special assistance in contacting the staff at Warm Springs, to whom I owe a vote of gratitude—to Robert Chaplin, Betty Brown, Duncan Cannon, Woodall Bussey, Horace Maddox, and H. M. McRae. (To the last-named I am indebted for much information concerning Roosevelt's braces.) Mr. Charles A. Phelan, of the Little White House Memorial Commission, was also most kind and helpful. To all of these, and many others who contributed to my general knowledge of the subject, I offer my appreciation and admiration.

J.G.

Contents

A GOOD FIGHT

CHAPTER I

The Attack

ON THE EVENING of July 18, 1921, Franklin D. Roosevelt was working tensely to complete a crucial and dramatic statement to the press. It was a quarter to eight—he had fifteen minutes.

He had been given only ten hours to refute the testimony contained in fifteen volumes—6,000 pages—of a Senate subcommittee investigating the administration of naval affairs during World War I. Roosevelt, the particular target of the investigation, had been Assistant Secretary of the Navy. At ten o'clock that morning, the two Republican Senators, who had already written their "majority" report without giving him the hearing he requested, had granted him the opportunity to go through the fifteen volumes of testimony and submit a statement by eight o'clock in the evening. If he had not been so outraged, he would have laughed in their faces: it was like being told to empty the sea with a sieve. As it was, however, he accepted the challenge. He got hold of Steve Early (who had been one of the advance publicity men in the vice-presidential campaign Roosevelt had made as the running mate of Cox the year before) and they rolled up their sleeves and went to work.

Washington in mid-July is historically hot as a firecracker, and the summer of 1921 was no exception. It was a sweltering

1

day and, as the two men labored through volume after volume of repetitious statements made by the thirty witnesses who had come before the subcommittee, they grew feverish with the heat and mounting indignation. Roosevelt—slim, tall, and taut as a live wire—kept jumping up every now and then, pacing back and forth in his old office in the Navy Building, which they were using for the study. Overhead a fan buzzed, but it did little more than create a sirocco-like breeze through the room.

"Damn it, Steve, this whole business is nothing but dirty politics; that's the point we've got to emphasize." He had been clenching a short-stemmed pipe between his teeth, but now he took it out to punctuate his remarks with short angry jabs at the air.

Early nodded. "I get it."

Roosevelt sat down, taking up a pencil and some legal foolscap. "We'll make that subcommittee look sick."

All day long they had sweated over the mountainous pile of hearings; at lunchtime they had sent out for sandwiches and cold drinks (which had grown tepid by the time the bottles reached the office). Both men had loosened their ties and opened their shirt collars; it must have been one of the hottest days on record . . .

At four o'clock, as the statement was beginning to take shape, the phone rang. It was the reporters: they thought Mr. Roosevelt should know "that the majority report was in the hands of all the papers for release the next night and that Senator Ball (the committee chairman) had declined to hold it back or amend it in any way."

"Thanks, boys." He hung up, white with anger. The opposition Senators wouldn't even wait to hear him! They probably never expected him to show up at eight o'clock; their move "proved the futility of trying to get any fair treatment." Well, he would keep on with his statement; and, after he had given it to the majority Senators, he would give it to the press; and he would request an open hearing before the full Senate Committee on Naval Affairs.

The hours ticked by while the two men wrote, consulted the files, crossed out, and rewrote. The sweat rolled off their faces, and their fingers stuck to the copy pencils. After the phone call came, they wrote more with the press in mind than the sub-committee.

As he and Steve finished whipping each paragraph into shape, his secretary, Marguerite LeHand—"Missy," as she was familiarly known—typed it into the official statement. Missy, like Steve, had been part of the 1920 vice-presidential campaign staff, and Roosevelt had been so impressed with her efficiency and personality that he had retained her as his private secretary. The three had worked together often during the campaign and were able to co-ordinate their efforts easily now.

The next completed paragraph read, "In September, 1919, I, as Acting Secretary, and Captain Leigh, as Acting Chief of the Bureau of Navigation, were, for the first time, informed by two friends of a local Newport minister, who had been tried in a local court and acquitted, that some of the members of the investigating squad had used highly improper and revolting methods in getting evidence. Immediate orders went out from me and Captain Leigh that day to stop it. There is no charge that any wrong-doing occurred after that. That is all there is to the Senators' unwarranted deduction."

It was getting late; there was no thought of stopping for a bite of supper; they pushed on. Seven, seven-thirty, a quarter to eight. . . . The succeeding paragraphs amounted to a denunciation of the Senators' "perversion" of the facts and their accusations against Roosevelt. The language was simple and strong:

"Their insinuations that I must have known, that I supervised the operations, that I was morally responsible, that I committed all sorts of high crimes and misdemeanors, are nowhere supported by the evidence directly or indirectly. The Senators cannot cite the evidence in their support.

"Throughout their report I accuse them of deliberate falsification of evidence, of perversion of facts, of misstatements of the record, and of a deliberate attempt to deceive."

The conclusion of the statement was a stern, forceful protest:

"This business of using the Navy as a football of politics is going to stop. People everywhere are tired of partisan discussion of dead history. If these Senators want to go on with the question of how effective our Navy was in the war, then take it out of the Senate, out of partisanship, and put the facts up to any good, average jury of twelve men in any court in the land. I am quite willing to abide by the result. I only ask fair play."

As Missy was typing, Roosevelt added a final dart:

"The facts in complete answer to the subcommittee's majority report will be immediately filed by me with the Senate Committee on Naval Affairs."

Missy scarcely had time to pull the last sheets from the typewriter before her "boss" and Steve Early grabbed them, put them with the rest, and rushed across to the Senate Office Building. It was eight P.M. on the dot!

Two days later Roosevelt was ready to leave Washington for New York to complete some private business and join his employer on a cruise up the Atlantic. He gave Missy some last-minute letters and instructions regarding the statement, the hearing, the forwarding of mail, and the other matters. He seemed worn and tired; she could not remember ever having seen him look tired before. And she noticed that his skin had an unusual pallor . . . but perhaps it was only the heat and the strain he had been under. . . .

She promised to take care of everything. "And Boss," she added to her own surprise, "you take care of *yourself*."

"Yes, *Ma'am*." He was going to attend a Boy Scout rally before he left New York, and, clicking his heels together, he gave her a snappy salute. They laughed; a minute later he left the office with his usual rapid strides. Missy could not know then that it was the last time she would see him walking at that lightning pace.

Cool and green, the island of Campobello rose out of the mists like a mirage. But it was not a mirage—and, to the man who had been standing at the wheel of the *Sabalo* for many hours, its rocky coves crowned by wooded heights represented a haven of relaxation and rest. He had been coming to the island every summer since he could remember, and now, in the first week of August 1921, it beckoned him like a veiled mistress, half displaying, half concealing, the delights that would frame a long-overdue vacation in the weeks ahead. His keen blue eyes, intent on navigating the ship through the tricky, fogbound Lubec Narrows separating the island from the mainland, were alight with eager anticipation and a joyous, ironical good humor. He was thirty-nine and he was in love with life.

The owner of the *Sabalo*, Van Lear Black, stood watching the helmsman with a slight apprehension. He had known Franklin Roosevelt for some time and had offered him a post as head of the New York office of his insurance firm; but, as for the man's ability to steer them through this treacherous thoroughfare of water between Lubec and that beautiful island in the distance, he still had doubts, although the fog seemed to be lifting a little. They had run into dirty weather just off Maine and, when the captain confessed he did not know the coastline well enough to go through the Narrows, Roosevelt had taken over immediately and remained on the bridge ever since; he must surely be growing tired from the strain. . . . Black gazed rather fearfully at the sculptured profile of his friend.

Not without reason had Roosevelt been called a "twentieth-century Apollo": his incisive features stood out with cameo-like clarity against the rushing waters of the Bay of Fundy, a seaway of titanic, swiftly-moving tides. He was a damn sight handsomer than any man had a right to be, Black thought, and he had a devil-may-care recklessness in his face at the moment, as if this was an intriguing game, with the edge of danger giving it added spice.

"Cheer up, Van," he said with an upward toss of his head that was characteristic of his manner; "I'll make it! I've taken a destroyer through this passage more than once and never scraped her bottom." He chuckled. "First time I tried it I thought the lieutenants would have heart failure."

"I should think so," Black said. "A destroyer!" He watched Roosevelt's hands, marveling at the ease with which they maneuvered the boat—the grip of one was strong as steel; the other played lightly on the wheel, supple as the bow hand of a violinist. Somehow they symbolized the nature of the man, sturdy and sensitive at the same time. His tall slender body was not tense, but taut and alert, vibrant as a stringed instrument.

He began recounting further exploits and escapades of his recent years as Assistant Secretary of the Navy, and one or two other members of the party came up to listen. Franklin Roosevelt was a great storyteller whose compelling voice could attract an audience out of nowhere. He kept up a steady stream of anecdotes, while his hands expertly steered the *Sabalo* through the pass as if they were acting independently; yet a quick twist every now and then showed that his mind never left the navigation nor relaxed its sharp vigilance until they were well out of the Narrows.

"Welchpool Harbor ahead!" he sang out exuberantly.

Presently the shore came into view, and then the docks, where a small crowd seemed to be gathered.

"Just the family," Roosevelt grinned, returning the wheel to the captain of the *Sabalo* and waving both hands above his head. "Now tomorrow we'll try these waters and I'll prove that we have some of the finest deep-sea fishing in the country here."

He was the first to leap onto the dock, lithe and swift as a diver, and was immediately surrounded by half a dozen children, five of them his own: Anna, the oldest, and the only girl, a golden-haired "young lady" of about fifteen; James, a year younger;

Elliott, eleven; Franklin, Jr., seven; and John, five. The other child was Hartley Howe, small five-year-old son of Louis Howe, Roosevelt's political adviser and friend, who was expected at Campobello in a few days. The children swarmed around Franklin like friendly bees, and he seemed to take them all in at once: he gave an affectionate hug to Anna, or "Sis," as they called her; tousled the boys' hair; punched James playfully on the shoulder; rubbed the back of young Franklin's neck; and patted Hartley Howe on the head. With great pride he presented his "chicks" to the men in the party.

Up at the rambling, comfortable house, his wife, Eleanor, whom he hailed affectionately as "Babs," welcomed them graciously. Mrs. Howe was there, also; and Jean Sherwood, a young Vassar graduate who had tutored the older children, was visiting at Campobello with her mother. The Roosevelts were used to an overflowing household, and several guests more or less made little difference in the easy-going, smooth-running schedule Eleanor always managed to maintain, whether it was in Albany, Washington, or here on the island. She seemed to have the touch of being warm, efficient, and casual at the same time, so that no one suffered from overweighted hospitality, but merely felt comfortable and at home. She almost always wore white in the summertime, with a band of some sort around her head to keep her hair from blowing in the wind—such pretty hair, fine and thick, her husband thought fondly, watching her as she greeted the men— and what fine eyes she had, with that intent look in them, as if each word someone spoke was of the greatest interest to her. They were telling her about the fog and how Franklin had brought them safely through the Lubec Narrows to the harbor.

He laughed off their admiration. "I knew I could do it, but I'll bet Van thought his precious *Sabalo* would end up in Davy Jones's locker!" he teased. He went on briskly, "We'll want to push off around dawn. We stocked the boat at Lubec, so we're all set."

If his wife felt that he should rest a few days before starting on a strenuous fishing trip, she said nothing. Franklin had always been a man who knew his own mind and strength, and the most arduous sports only served to relax him. When the war was over, he had hardly wound up his affairs in the Navy Department when he became the vice-presidential candidate and undertook the most demanding campaign schedule all across the country. He had made a total of eight hundred speeches, many of them for James Cox, Governor of Ohio, the presidential candidate. On the last swing, he had covered twenty states in eighteen days, sometimes making seven or eight speeches a day, from early morning (seven A.M.) to late at night (midnight). Right afterward he had gone on a hunting trip in Louisiana that would have exhausted a much huskier man; yet he came back apparently refreshed and plunged into the business world without stopping for breath. He had written her a long account of his trip to Washington and the way he had refuted Republican charges. She marveled that within the space of a few hours he had perused the huge Investigating Committee report, written a burning statement refuting the charges, and presented it to the Senate subcommittee on the dot of eight o'clock in the evening, the promised hour. Eleanor often wondered how he kept going, but he had so much vitality and energy that she did not worry about it.

The boys claimed his attention, the minute introductions were over, with the model sailboats they had completed while he was away. They were beauties, he said, trim little sloops with jibs and mainsails neatly rigged; a regatta would be held soon to test the new models for seaworthiness and speed. This was one of his favorite hobbies: he loved building and sailing small craft almost as much as handling or being aboard any kind of boat. Anna had a special problem for "Father" to figure out, and Chief, the pet police dog, was romping around him, jumping up on his legs. Mademoiselle, the French governess, called to the little ones to get ready for supper, but they swung on his arms, begging him to wrestle with them.

"Later," he told them, laughing. He was in the habit of rough-housing with the boys on the floor after supper. He didn't seem to mind the confusion at all, but enjoyed and even fostered it.

Supper was a lively affair, served at a long table, with all the children present, joining in the general conversation and engaging their father in heated arguments on a wide variety of subjects, ranging from ornithology to Shakespeare.

The next few days were spent on the water, deep-sea fishing in the Bay of Fundy, sailing in the harbor; one night they heard the sound of the weir watchman's horn and raced to the scene of the seining in the *Sabalo's* tender. The visitors were fascinated at the sight—the weir itself, built by the fishermen to snare the schools of fish wandering by or chased into its circle of posts by larger fish; the nets around the edge of the circle, which had been dropped at sunrise and were now being raised; the fishermen in their oilskins and rubber boots, dipping their hand nets into the seines of flopping fish and filling the wells of the little boats. The red glow of the flares used in night-seining lit up the men's faces with a fierce warmth and lent an unearthly atmosphere to their picturesque labors. There was a catch of herring that night, sold by the packing companies as domestic sardines; after several hours, the little boats left the fishing grounds with brimming wells and made for the commercial docks to "weigh in." The spectators dispersed for a few hours' rest before dawn and the next day's casting.

On the last morning of the *Sabalo's* visit, the sun shone bright and clear, bringing a spell of hot August weather. "Perfect for cod-fishing," was Franklin's verdict, so they took the tender and went to a spot he considered most likely for cod. As usual, he supervised the project, exerting himself strenuously to make sure that everyone else was enjoying it as much as he. He baited hooks constantly, "alternating between the fore and aft cockpits of the motor-tender, crossing beside the hot engine on a three-inch varnished plank," paying no attention to the heat of the

midday sun beating down on them all. On one of the trips back
and forth, he suddenly slipped. Overboard! The water felt
like ice! He grabbed hold of the side of the tender with one
hand while his friend Van grabbed the other and helped him
to haul himself out of the ocean, gasping for breath.

"Franklin, are you all right?"

He nodded, too shaken by the swift chill to speak for several
moments. His teeth chattered and a tremor swept down his
spine. Someone seized a beach towel and handed it to him, but
his head was scarcely even damp. Later he said, "I'd never felt
anything as cold as that water! I hardly went under, hardly wet
my head, because I still had hold of the side of the tender, but
the water was so cold it seemed paralyzing. This must have been
the icy shock in comparison to the heat of the August sun
and the tender's engine." That was the only way he could figure
it out. He had been swimming in the Bay of Fundy a thousand
times, had dived into its cold depths from rafts and from boats,
and never before had it been such a petrifying experience.

The *Sabalo* and her party left. Roosevelt was still not quite
himself again, but he thought a few days more of open-air exercise would fix him up. Wednesday, August 10, continued sunny
and very warm—much hotter than Campobello usually was, even
in dog days. In the forenoon he played a round of golf. He was
not quite up to par on the links, either, but he was only a few
points off, so he was not going to fret about it. He loved the
game, loved the course—which he himself had laid out on the
island and helped to develop over a score of years before, while
he was at Groton. One summer he served as secretary and treasurer of the golf club and put over the "new" sport among the
sedate families who vacationed every year at Campobello.

Before lunch Eleanor and the boys wanted him to inspect the
tents and other equipment they were taking on a camping trip
the next day. Captain Calder, a native of the island, who had
long been a friend on the water and ashore, was to be in charge
of the party, which included the older children and any of the

adults who wanted to go. They were to travel up an island river to inland fishing grounds where there were a campsite and a number of shacks in the woods. Franklin, Jr., and John begged to go along, and Hartley Howe joined in, but all the parents thought they were too young. In retribution, the three little boys jumped on Franklin's back and pulled him to the ground for a tussle. Laughing good-naturedly, he took them all on at once, and soon had them crying "uncle."

He had just lit his pipe, settling on the side-porch steps for a few minutes after lunch, when Elliott suggested, "How about another sailing lesson, Pops?"

"That's a grand idea, Bunny." His father stood up, stretching his long legs. "Is the *Vireo* in good shape?" He had bought the small craft to replace in part his eighteen-ton schooner yacht, *Half-Moon II,* which he had turned over to the Government during the war. He wanted the boys to know early the rudiments of handling a boat.

"You bet." Elliott banged open the screen door. "Anybody for a sail?" he yelled, and they all appeared like magic, bounding out of the house with whoops and calls or coming around the corner of it on the run. In the end, the older ones trooped down to the dock with Jean Sherwood and their mother and father. The wind was right, and they set sail in high spirits. The children must each have a turn taking the tiller, and they all had to learn how to dodge the boom or get their heads bumped.

On the way back, they noticed a blue haze over a good-sized stretch of shore on one of the islands; and a sudden breeze from land brought a pungent odor with it.

"Burning spruce," Franklin declared as soon as he caught a whiff. "Let's go, boys!"

They made for shore as fast as the *Vireo* would take them, beached the boat, and jumped out. With the hunting knife he always carried on trips like this, Franklin cut wands of evergreen for all of them, and they began beating back the flames which were curling and spreading around a grove of spruce. It was hot, tough work, and they flailed with might and main at the red tongues licking the life from the trees. They called encouragement to each other, brushed away the sparks that flew out against their arms, and kept right on beating, beating, until the last flame was smothered and only a lagging trail of smoke drifted up from the blackened trees.

Satisfied that the fire was under control, they set sail for home, bleary eyed and exhausted. Their faces were grimy as a bunch of chimney sweeps, and they smarted all over with spark burns; an acrid smell of woodsmoke clung to their clothes. It was a hot, disheveled, and weary group that trudged back up to the house at Campobello around four o'clock in the afternoon.

"I think the remedy for this condition is a nice, cool swim at Glen Severn," Roosevelt declared—a suggestion that was hailed with delight by all the children. The landlocked lake on the other side of the island was one of their favorite spots. Their mother decided to stay home and rest, but the younger boys and Hartley Howe were going, and there was a great scramble to hustle out of their clothes and into bathing suits. "Last one downstairs gets a ducking in the lake," Jimmy flung at the others as they all ran up to change.

The water felt wonderfully cool and refreshing after the hike to the lagoon; they splashed, swam, and played water ball for over an hour. Then the boys and their father took the hot, dusty road at dogtrot all the way back across the island. They were out of breath and almost as warm as before by the time they reached the Bay of Fundy side. Roosevelt could not resist a quick dip in the ocean before going up to the house.

If he remembered his chill in those waters the day before, he put it out of his mind or was determined not to let an accidental experience interfere with the pleasure he always got from plunging into the stimulating waves; moreover, he was not the sort to be intimidated by an isolated shock: merely because he had been shaken by a severe chill one day was no reason for being afraid of the same water the next. In all probability he did not give the matter a single thought—he was a man of action.

He sprang into the foam with a bounding leap, like some mythical sea god, taking the waves in rapid rhythm, and then swam with swift, vigorous strokes. When he came out he ran all the way up to the house.

The mail was in—a batch of letters and several newspapers he hadn't seen; he had not taken the time to read while the fishing party was there. The children were already upstairs changing into their clothes (he could hear Jimmy and Elliott arguing about the way to head close to the wind and still keep the boat from heeling too far over), but for some reason he felt too tired to go up and dress. It was strange—he usually was exhilarated by a quick dip and a fast run like that; the glow he had expected had not come. The tiredness persisted; he had never felt quite this way before.

His suit was still damp and he was slightly chilled, but he sat there reading, scanning the papers for reports of his recent bout with Congress. On July 20 the *New York Times* had carried a screaming headline: "LAY NAVY SCANDAL TO F. D. ROOSEVELT"—"Details Are Unprintable." But would it proclaim in as loud a voice that he had been the target of a scurrilous attack, that the Investigating Report contained "a conscious perversion of facts"? The statement had been printed, but there were no editorials justifying his position. He was deeply disturbed by the whole sordid affair, even though he knew that the charges against him were untrue and that, as he wrote privately in a letter to his office manager during the vice-presidential campaign, "in the long run such low-down stuff will only hurt those mean and dishonorable enough to stoop to deliberate falsification for the sake of politics." Newspapers, even the generally reserved *New York Times,* were quicker to flash a man's possible guilt than his innocence. He found no further mention of the investigation or his refutation of the charges. Evidently the Republican Senators were letting the matter drop.

He frowned and turned a page, looking, too, for the latest news on the League of Nations, struggling for permanent establishment even without the support of the United States. This was a project dear to his heart, one he had pushed constantly during the campaign; he was almost as close to it as its creator, Wilson, had been. As he sat searching for news of its progress, his long, lean face, lengthened even more by the pince-nez he always wore for reading, seemed to take on a resemblance to Wilson, as if the spirit of the man who conceived the Covenant was breathed into Franklin Roosevelt, molding his actual features as well as his inmost feelings.

Eleanor came into the living room and brought him abruptly back to the fact that he was still in his damp suit and that he had better change before supper, which would soon be served.

"I'll go up right now," he said, folding the paper, but he made no move; it was an effort to think about dressing. "I don't know what's the matter with me," he went on. "The loginess I told you about lingers with me in spite of all the exercise. That swim didn't do a bit of good! And I'm cold, Babs. I can't understand why I don't warm up." Even as he spoke a sharp shiver ran down his back, almost as penetrating as the one that had followed his fall the day before. "Ooo-oh!"

"Franklin, what is it?"

"Another bad chill." He stood up as the shivering continued. "See here, I think I'd better not eat supper with the rest of you; I'll go right to bed and get warm, so I can avoid having a cold, if possible. I don't want to spoil my vacation." He smiled at her. "What do you say?"

His wife thought he was probably wise in going to bed and said she would send him up a tray.

In spite of heavy woolen blankets, the chill lasted all night; and the next morning, when he "swung out of bed"—or started to, in his usual fashion—his left leg lagged behind, sluggish with a heaviness he couldn't identify; it ached, too. He might have strained the muscles in swimming, but he couldn't recall doing anything out of the ordinary. He managed to move around slowly and shaved himself; perhaps the trouble would disappear as he used his limbs and the circulation loosened things up. He had had a touch of lumbago at various times; perhaps this was nothing more.

But the ache did not disappear and, when his wife took his temperature, the mercury registered 102 degrees. She suggested that he stay in bed for a day or so, and he was feeling too miserable to object. Yet, when Anna came upstairs with his breakfast tray a little later, he had a smile and a cheery greeting for her. "Come in, Sis. I think old age must be setting in; my legs won't behave this morning!"

His daughter was worried. "Mother says you have a fever . . ."

He nodded. "I've had 'em before, too. Now don't fret about me. How are things coming along for the camping trip?"

"All right, only we don't want to go without you, Father."

"Well, we'll see; perhaps I'll feel better by tomorrow."

But, after Anna had gone, he lay back limply and closed his eyes. He took a few swallows of coffee, but felt too tired to eat his breakfast.

In the meantime, since there was no phone in the house at Campobello, Mrs. Roosevelt had sent one of the islanders to Lubec in the launch with a message for their family doctor during the summer, their faithful friend, Dr. Bennett. He was there by ten o'clock, full of concern. He examined the patient thoroughly, watched him walk across the room; Franklin could move his legs, though it was more difficult than it had been even two hours earlier, because the pain was greater: his whole back ached now.

"What do you make of it, Doc?" he asked.

Dr. Bennett was puzzled, but if he thought his friend's condition was serious, he gave no sign. "I think it's probably an ordinary cold, as they say," he smiled, "but a severe one. Stay in bed till the fever comes down." He turned to Eleanor. "I think this boy's worn himself out. See that the house is as quiet as possible, and keep in touch with me."

She nodded. She was worried, because she had never seen her husband so listless, but she was composed. It did not take her long to decide to send all the children, even the little ones, off on the camping trip. She could not possibly go; Franklin's illness, whatever it was, appeared to be serious; she asked Mrs. Sherwood to take charge of the group as a whole. Jean could help with the younger boys, and Mrs. Howe decided to go along to look after small Hartley herself. It seemed a shame that they should all go off without Franklin on the camping trip he had suggested in the first place and had been looking forward to as much as the children. But it could not be helped; and this way there was less chance that any of them would catch his cold . . .

None of them, including Dr. Bennett, had any idea then that the dread virus poliomyelitis had invaded a victim who was destined to become its mortal enemy . . .

Eleanor, after she had helped the campers pack the boat with the necessary food and equipment, waved good-by at the dock, confident that they would all be safe with Captain Calder. Then she turned and went back up to the sickroom. Franklin was dozing uneasily.

CHAPTER II

The Siege

BY NIGHTFALL THE FEVER had superseded the chills and he slept
fitfully through the long hours, wakening every now and then
in a burning wave of heat. Shortly after dawn he awoke again,
suddenly aware of pain and tenderness in the forepart of his
thighs. He could hardly bear the weight of the covers. With
an inward groan, halfway between despair and disgust, for he
knew in his heart that he was in for some sort of a siege no
matter what Bennett had said about an "ordinary cold," he lay
quietly for some moments, thinking. The house was still; usually
at this hour, though the sun was scarcely up, the youngest boys
were reveling in a pillow fight or jumping up and down on their
beds until they heard the cook in the kitchen and it was time
to get up. The quiet seemed unnatural to Franklin until he
remembered that they had all gone off on the camping trip; for
a moment he felt lonely and deserted, but then he was relieved
to realize that they would not be exposed to whatever malady he
had picked up. He was always afraid they would catch some
contagious disease.

They had all come down with the flu, himself included, in
the terrible epidemic that swept the country toward the close of
the war; only Eleanor had been spared, and she had certainly

17

had her hands full, especially when three of the servants had to take to their beds. Elliott's case had turned into double pneumonia and the baby, John, had had bronchopneumonia. It was a wonder they had all survived. But, more than colds or the flu, Franklin, who knew few fears, had always been terrified at the thought that his children might contract infantile paralysis. During the last severe epidemic, in 1916, just before John was born, he had insisted that Eleanor and the children stay at "Campo" all through September and into October to avoid contact with the paralyzing illness that was striking down little children all over the country. Even then, he made arrangements to take the Navy ship *Dolphin* up to the island, where he put the whole family aboard, sailed down the Atlantic to the Hudson, and landed them on the Roosevelt dock at Hyde Park to avoid the risk of riding on crowded trains. Whenever there was news of a fresh epidemic, his vivid imagination conjured up the horror it would be if Anna or any of the boys could no longer move their supple limbs or had to be burdened with braces and crutches. His outlook, so cheerful and optimistic on most counts, was practically morbid on this subject, and he knew it; nevertheless, he always took the utmost precaution to keep his children in the fresh, pure, almost distilled air of Campobello until the danger of the hot months, the rampant season for infantile paralysis, was well past.

His disgust came from the prospect that he was going to be laid up for a few days, and he hated to be in bed when there was so much he wanted to do. With a gesture of impatience, he flung back the covers and tried getting up again. This time his right knee buckled when he started to put his weight down! What in thunder could be wrong with him? Discouraged, he lay down again and closed his eyes, suddenly weak with pain and fever.

His temperature stayed at 102 all that day and the next; his muscles became more and more sensitive; and his legs were so heavy he could hardly move them. Eleanor and he tried to make jokes about the situation, but they both knew it was nothing to laugh at. She decided to sleep on the couch in his room in case he should need her at night. By the time the campers returned the following day, his legs were completely paralyzed and his back was a belt of pain.

Anna and the boys, bursting with vigor, full of the adventures of the trip, were ready to rush upstairs and give their father a complete account; it was only the firm tone of their mother's voice telling them not to go near the sickroom, admonishing them to be as quiet as possible at all times that restrained the impulse. She could not tell them what was wrong—Dr. Bennett himself wasn't sure, she said; he wanted to have a consultation with a specialist, if one could be found in the neighborhood.

Louis Howe arrived in the afternoon, and no one could have been more welcome just then than this gaunt, emaciated little man with his asthmatic cough, his gnome-like face (from which his burning eyes snapped at the world with whiplash intelligence), and his droll, sardonic sense of humor. Deeply concerned about "Franklin," he galvanized the household into action. With Eleanor and Dr. Bennett, he canvassed the nearby resorts for a likely doctor; and, when they located a prominent, elderly diagnostician, Dr. W. W. Keen, who was vacationing at Bar Harbor, Louis went with Captain Calder to fetch him in the launch. "We can't do much good just standing around," he said to Eleanor; "we've got to find out what's wrong!" He flicked his cigarette impatiently and his raspy cough sent the ashes flying over his suit.

(Louis was always smoking, and he managed to time his cough so that this frequently happened; but, since his clothes usually looked as if he had slept in them, it did not make much difference.)

Dr. Keen examined the patient thoroughly. By now Roosevelt was completely paralyzed below the waist; above his chest he could move, but his arms felt heavy, and the muscles in his thumbs were so weak he could not even hold the pen when he had to write some notation on a scrap of paper that morning. "I couldn't even sign a check at this rate." He grinned feebly at the doctor.

The physician nodded solemnly, ignoring the remark. After some deliberation, his verdict was that " a clot of blood from a sudden congestion has settled in the lower spinal cord, temporarily removing the power to move, though not to feel." He prescribed vigorous massaging of the patient's thighs and legs. "I think he will recover," the doctor went on, "but it may take many months." He suggested that the massages begin right away.

Eleanor wired to New York for a masseuse; but, until someone could get to the island, she and Louis Howe together took on the job of rubbing Franklin's feet and legs as best they could. The muscles were so sensitive he jumped at the slightest touch. The heavy kneading was extremely painful, they knew from his grim face, his set jaw; yet he did not utter a word of protest nor tell them to stop. As much as he could, he sought to help by trying to move his toes; he concentrated on his great toe for two hours until he was able to "wiggle" it a fraction of an inch. Yet in the next few days his general condition did not improve and even seemed to get worse. It was most discouraging.

Sunday morning the children were told not to go to church, but to stay around the house and always to be quiet; they had known from the constant shushing, the drawn shades, and the tiptoeing in their father's room that he must be very ill, but now they realized how serious it must be, though nobody seemed to be able to tell what the trouble was. One of the older boys was of the opinion that it must have been a heart attack. Anna was frightened and worried.

Some word had to be sent to the relatives. Franklin's mother was in Europe, but would soon be leaving for home. On August 14 Eleanor managed to snatch a few moments to write "Rosy" Roosevelt, Franklin's half brother: "We have had a very anxious few days, as on Wednesday evening Franklin was taken ill . . ." She told him all the facts, simply, not wanting to sound hysterical or to alarm anyone unnecessarily. She paused, as if she were choosing the next words with extra care. She was dead for sleep. Franklin was completely helpless: he would have to be catheterized for several weeks, the doctor thought, and he had only partial control of the bowel muscles; he required constant attention and no small skill to care for him. (She was glad now of the knowledge she had picked up from Miss Spring, a trained nurse she had always called in when the children were born or when some member of the family was seriously ill.) After a few seconds' deliberation, she continued rapidly: "I have only told Franklin he (the doctor) said he could surely go down to New York the 15th of September . . . but it may have to be done on a wheel chair. . . . Do you think you can meet Mama when she lands? She has asked us to cable just before she sails and I have decided to say nothing. No letter can reach her now, and it would simply mean worry all the way home."

She wrote much the same letter to Franklin's uncle, Frederic Delano, his mother's brother and one of his favorites among the Delano clan. She knew Uncle Fred would have some ideas on the mysterious malady and perhaps could suggest some means of help which had not occurred to them. By the next day Dr. Keen had changed his diagnosis of the case: it was not a clot on the spinal cord, but a "lesion" in the cord, that was causing so much trouble. Directly after this information, he sent a bill for $600! Eleanor showed it to Louis Howe, aghast.

"No wonder he said yesterday that Franklin could sign a few letters every day," he commented drily.

Eleanor had not yet told her husband the doctor's verdict that it might be many months before he could walk. In spite of his pain and distress, Franklin was beginning to show signs of impatience at the limitations caused by his illness. In a letter he had dictated that morning, he had said with good-natured grumbling: "Thanks to a severe chill which I lay to the vagaries of the Bay of Fundy climate, which has more tide and more kinds of weather than any other place in the globe, I am spending a considerable longer vacation than I intended under the stern eye of a doctor who refuses to allow me to more than look at my mail and sign a few letters each day." If he felt that way after little more than a week, how would he face the fact that it might be months before he could resume a normal life? His wife wondered how she could tell him. She wrote to his half brother: "Yesterday and today his temperature has been normal and I think he's getting back his grip and a better mental attitude, though he has of course times of great discouragement. We thought yesterday he moved his toes on one foot a little better, which is encouraging." She spoke of the doctor's gloomy prediction and continued confidentially: "I dread the time when I have to tell Franklin and it wrings my heart for it is all so much worse to a man than to a woman . . ."

Uncle Frederic, as she had expected, was not at all satisfied by Dr. Keen's diagnosis and set off for Boston to consult a well-known specialist, Dr. Robert W. Lovett, who was out of town, but expected back in a few days. While waiting for his return, persistant Uncle Fred made inquiries and went to see one of Lovett's most emminent colleagues, Dr. Samuel A. Levine. As soon as Dr. Levine heard the symptoms and the subsequent stages of Franklin's illness, he immediately pronounced it to be infantile paralysis and suggested that the massages be stopped at once as they were probably doing more harm than good! Unfortunately he was leaving town the next day, but he was sure Dr. Lovett would be back soon and would consent to go to Campobello if the Roosevelts wanted a consultation; and Dr. Levine strongly advised it.

All this Uncle Fred included in a letter to Eleanor, who, in turn, passed it along to Rosy and added, as if she were "thinking out loud": "On Uncle Fred's urgent advice, which I feel I must follow on Mama's account, I have asked Dr. Keen to try to get Dr. Lovett here for consultation to determine if it is I.P. or not. Dr. Keen thinks *not* but the treatment at this stage differs in one particular and no matter what it costs I feel and I am sure Mama would feel that we must leave no stone unturned to accomplish the best results."

To her mother-in-law she wrote a cheerful, loving note, merely hinting at Franklin's condition: "Dearest Mama," she began with her usual greeting, "Franklin has been quite ill, and so can't go down to meet you on Tuesday to his great regret, but Uncle Fred and Aunt Kassie both write they will be there so it will not be a lonely home-coming. We are all so happy to have you home again, dear, you don't know what it means to feel you are near again." She spoke of the children, the weather, the island, and ended, "Franklin sends all his love and we are both so sorry he cannot meet you." That was all. She knew that to Sara Delano Roosevelt the mere fact that Franklin, always so devoted to his mother, was not able to meet her was enough to convince her that her son must be very sick indeed!

Sealing the envelopes, Eleanor stopped in the sickroom on her way downstairs to see if Franklin had any mail to go. He was dictating a few letters to Missy LeHand, who had arrived the day before. Eleanor had written her about his illness and she had offered to come to Campobello at once, if she could be of assistance. Small, delicate, even frail in appearance, she possessed an amazing capacity for work and was such an appealing person that she had become a family friend soon after accepting the position of private secretary.

"Don't let him wear you out, Missy!" Eleanor warned, sticking her head in the doorway.

"We're just about through, Babs," her husband said. "I've only got to tell President McCracken of Vassar that he can put my name on his committee for an endowment drive this fall, and we will have cleared up all the correspondence." He turned his head to smile at her, and his eyes were bright and clear; there seemed to be no doubt in his mind that he would fulfill his commitment.

"Fine," Eleanor nodded. "If you have any letters ready to go, I'll send them along with these."

Missy handed her two or three, and she went downstairs. Louis was in the living room talking to the newspaper reporters again. Ever since Dr. Keen had been called in for consultation, the papers had been sending some of the staff over from Eastport every day, trying to get the details of Franklin's illness. Louis, a former newspaperman himself, had always been sympathetic toward reporters and had won a reputation among them for honesty and truthfulness. Now, however, he was hedging, putting them off every day with a different story: "Mr. Roosevelt has been suffering from a severe cold." "Mr. Roosevelt has a slight touch of lumbago, which has delayed his recovery." "Mr. Roosevelt has a congestion of an unusual sort, which complicates his condition."

He patted the boys on the back, thanked them for their interest, promised to give them all the facts as soon as he could, and sent them back to Eastport in the launch.

"I don't want anyone to know how sick Franklin is until we're sure ourselves. And I'm not going to mention the word 'paralysis' unless I have to," he grumbled. "If it's printed, we're sunk. Franklin's career is *kaput*, finished." He paused to dig into his vest pockets for a match. "You know how the public mind works."

"I see what you mean, but . . ." Eleanor began, but Louis would not let her finish. He was staring at her.

"Why the devil don't you get some sleep for an hour or so?" he demanded. "Your eyes are like sockets."

"I'm all right; I had a few cat naps last night." She smiled at him. "What about you? I heard you pacing up and down most of the time."

"Oh, I haven't slept a night through for years," he said shortly. "Anyway, I was trying to make up my mind about that oil job." He hesitated, and then announced crisply, "I'm not going to take it. Franklin's career is more important."

She was moved. Louis Howe had stayed on in the Navy Department until now to wind up Franklin's affairs there and be on hand to give any necessary help to the incoming Assistant Secretary, Colonel Theodore Roosevelt. When Louis was ready to leave the Department at last, he received an offer of a public relations job for a large oil company at a rather lucrative salary. He was still considering the position when he left for the island; he could decide during his vacation whether or not he would accept. Then events at Campobello had shaped his decision within those few days.

Picturing her husband as she had seen him in the last two weeks, lying helpless on the bed, Eleanor marveled at the loyalty of the little man now hunched in a wing chair near her and at his faith in Franklin's future.

"I know you believe as I do, that Franklin will recover," she began.

"I'm sure of it," Louis snapped. "I can tell by his eyes."

"Yes, the light is back, just the last couple of days," she agreed. "But do you think he'll be able to campaign, and hold public office again?"

Louis nodded. He said slowly, "I've felt for a long time that Franklin could be president of the United States some day. I see no reason why this illness should change that belief."

Dr. Lovett was located at Newport and consented to come to Campobello at once. He arrived on the twenty-fifth of August and made a thorough examination of the patient, after which he told Eleanor and Dr. Bennett that Franklin undoubtedly had a "mild case of infantile paralysis." He added that the weakness in the arm muscles would probably clear up in a few days; the legs would take much longer.

So it *was* infantile paralysis! In spite of the fact that they had discussed the possibility, Eleanor had a moment's panic at the thought of the six children in the house. Would any of them come down with it?

The doctor reassured her almost at once. He asked if any of them had been ill and, when she recalled that Mademoiselle had reported one or two minor upsets but nothing out of the ordinary (headache, a slight sore throat, a "sour" stomach), he said calmly that they were probably immunized by now since none of them was critically ill. "Chances are none of them will ever have it," he concluded, to her vast relief.

Dr. Lovett, like Dr. Levine, said the massages must be stopped at once, before any more damage was done; but he had little treatment to recommend outside of warm baths, if these could be managed. He wrote to Dr. Bennett as soon as he got back: "Drugs I believe are of little or no value, and not worth giving if they impair appetite. Bromide for sleeplessness may be useful. Massage will prolong hyperesthesia and tenderness, and the high sensitiveness should be watched from this point of view. There is nothing that can be added to the treatment, and this is one of the hardest things to make the family understand. The use of hot baths should, I think, now be considered again, as it is really helpful and will encourage the patient, as he can do so much more under water with his legs. There is likely to be mental depression and sometimes irritability in adults, as you heard me say to Mrs. R. I should have the patient sit up in a chair as soon as it can be done without discomfort."

When Eleanor told Franklin what Dr. Lovett's diagnosis had been, his first thought, like hers, was for the children, and she relayed the information the specialist had given her. "He says scientists still don't know how the disease is communicated," she went on. "He changes all his clothes when he goes near his own grandchildren after visiting an infantile paralysis case, but he thinks it's entirely useless. Anyway, he says the danger of any of the children here catching it at this point is completely past."

"Thank God they were spared!" Franklin murmured, closing his eyes for a moment; then he opened them. "He said my case was '*mild*,' did he?"

She nodded. "That's right."

He clung to the word. "Then I don't see any reason why I can't lick it," he said confidently. "Babs, will you move my legs again? They're like two loads of cement."

So she moved them for the *nth* time, and he told her that the doctor had commented on the excellent care he had received. "I know," she laughed. "I'm sure he didn't know I was the only nurse you had. I'm so flattered I don't think I'll give up the case!" And she did not, for the most part.

She had, however, already sent for a nurse to help out, a Miss Rockey, who came up from New York in a day or two. Mrs. Howe and little Hartley left the first of September (there was no thought of Louis' going with them—they all saw how much his help was needed at Campobello), and the next day brought "Mama"—Sara Delano Roosevelt—bustling into the household, full of anxiety and concern for her only child.

Franklin greeted her with a wisecrack and teased her with a boyhood nickname, but she was too overwrought to see the humor and, in her dowager way, wrote a dramatic account to Uncle Fred: "I got here yesterday at one-thirty, and at once . . . came up to a brave, smiling, and beautiful son, who said, 'Well, I'm glad you are back, Mummy, and I got up this party for you!' He had shaved himself and seemed very bright and keen. Below his waist he cannot move at all. His legs (that I have always been so proud of) have to be moved often, as they ache when long in one position. He and Eleanor decided at once to be cheerful and the atmosphere of the house is all happiness, so I have fallen in and followed their glorious example. . . ." As she was writing, the doctor came, and she listened awhile to find out if there was any further bit of information she could give her brother. She continued, "Dr. Bennett just came and said, 'This boy is going to get all right.' They went into his room and I hear them all laughing. Eleanor is in the lead."

She herself found it difficult to act as lighthearted, but she did her best to be cheerful. The children, as always, were happy to see "Granny" again, and she made a great fuss over them.

(Anna called her "Gran'mere," and was able to converse fluently with her in French, to her great pleasure.) She had brought them all souvenirs from abroad, as usual. She went to Europe nearly every year, and she never forgot them.

She stayed only a few days, however. There was little she could do here for Franklin, but she could get the twin houses she had built in New York ready for herself and the family when they came down. The doctor said Franklin could probably leave the island by September 15, but he would need hospital care for several months after that. He suggested the Presbyterian Hospital in New York.

As for the patient himself—he showed remarkably little of the irritation and mental depression Dr. Lovett had warned Eleanor against. He was relieved to have the massaging end, but his legs were still so sensitive and leaden that he had to have his knees propped up with big pillows under them. He was tired of the persistent pain and the fluctuating fever—sometimes his temperature was normal and even subnormal, at others it flared up again—yet he could be cheerful with those around him, he could be lighthearted in the letters he dictated, because he somehow knew that he would be well and strong again, that he would once again take up the career that showed such brilliant promise in San Francisco.

He received a letter from Uncle Fred that expressed something of this outlook. Dear Uncle Fred, in his deep concern for his nephew's state of mind, had been almost apologetic in approaching the subject. He had not given out with self-righteous advice, but was, he said, merely offering an old man's "philosophy" in the hope that it would help Franklin to face the struggle ahead. He had made it a point not to worry about anything, he said, because he had learned through experience that worry could be more of a hindrance than a help; he never looked backward, but always forward—not merely to the immediate future but to a time when the greatest constructive possibilities of the present would be realized. . . . It was a touching letter, full of warm family feeling as well as strong conviction, lightened by an underlying sense of humor that made it completely acceptable; and the lines carried a courage that must have existed since the days the first De LaNoye "immigrants" ventured forth to settle in a new land in 1621.

Yet, even before his uncle's letter came, Franklin was aware that he would grow well and move forward to a goal still undefined but greater than any he had envisioned. Only long afterwards did he recall what actually happened, and even then it was difficult to explain what was in a sense a spiritual experience.

It occurred about a week after the attack had seized him, on the day his temperature had first gone down, and Eleanor noticed that he "was getting back his grip and a better mental attitude." During the first few days he had been full of despair, so wracked with pain and fever that he was nearly bereft: his faith was gone; he could not help feeling that God had deserted him and that there was no hope of his being saved. (He never spoke a word of this and, often, when he felt the fiercest stabs in his legs, he made the most flippant remarks and much of the time was able to cover up his utter depression.) But early one morning, when he realized that the fever was not raging inside him, he experienced a soaring of spirit such as he had not known since before the first chill. It was as if, in the early morning light, a revelation had been given to him. His faith in God returned, and he knew, with a visionary instinctiveness, that he would not only be saved from a miserable and untimely death, but that his life was being spared for some *purpose*, he knew not what. He did not question further. His trust in God was once more serene and complete.

He would do whatever he could and must do himself to bring back a normal life. The main thing was to recover from this "humiliating" illness—infantile paralysis!

CHAPTER III

The Retreat—Part I
Springwood and School Days

HE WAS, IF ANYTHING, impatient with medical science for its
meager knowledge of the disease, the cause of it, and the cure
for it—if there was such a thing. He himself was determined, at
this early stage, to overcome the paralysis, no matter what he
had to go through. He was not going to let it get the better of
him, an adult thirty-nine years old.

"It's ridiculous to tell me a grown man cannot conquer a
child's disease!" he exploded one day when he and Louis were
talking over the prospects for his recovery. He had just accepted
membership on the Executive Committee of the Democratic Party
in New York State for the coming year, and he hated to think
that it might be in name only. (Louis had been telling him of
the ruses he used to get rid of the newspapermen, exaggerating
his own exaggerations—as to the "minor" illness "Mr. Roosevelt
had suffered"—and Franklin was hugely enjoying the account
of his inventions to avoid admitting the truth.) He would soon
be going to New York for special treatment in the hospital, and
surely there they would be able to do more for him than the
doctors had been able to manage here.

"We'll have to figure out a way to give the press boys the slip when you leave the island," Louis continued, frowning. "If they see you like this, they might think I'm a prevaricator!"

A private train, which Uncle Frederic had arranged for, was to pick up Franklin and the family at Eastport and take them to Boston, where it would be switched around so they could go straight through to New York without making any change. The problem was to transport the patient from Campobello across the Bay to Eastport without letting him be seen by the crowds that would certainly be waiting to catch a glimpse of him—not to mention the reporters, who were ready by this time to pounce on any detail for a sensational story.

"How do you expect to do it?" Franklin challenged; "make me invisible?"

His friend grinned. "I might."

Franklin reached for a cigarette from the pack on the bed table and slowly fitted it into one of the white paper holders he kept nearby. Lying flat on his back forced him to perform the smallest act with great deliberation. "You may be a wizard in politics, Louis, but that doesn't make you a magician."

The little man crossed over to the bed to give him a light. "Give me time—I'll think of something."

Unexpectedly his protégé chuckled. "I don't doubt it, at that."

It was ironic, in a way, that little anemic Louis should be the one to plan this physical move for Franklin Roosevelt—he who had never thought twice about sprinting a block or two to jump aboard a moving streetcar. It was a terrible disease that could render a man as helpless as an infant. He thanked Heaven again that none of the children had caught it; the thought of growing children often crippled for life at a time when the sweet freedom of motion was at its peak filled him with horror.

He remembered the deep pleasures of his own childhood—the forest rambles with Ed Rogers, neighbor boy and friend; the "crow's nest" they built in the hemlock tree, shinnying up the trunk, agile as monkeys. He remembered the horseback rides through the hills with his father and the bike rides along the country roads with a neighbor girl, Mary Newbold. "No hands," they used to say, showing off to each other as they pedaled around the driveway. He recalled many more scenes of those early days in Hyde Park, the village a mile and a quarter from *Springwood,* the house where he was born on a wintry day, January 30, 1882. (That morning his father, James Roosevelt, an elderly country squire of fifty-four, whose muttonchop whiskers framed a kindly face, wrote happily in his diary: "At a quarter to nine my Sally had a splendid large baby boy. He weighs ten pounds without his clothes.")

It was a pleasant house, set on a green rise of ground above the Hudson River, with narrow, vine-covered porches around three sides and a squat tower jutting up in front. One of Franklin's earliest recollections was the playroom his mother fixed up for him in the top of the tower as soon as he was old enough. It was over his mother's bedroom and also served as a schoolroom. Here he kept all his "things" and conducted his projects (among them bird-stuffing), so that his bedroom, with its narrow brass bed, white wardrobe, and small white bed table would stay neat and uncluttered.

From the beginning, Franklin (he was named after his mother's uncle, Franklin Delano, and was the first Roosevelt by that given name) was a great joy to both his parents. His mother, who was the beautiful, imperious Sara Delano, one of the five "fascinating Delano sisters," wrote in her diary that the baby was "plump, pink, and nice." She loved to bathe him and take care of him herself and would not consider having a nurse for him while he was a baby.

His father was old enough to be his grandfather; he had been a widower before he married "Sally" Delano, with a son, James Roosevelt Roosevelt (the "Rosy" to whom Eleanor had first sent word of Franklin's illness) exactly the age of his bride, twenty-six years old. When Franklin was born, he already had a small niece and nephew older than himself! Nevertheless, his father took great interest in him: before young Franklin was two, he carried him around on his shoulder, like any doting young father; when Franklin was three, he went "sleighing" with "Papa"—just the two of them coasting down the sled run on the Roosevelt land.

Sometimes the whole family went tobogganing on the Rogers' long, sweeping, three-level run, the most famous coasting hill in the countryside, where all the river people gathered when winter set in and the snow was hard-packed and smooth. *Crumwold,* the Rogers' estate, offered many attractions for young and old, with its pond, ideal in winter or summer, for skating, ice-boating, sailing, or swimming; its stables; its many-turreted, mishmash chateau, with "a porch put around to squash it down," Franklin used to say; and its merry parcel of children, ready to venture forth on any scheme that was likely to hatch in Franklin's fertile brain.

The crow's nest in the hemlock was his idea, along with the fierce naval battles fought from below. He remembered with slight chagrin another plan he initiated, which was not so successful. He and Ed, the Rogers boy closest to his age, only six months younger, had built a raft from logs they cut in the woods—with Mr. Roosevelt's permission. It took them several weeks, and they were set to float it up the Hudson like the river barges that plied between Albany and New York. They stocked the raft with provisions out of the pantries at *Crumwold* and *Springwood,* invited the members of both families to witness the grand launching, waved a fond farewell to those on shore—only to feel themselves sinking after about ten feet! The poor raft submerged like a leaden pipe; he and Ed found themselves splashing around in the water, while the food drifted along on the current. After that, his father taught him something about ballast and how to build a craft, model or otherwise, that would stay on top of the water.

His father taught Franklin the lore of the woods—the names

of trees and the care of them, for the forests must be preserved and protected; a knowledge of birds, which the boy himself enlarged; the cultivation of the land; the love of horses and dogs. Franklin had a red setter puppy, "Marksman," which he cared for himself; and on his seventh birthday his parents gave him a pony of his own, "Debby," with the proviso that he groom her himself.

He loved Debby and he loved the rides with his father—to his half brother Rosy's house, a mile or so away; or as far as *Algonac*, Grandfather Delano's home north of Newburgh, where they would spend the day, riding the twelve miles back in the twilight. Once he became too ambitious for poor Debby; he was out alone and came upon Colonel Rogers' fox hunt, in which his father was riding; on the instant, he joined the hunt at the fringe and followed the horses as fast as the pony could gallop, bringing her in at the finish with foam-covered jaws and a pounding heart. One look and his father ordered him home. Debby had suffered a bad chill, he remembered now, ruefully; it took a week of careful nursing to bring her back to health.

His father taught him to shoot, to fish, and, above all, to sail a boat. From his earliest days, he was fascinated by ships, sailing vessels of all sorts, anything that rode the waves. He liked to sit gazing at the print that hung on the wall in the study—a square-rigged clipper, like the *Surprise*, which had taken his mother and her brothers and sisters all the way to China when she was a little girl. Grandfather Delano had been in the "China trade" and wanted to have his family with him; young Franklin never tired of hearing his mother tell of that four-month journey around the Horn to the Orient. The lure of the sea lay hold of him then, never to leave him, though it took the outward expression of a collector's interest, rather than a rover's. Prints, documents, ship models, naval histories, logbooks, and diaries piled up in his collector's store house, particularly during his years as Undersecretary of the Navy. (He had never properly catalogued all of the items; if he was going to be laid up for awhile, this might be the time to compile a permanent record of his treasures.)

It was his mother who first inspired and then fostered his instinct for amassing all manner of material on a subject that aroused his interest. Sally Delano had a reputation for never throwing anything away, and she kept things in a neat and orderly fashion. She had started a stamp collection when she went to China as a small girl, later giving the album to Uncle Frederic, who was her younger brother. When Franklin was no older than she had been at the time her hobby began—about five or six—his mother showed him the stamps that came from distant places and saved them for him. He was at once fascinated with the pictures and the symbols that denoted the culture of different countries all over the world; by the time he was nine, his interest was so great that Uncle Frederic had made him a present of Sally's early collection, which he had enlarged to a fairly sizable set of albums. From then on till the end of his life Franklin Roosevelt was an ardent philatelist. A year after he acquired the albums he had become a real "professional" and could spend hours sorting and pasting stamps. Uncle Frederic traveled a lot in those days and would always send his nephew a batch of postage from whatever country he was visiting.

One night ten-year-old Franklin was lying on the floor in his mother's sitting room listening to her read a story about the pharaohs while he "matched up" and pasted in a fresh package of stamps that Uncle Frederic had just sent from Egypt. He was completely absorbed with the job, turning the album pages, shuffling through the stamps, checking the album again; but suddenly he realized that his mother had stopped reading. When he looked up at her questioningly, she explained tartly, "I don't think you've heard a line I've read in the last ten minutes."

With a perfectly sober face, and the merest suggestion of a gleam in his eye, Franklin repeated the last two sentences she had read, word for word.

His mother was astonished. "I don't see how you do it!" she

marveled. "You seemed so wrapped up in those stamps."

The gleam brightened. "Why, I'd be ashamed if I couldn't do at least two things at once," he told her.

He was half joking, but it was true that he had a facility to give his attention to several things at the same time. As a boy he had a number of hobbies, all of which he carried through thoroughly. When he began to collect birds, he took only one of each kind, and he turned taxidermist for several weeks till he could mount the specimens himself, although his face was sometimes a sickly green when he came down from the tower room. He stuck to the job till he had mastered it; after that, the specimens were mounted at the local taxidermist's shop in Hyde Park. He started this hobby when he was eleven and, before he was fourteen, had collected over three hundred different kinds of Dutchess County birds. His parents had a special glass case built into the front hall to display his collection, and his grandfather Delano gave him a life membership in the Natural History Society. (Much later he gave a few specimens to the Museum of Natural History in New York when it lacked certain varieties of New York State birds.) He knew every birdcall, could identify every variety from no more than a flash of wings in the forest primeval, where he and Ed Rogers and sometimes the farm boys played Indian, stalking imaginary tribal enemies. He was always active, always coming up with new diversions for the boys, so it was natural for him to give the orders, which were usually carried out with a will. One day his mother heard him bossing the job of digging a fort and she decided it was time to say something about this habit of his, which she had noticed before.

"My son, don't give the orders all the time," she protested; "let the other boys give them sometimes."

His face streaked with mud, he looked up and gave her what seemed to him a perfectly obvious answer: "Mummie, if I don't give the orders, nothing will happen!"

He was right. Boy or man, he was a person who made things happen, and it was this quality as much as any other that in-

spired his determination to override his illness: he had to accept
the destiny of being struck down, but no creator of events, such
as he had been, could remain lying down for long . . .

He remembered with half a smile how he used to "predict"
his illnesses, especially on snowy Saturdays, when there was the
prospect of having to get up early for church the next morning.
Like the boys of most "river families," Franklin was tutored at
home until he was about fourteen (except for a two-year period
when he and two other boys besides the Rogers had their lessons in the round, glassed-in schoolroom on the top floor at
Crumwold). He had several different governesses through those
years, but the one who stayed the longest and stood out most
clearly was Mademoiselle Sandoz, a Swiss teacher, whose French
was impeccable.

His parents were away for a few weeks in February 1892 and,
although he missed them, he kept his affectionate letters bright
and comic. "My Darling Mumkin and Pap!" he addressed them
on Saturday after they left. "Good morning I hope you have
used Pear's Soap & are flourishing now. I am dying of school
fever and you will be horrified to hear that my temperature is
150°. But really I have got a 'Petit rhume' only I am in the
hands of the celebrated Dr. Sandoz. ——He came up to see me
this morning and ordered 5 drops of camfer on sugar twice in
the mornin; a hot toe bag, breakfast in bed & stay home all
day tomorrow and today if not clear of the disease. I went to
play with E, yesterday and rided over there. ——Today the whole
army of carpenters come to lunch. ——We got twelve eggs yesterday and there is no clocking hen. I can't write any more, So
Good-bye. Your affectionate Roosevelt Delano Franklin." (He
liked to switch his names around; sometimes he spelled them
backwards, too.) "P.S. The thermometer went down to 10° last
night. High wind all night."

On the back of his letter, Mademoiselle Sandoz had written
in French:

"Do not concern yourselves in the least, I won't let Franklin go out and will take good care of him; he is gay as a finch and actually he is hardly sick at all. ——He changed his clothes yesterday when he came in and I couldn't see that he had a cold but he said he had one. ——I was a little distrustful because yesterday he had told me laughingly that he would be ill and wouldn't be able to go to church."

When his teacher went home for a visit the next year, he wrote to her:

Dear Mademoiselle:

What sort of trip did you have? Was the sea rough? How many and what sort of people did you have in your cabin? And how much did the trip cost? Were you seasick? I hope you found your friends well in Switzerland. Miss Inkstand is not at all nice. She comes from China . . . I would very much like to know who is the President of Switzerland? Is there a representative of each canton in the Federal Assembly and how many Senators for each Canton? I have to go out now. Hoping that you will reply to all my questions, I am your faithful

Tlevesoor
Roosevelt spelt backwards

Besides the life at *Springwood,* Franklin's childhood had included a trip to Europe nearly every year from the time he was two until he was about fifteen. His parents enjoyed spending part of every winter "season" at the fashionable resorts in Germany, famous for mineral springs, and young Franklin accompanied them.

In the heat of the summer, usually after the Fourth of July, they always went up to the island of Campobello, a "discovery" of Mr. Roosevelt and several other river families, who bought or built homes there and became "permanent summer people," as the native fisherfolk called them. To Franklin, the island was a second home. Here he first learned to sail, under his father's direction, in the family schooner, until he could maneuver in and out of every cove and inlet of the rocky coastline, including the Lubec Narrows. When he was sixteen, his father gave him his own twenty-one-foot knockabout, and, when he went to Harvard, presented him with a forty-footer, the *Half-Moon*. He learned deep-sea and fresh-water fishing at Campobello, and roamed over every inch of the island, scaling the cliffs like a mountain goat.

He had had a singularly happy childhood, and much of its serene pleasure, he realized now, lay in the wide variety of physical activity so close to every boy's heart. He liked to read, it was true—one morning, when he was about ten, his mother found him propped up in bed, poring over the big dictionary that usually stood on the stand in the library: he had read halfway through and found it "very interesting"—he enjoyed study because of his enormous curiosity. But equally as important to him was the swift and skillful use of his body—arms, hands, legs, and feet.

At fourteen, when his parents finally decided it was time for Franklin to have formal schooling, he entered Groton, the boys' school on the Hudson started by its headmaster, the Rev. Dr. Endicott Peabody, some twelve years before. Here again, as much emphasis was placed on "muscle" as on mind and character. Franklin was by no means a great athlete, but he excelled in running and jumping, and the zeal with which he tried out for all sports was admired by students and faculty alike.

Dr. Peabody ran his school with the Spartanlike attitude of a British headmaster, with some of the flavor of Puritan New England thrown in for good measure. If the students at Groton had come from poorer families, their way of life here would have been "deprived." As it was, since the boys were not only rich but well-born, Dr. Peabody's strict regimen was considered "character building."

To Franklin, the first term was lonely, strange and bewildering. Most boys entered the school at twelve, so he was two years late in joining his class, in the third form rather than the first. An only child, used to his own bedroom, playroom, and schoolroom, he found it difficult (and even frightening at first) to be thrust in with a floorful of boys; to sleep in a tiny, walled-off cubicle, doorless and airless; to get out of bed before seven every day and shiver under a cold shower; to study under the stern eye of a master all the time; to attend chapel services every day in the week and twice on Sunday (no "excuses" like a "petit rhume" permitted here!); to dress in a stiff white collar for dinner every night; and to bid the Rector and Mrs. Peabody a formal good night before going back up to his little cell. He had always felt that he missed the company found in a houseful of brothers and sisters and cousins—like the Rogerses or the Warren Delanos—but this was hardly what he would have selected for himself.

He remembered with a stab of irony his initiation into the exclusive student body of "Grotties," his first experience with mob psychology—albeit adolescent—his hazing in the opening week of school.

He was an exceptionally good-looking boy, whose neat, straight features, deep-set blue eyes, and blond, plastered-down hair gave him almost a prissy appearance, until he smiled or began to speak, when his liveliness and good-natured warmth dispelled the first impression. Overwhelmed on his arrival by the clamor of a hundred boys reuniting after the summer vacation, laughing, greeting each other with shouts of recognition, swapping experiences, and arguing about them, he had been somewhat abashed and had fallen into an unusual reserve. He was standing in the hall after classes the second or third day, watching the boys in the upper form come in from a hockey game, when one of them spied him.

"What do you think you're doing?" his senior demanded accusingly. "Listening in on our conversation?"

"No, sir," he said, smiling. (It had not taken him long to realize that upper-form boys required respect from those in the lower, especially of "new" boys.) "I wasn't even hearing."

Ignoring his remark, the boy gave him a shove down the hall. Another jabbed at his ankles with a hockey stick and he took a quick step to avoid being struck.

"Look at him dance!" a third boy jeered. "I'll wager you went to dancing school, didn't you?"

"Of course—didn't you?"

The boy paid no attention. "This is Uncle Frank, fellows— 'Rosy's' uncle——" He was referring to Taddy, Franklin's half nephew, who had been at Groton two years already. "And he hasn't been hazed yet. Let's make him dance!" he called out gleefully, proud of his inspiration.

"Yes, yes, dance for us!"

"Give us a two-step."

"A waltz!" several of them chorused, and the instigator cried out, "In the corner, in the corner!"

Like any mob, they converged upon him, caught up with the enthusiasm of the ringleader, and backed him into the corner of the hall with their hockey sticks and shouts of "Dance, kid, dance!"

He had never been the victim of an attack, playful or otherwise, and, although this was half in fun, he realized it was a test. If he was disturbed, he gave no sign, but laughingly went along with the gag. He used mimicry and satire, pretending to talk to a partner, exaggerating the dance steps. His persecutors called out the steps and commands of "Faster!" "Slower!" —punctuating each with a sharp whack at his whirling legs with their hockey sticks. He neither stopped nor uttered a cry of pain or protest, but kept right on, acting as if he were a part of their sadistic tomfoolery.

Because of his serenity, his hazing was over much sooner than most of the boys'. After a short while his tormentors grew tired of their sport and left in disgust, searching for better prey. Nevertheless, Franklin knew as he rubbed his smarting ankles that he had won the respect of all upper-form boys by not howling, and he was right. They did not bother him again. The nickname "Uncle Frank" stuck, but it didn't bother him especially. As he wrote in one of his daily letters to his parents: "I would sooner be Uncle Frank, than Nephew Rosy, as they have been calling Taddy!"

Indeed, most "Grotties" soon accepted Franklin Roosevelt as one of themselves. The single fact that set him apart was that he was the only Democrat in the entire school. This they could not quite understand, but he was so genial and well-behaved that they let him alone. He was never "put in the boot box" nor "pumped" for being "fresh" to upper-form boys, though for awhile he lived in dread of being made to lie doubled up and cramped in his stumpy boot box down in the dormitory basement until his captors saw fit to let him out; or, even worse, he dreaded being dragged out of study hall into the lavatory, where basins of water would be poured over his head and down his throat till he practically drowned—more than one boy nearly choked to death during this form of private punishment by the students. Both were permitted by the faculty as a means of keeping the boys in hand.

Another method was a system of black marks, worked off by the students in extra study periods after class, or on the Saturday half holiday. (Too many black marks could lead to a notice to "see the Rector in his study.") Franklin saw to it that he received very few black marks, mostly because he didn't want to miss out on athletics by having to sit in study hall. To discourage tardiness, which was frowned upon as a serious infraction, the school offered a prize for punctuality—and for three of his four years at Groton, Franklin won that prize; it was easy to be punctual after fourteen years in his mother's well-run household; Sara Delano had been taught punctuality at meals, lessons, and church when she was little, and as Mrs. James Roosevelt she demanded strict adherence to the traditional schedule.

On Franklin's first report card, which placed him fourth in his class, the Rector wrote: "Very good. He strikes me as an intelligent and faithful scholar and a good boy." He was by no means brilliant, but he was quick; he wanted to do well and he wanted to be liked by his classmates. A month after he had come to Groton, on October 1, 1896, he was able to write to his mother and father: "I am getting on very well with the fellows although I do not know them all yet."

By the second term, he was well settled in the ways of the school, outwardly as much a "Grotty" as any of the boys. He went out for sports with a will—football and hockey in the fall, baseball in the spring (along with swimming and canoeing, which he did for sheer pleasure). He never made the first team in any sport, but in his senior year he became manager of the baseball team, a post he seemed to enjoy. The only athletic prize he ever took, he remembered with a sigh as he tried to shift his leaden limbs an inch or two, was the medal for the high kick. What a red-letter day it had been when he kicked the tin pan, suspended on a wire from the ceiling in the gym and moved higher and higher each time the boys touched it with no more than a big toe, at a height of seven feet three and one half inches, an inch above that of his chief competitor in the contest. The boys had cheered, and the Rector, who encouraged all sports and even took part in them himself, congratulated Franklin on his success.

In the evening of that same day he had scored another hit, in the very different field of debating. (He had become a regular member of the team, and soon stood out as one of its stars.) He was on the side arguing for the expansion of the United States Navy, and his eloquent six-minute speech, three times longer than most of the boys', won a victory of twenty-seven to three (out of thirty votes cast) over the opponents. His cousin, Theodore, who was Assistant Secretary of the Navy then, had been agitating for a larger Navy, but young Franklin needed no such stimulus to take the side of the affirmative. With his love of ships and sea, he had sailed into the argument like a veteran, easily winning the decision.

In this respect he was not like most "Grotties." He thought a good deal more about current events than they did, although, outside of the debates, he did little spouting in front of the other boys. He did not want to get a reputation as a "worm," grubbing every minute; toward the end of his second year, he wrote home: "I have served off my very first black-mark today, and I am very glad I got it, as I was thought to have no school spirit before." As time went on, he received a fairly respectable number of black marks, enough to keep him in good standing with the students and still out of trouble with the masters. Nevertheless, he could not deny his interest in geography, history, and world affairs, which shone like a searchlight through his well-constructed arguments in debate.

Two weeks before his sixteenth birthday he took the negative side of the question, *"Resolved,* That Hawaii be promptly annexed," following a formidable opponent in the person of Dr. Peabody himself; several of his statements were so remarkable as to seem in later years an insight into the future. He started boldly by saying: "Mr. Peabody has told us that our country cannot be safe without Hawaii. I shall try to disprove this." Among other things, he pointed out that "the United States and Russia are the only two countries no part of whose territory can be cut off by a naval enemy," and that "it is a little known fact that Pearl Harbor, a port in one of the islands, belongs to the United States. All that is needed is a little inexpensive dredging and we shall have a coaling-station (without annexation)." He continued: "What we want is a favorable trade treaty with the islands, and this we have already, for everything of commercial value is provided for in it."

In the spring following this debate, the Spanish-American War broke out, causing great excitement among the boys. The fact that two cases of scarlet fever broke out in the infirmary on the same day was soon forgotten; waves of patriotism swept over the school, and Franklin was among the first to be caught in the current. With Lathrop Brown, one of his closest friends in the form, he plotted to escape from school in the bakery wagon that came to Groton every Friday. The boys planned to hide in the back while the pieman was selling his wares in the kitchen. Hidden under the baskets and boxes of baked goods, they would ride into Ayer, where the nearest recruiting station was located. By the time the masters discovered they were gone, the boys would have enlisted in the Navy and it would be too late. They might have succeeded in their scheme, but on the day they were to make their getaway, both came down with scarlet fever! Instead of joining the Navy, they had to join the other boys in the infirmary. By the time they recovered, the war was over, but if it had not ended so quickly, Franklin would probably have made another attempt to get into the service, for his young blood was warm with patriotic fervor.

When Hampton Institute sent a Negro quartet, an Indian soldier, and a Negro lawyer to present a program on behalf of the Institute and its work, Franklin suggested taking up a "subscription" to promote the educational work of the school for Negroes and Indians; the students succeeded in raising $124, which was sent to Virginia soon afterwards. The words of Booker T. Washington, another speaker who came to present the problems of the South at Groton, also aroused Franklin's concern for those less fortunate than he.

Inwardly he was quite different from his fellow "Grotties," though few of them realized it. For one thing, he listened to Dr. Peabody's sermons instead of just sitting through them, and many of the Rector's precepts made a lasting impression on him. The idea of a life of public service, which the Headmaster constantly expounded, appealed to Franklin Roosevelt, and, although its ultimate expression years later was far removed from the form the good doctor had intended, his teaching and his personality left an indelible mark. Franklin stood somewhat in awe of the Rector, but he also admired him greatly. His first true spiritual feeling came from the chapel services as he sang in the choir and listened to the words of God as Dr. Peabody pronounced them. He never analyzed his religious feelings, but let them become part of his being; and, except for his black despair during the first days of this illness, he never doubted the existence of God throughout his life. And he was always to turn, in events of great moment, to the man who showed him the faith to be found in divine teachings.

During his last year at Groton, Franklin became a "full-fledged dormitory prefect" and an editor of the school paper, the *Grotonian*. He took part in the senior play and was generally as important a figure as a "VI-Former" was supposed to be. On the closing day he "was somewhat taken aback" when his name "was called for the Latin prize" and he received a forty-volume set of the Temple Shakespeare. He was eager to be off to Campobello with his parents the next day, but found to his surprise that he was sad at the thought of leaving the school for good. He and Lathrop Brown, who was to be his roommate at Harvard the following year, took two of the little Peabody girls canoeing on the river after the prize-day awards were announced; and, when they returned their small charges to the Rector and his wife, Franklin realized with a pang that this might be the last time he would be receiving the warm good-night handshake of the Peabodys. (Formal as it had seemed at first, the little ceremony had become one of the pleasantest features of the school routine.) The unconscious thought came to him that he must not lose touch with his mentor.

For his part, Dr. Peabody was not then aware that his pupil held him in such high esteem. On Franklin's final report card (which amounted to a "B" average) the Rector had written with his customary conservatism: "He has been a thoroughly faithful scholar and a most satisfactory member of this school throughout his course. I part with Franklin with reluctance."

When Missy LeHand came into the bedroom a few minutes later to consult the "boss" about a certain letter, she turned around and tiptoed out because she thought he must be asleep: his eyes were closed and a peaceful smile was on his face.

He let her get just beyond the door, and opened one eye. "Missy!" he called, startling her to a halt. "Take a letter to Dr. Endicott Peabody!"

CHAPTER IV

The Retreat—Part II
The Crimson Banner and Cousin Eleanor

IN THE FALL of 1900, Franklin recalled with a kind of nostalgia, he had entered Harvard. His own choice had been the U. S. Naval Academy, but his father, who had been ailing for some time, persuaded him to follow in the path of most Groton graduates —since Cambridge was much closer to Hyde Park than Annapolis and there would be no danger of his going off to sea. Franklin had secretly longed to become a naval officer, but in the quiet family talks at Campobello during the summer of 1899 he could see that his father dreaded the idea of his being so far away that he couldn't come home in a few hours. He was deeply fond of both his parents, to the point where he would put aside his own wishes to gratify theirs, and so he had "agreed" to try Harvard. Early in his last year at Groton, toward the end of October, he and Lathrop Brown had decided to room together and had gone to Cambridge to pick out their quarters. (Once he had made his decision, Franklin was able to put aside his longing for a life of the sea and enter into room-hunting with enthusiasm—a happy faculty he always possessed, and one which served him well in later years.)

The boys had found the "pick" of Cambridge student apartments, a first-floor corner at 27 Westmorely containing two bedrooms, a bath, a sitting room, and large hall, and here they both spent four college years. (Franklin was to take his degree in three, but stayed on another couple of terms doing graduate work.)

Life at Harvard was relaxed and pleasant; Groton students came so well prepared that Franklin, outside of his major in American political history and government, could elect a wide variety of courses; there was no strict daily routine there and more time for socializing outside of school. Looking back on it, he thought perhaps those first few months of college were among the most carefree he could remember. Others may have been happier, more exciting, or thrilling, but none were so untroubled. He tried out for football and became captain of one of the eight scrub teams—the only freshman captain. His greatest aim was to be elected to the staff of the Harvard *Crimson*, and he succeeded by means of a spectacular scoop, which, if he had been less intrepid, he would never have received. One of the burning political questions on campus (and outside of it) was President Charles Eliot's vote in the coming presidential election. Bryan was running against McKinley (whose running mate was Teddy Roosevelt, then Governor of New York) and as Eliot had criticized both candidates in a magazine article, there was speculation about which one would receive his vote. Franklin decided to find out. There was a rule forbidding contestants for the *Crimson* staff to interview the president, but, as a green freshman, Franklin had never heard of it, or, at any rate, he didn't bother to check. He went straight to Eliot's home, asked to see the President, and put the question directly to the great educator. Eliot, perhaps taken with such artlessness, gave him just as direct an answer: "I intend to vote for President McKinley, Governor Roosevelt, and Representative McCall, and I have never had any other intention." The *Crimson*, though it rebuked the would-be reporter for breaking rules, headlined the news the next day, and it was picked up by publications everywhere, much to

Franklin's delight. Shortly afterward he was elected to the staff. He was invited to join one of the social clubs, *Fly*, and he became a member of the Political Club. He was almost too busy to write to his beloved parents.

And then, on December 8, his father died. Franklin had been worried when he received the news a week earlier that his seventy-two-year-old parent had been seized by a severe winter cold, but he did not think it would be fatal. He stayed with his mother until after the New Year before returning to Harvard, where he plunged into work and the assignments he was given for the *Crimson*. He did not accept many social engagements for the rest of the winter, and his letters were all written on black-bordered stationery. He wrote to his mother only once a week, instead of twice or even three times as he had at Groton, when he had sent semiweekly reports to both his parents; and he was much less effusive. This was not only because he was very busy with campus affairs (and more adult), but because he realized soon after his father's death that his mother was ready to shift her whole life interest from her husband to her son, and something in him drew back. He did not care to be the sole center of his mother's attention, nor a substitute for her husband's companionship.

Not that he expressed himself in so many words; the difference in his attitude was as subtle as mist in the morning air. To judge by his mother's actions, he gave no outward indication, or so little that it did not prevent her from taking an apartment in Cambridge during the winters of 1902 and 1903 in order to be near Franklin. (In the summer of 1901, they took a European trip together, accompanying his cousin, Teddy Robinson, and some old family friends on a North Cape cruise; Franklin had even urged his mother to go, so that she would not be alone the first summer after his father's death.)

The change came within himself and was due in part to a growing interest in Eleanor Roosevelt, one of the many cousins whose company he enjoyed. He had singled her out at an

Orange Christmas party several years before, while he was still at Groton; her shy, serious look set her apart from most debutantes, who, he thought, were "pills." He had asked her to dance a number of times that first evening and discovered that they were fifth cousins; that her father, Elliott Roosevelt, had been his godfather; and that the famous Teddy Roosevelt was her uncle.

His second recollection of Eleanor was his chance meeting with her on the train going up the Hudson from New York to Hyde Park. (She was going a little farther, to Tivoli, where she lived with her grandmother.) He was walking through the coach when he noticed her; she was sitting by the window, her nose so deep in a book that she jumped when he called "Howdy!" And he had laughed and sat down beside her. They were soon deep in conversation on all manner of things; after awhile he realized that his mother, who was in the pullman a few cars back, would be wondering where he was, but he hated to leave Eleanor; so he took her back with him and the three of them talked all the way up to Hyde Park. His mother had recalled that Eleanor had been brought to *Springwood* by her parents when she was a very small girl and that Franklin, who was not much older, had given her a ride on his back all around the nursery, a story at which they laughed a little self-consciously. All too soon they had reached Hyde Park, where he and his mother got off, and Eleanor returned to her seat in the coach. Afterward, on the ride to the house, he had asked his mother more about his cousin's childhood and had been told that poor Eleanor and her brother, Hall, had been orphaned by the time she was ten and that she had lived with various relatives, principally her Grandmother Hall. (He gathered, from his mother's tone of voice, that she saw Eleanor in a much different light from the shining aura he saw her in, so he kept his impressions to himself.)

In December, while he was in his third year at Groton, he wrote casually, suggesting guests for a house party his mother was giving: "How about Teddy Robinson and Eleanor Roosevelt?

They would go well and help to fill out the chinks." From then on, although he saw her more and more frequently, especially after he went to Harvard and his father died, he made no mention of his growing interest in Eleanor when he wrote to his mother and maintained an attitude of cousinly friendship, so far as Sara Roosevelt could see. During his first year at Harvard he often went to Groton for weekends along with other alumni, and he usually wrote to his mother about the delightful time he had had; but he neglected to say that one of the people he usually saw there was Eleanor, who came to visit her young brother, Hall. When his mother took the apartment near him in Cambridge, she heard him mention Eleanor's name frequently, but no more often than his cousin Muriel's, or Mary Newbold's, or some of the other daughters of family friends whom he took to dances and parties.

It was a considerable shock to her, therefore, when, in November of his third year at Harvard, Franklin announced to her that he and Eleanor were going to be married. He had already asked his cousin, and she had accepted. Their engagement was a fait accompli, and his mother had had no inkling of it until that moment. Sara Roosevelt simply could not believe that this was her "boy Franklin," who had always turned to her for advice, who had more than once asked her to pick his dancing partners or accept invitations for him. Now he was telling her of a momentous decision like marriage in a way that left little room for protest on her part. Of course she tried: she could not bear the thought of his leaving her so soon after his father's death; and then they were both so young! Eleanor was so inexperienced . . . His mother might have said much more, but she could see the stubborn line of Franklin's jaw jutting forward (the Dutch side of the family coming out in him)—the same stubbornness that made him stick to a project until he had completed it when he was a small boy—so she kept her peace for the time being. She consented to see Eleanor soon.

The meeting on December 1, was somewhat of a strain for all

three, although none of them said anything that might create a rift in the family, least of all Eleanor. And the next day she wrote to her future mother-in-law:

Dearest Cousin Sally,

I must write you and thank you for being so good to me yesterday. I know just how you feel and how hard it must be, but I do so want you to learn to love me a little. You must know that I will always try to do what you wish . . .

It is impossible for me to tell you how I feel toward Franklin, I can only say that my one great wish is always to prove worthy of him.

With much love, dear Cousin Sally,

Always devotedly,
Eleanor.

On December 4, Franklin also sent an appealing note to his mother, but his told her in no uncertain terms that there was little she could do to change the plans of these two strong-minded young people. He said in part, "I know what pain I must have caused you and you know I wouldn't do it if I really could have helped it—mais tu sais, me voilà! That's all that could be said—I know my mind, have known it for a long time, and know that I could never think otherwise: Result: I am the happiest man just now in the world; likewise the luckiest——And for you, dear Mummy, you know that nothing can ever change what we have always been & always will be to each other—only now you have two children to love & to love you—and Eleanor as you know will always be a daughter to you in every true way——"

He could not take time for any more just then; he was in a rush to campaign for nomination to the office of marshal, one of three for the senior class. He did not get it, but was made chairman of the Class Committee (by unanimous vote of his fellow students), an equally important post. He was president of the *Crimson* that year, which meant that he had to write all of the editorials, besides his curricular work, rowing, and all the other things he tried to do. And every spare moment he could find, he spent with Eleanor. As he remarked in one of his letters, "It is dreadfully hard to be a student, a society whirler, a 'prominent and democratic fellow' & a fiancé all at the same time —but it is worthwhile, especially the last, & next year, tho' hard will be easier."

He wanted his mother to understand that no matter how busy he was, he had not lost sight of the fact that he still expected to marry Eleanor and attend law school in New York the following year. Sara, meanwhile, was so busy making her own plans that she scarcely paid any attention. She did not rent the apartment in Cambridge that winter. Instead, she invited Franklin and his roommate to go on a Caribbean cruise for six weeks, beginning the first of February. Both boys were far enough ahead in their work to make it up when they returned, and she hoped that during the cruise Franklin would think twice about his engagement, perhaps even forget Eleanor enough to break it off later on, never dreaming how obvious her purpose was to all concerned. Franklin, though he was politely enthusiastic about the sights in the West Indies and Latin America, and with his natural curiosity responded to each new country, wrote long letters to Eleanor and missed her more than at Cambridge, where he was occupied every minute.

Needless to say, the only purpose that journey served was to make the young couple more anxious than ever to be together. After his return in March, Franklin went to New York as often as possible; and in June Eleanor attended his graduation with his mother, who was beginning to see that further opposition was useless. Franklin, who had been so "reasonable" about going to Harvard, was adamant on the subject of his marriage; there was nothing his mother could do but try to be gracious about it. She went up to Campobello by herself that summer, opened up the house, and invited Eleanor to come up with Franklin for several weeks. He smiled when he thought how "proper" the daylong trip had been: Eleanor had to be accompanied by her maid, or her Grandmother would not let her come. And even on the island, where they had walked along the cliffs hand in hand, and sailed the *Half Moon II* along the coast, they were usually chaperoned by his mother and one or two others.

In the fall Franklin had followed through with his plan of entering Columbia Law School, and his mother obligingly rented a house in New York. The engagement was officially announced in December, but before then, on the twenty-ninth of November, Franklin had written to the Rector somewhat reticently:

My dear Mr. Peabody,

I think you will be rather surprised when I tell you that my engagement to my distant cousin Eleanor Roosevelt is about to come out. I know you will be glad for my great happiness and consider me a very fortunate man. . . . I am at the Columbia Law School, trying to understand a little of the work and of course I am going to keep right on. We hope to be married sometime in the late part of the winter and we both hope that you will be able to help us in the ceremony—it wouldn't be the same without you.

Always affectionately yours,
Franklin D. Roosevelt.

Would his old Headmaster accept? He wondered as he mailed the letter. But he need not have worried. Dr. Peabody was delighted to officiate at the ceremony and came up early on the day of the wedding.

It did not take place until March 17, because Eleanor's Uncle Teddy, who was giving her away, was coming up from the White House on that date to view the St. Patrick's Day Parade! (Just ten days before then, Franklin and Eleanor had been invited to Washington to see him inaugurated into his second term as President, a ceremony which gave them almost as much of a thrill as their wedding.)

Lathrop Brown had been best man because "Rosy" was traveling somewhere in the South; and while they waited in a little anteroom for Eleanor to make her appearance, the two graduates began reminiscing with Dr. Peabody about their old school, and all three almost missed their cue. The bride, on her uncle's arm, was nearly at the altar (in front of the fireplace in her Cousin Henry Parish's home on Seventy-sixth Street) before they realized the strains of the Lohengrin march were being played and rushed to their places just in time.

Franklin remembered other incidents: Uncle Teddy, saying just before he gave his niece away: "You do well to keep the name of Roosevelt." And then, after the ceremony, the guests following the President into the library, where refreshments were served, leaving the forgotten bride and groom standing alone instead of receiving well-wishers! After a few moments, they had joined the crowd and laughed with the rest at one of Uncle Teddy's anecdotes about his Rough Rider days, which he was, of course, famous for telling.

At the time Franklin had wondered how he would act in Uncle Teddy's position in the "highest office in the land"; now, flat in his bed in Campobello, he wondered whether he would ever have even the ghost of a chance of finding out.

CHAPTER V

The Strategy

THE WIZARDRY IN Louis Howe was at work, and before long he had devised a scheme to spirit Franklin away from Campobello without being seen by the newspapermen until he was on the train.

"Here's the idea," he said to Franklin one morning toward mid-September. "We'll have to get you down from here on a stretcher—right?" (He tried to make his voice as matter-of-fact as possible: they had had to abandon all notion of using a wheel chair, because the patient could not sit up as yet.)

Roosevelt nodded. "Frank is fixing up some sort of contraption." He was referring to Captain Calder, who had offered to improvise a stretcher so they wouldn't have to send for one from the hospital in Eastport, which would have been a real giveaway.

"Well, then . . ." Louis charted their course of action. "We'll put you in the bottom of the launch here, take you over to Eastport, up to the train, and slip the stretcher through the window. Then, when you're all settled, we'll call the newspaper boys over and you can give them a story from there—all they have to see is your head sticking out of the window."

Roosevelt rubbed his chin thoughtfully. "Sounds all right. But what's to prevent them—and plenty of curiosity-seekers—

from being on the dock when we land." He grimaced as he tried to shift his legs and failed. "By now people know I'm to go down on the fifteenth."

"That's so." Louis frowned, pondering. "I have it!" He snapped his fingers. "We'll give out a rumor that you're coming in at the *far* end of the harbor. People always believe a rumor quicker than a fact." He grinned wickedly, expanding his scheme. "What's more, I'll drop a hint that you're coming in later than you actually will be. That will give us plenty of time to get you settled before we notify the reporters."

The plan seemed logical enough—if it would work. On the day of departure Franklin's temperature was up again, and he was in a good deal of pain, for which Dr. Bennett gave him some pills. When Captain Calder and a couple of islanders came to put him on the stretcher and carry him down to the beach, he was able to compliment the captain on his ingenuity and joke a little with the men. But when they started down the path from the house to the stony beach below, he felt shaken with every step; the road had never seemed so rough before, nor so long! He thought they would never reach the motorboat. And although he knew his stretcher-bearers were strong young men, sure-footed and extremely careful, he shuddered to think of the consequences if one of them should slip or lose his grip just as they were lowering the stretcher into the launch.

During the two-mile ride across the bay he carried on a running conversation with Eleanor and Louis Howe to forget the fear . . . He wondered how the children were doing; they had gone ahead with Missy LeHand in another boat . . . It was good to see the blue sky overhead again, to feel the slap of the water against the boat, and to smell it! . . . How he loved to be on the water . . .

Then came another breath-holding moment at the Eastport dock, when they transferred him from the boat up the steep gangway to the dock and onto a wooden luggage dray, and started the bumpy ride up the rugged hillside road to the station.

Eleanor walked on one side of him and Louis on the other, slowly, slowly, as the cart was pushed; he tried not to let them see how painful every jolt was, like a sharp-edged dagger digging into his legs and back.

The car Uncle Frederic had arranged for was waiting, and they were just beginning to hoist the stretcher through the window of his compartment, when he spotted Franklin, Jr., who had broken away from the others to watch the proceedings, his small face a study in excitement mixed with terror. The expression was so much a mirror of his own feelings that Franklin suddenly smiled—a "tremendous sunny smile"—and he managed to wave reassuringly, as if he were not very sick after all.

Once the stretcher was safely through the window, everyone heaved a sigh of relief. Word was sent to the crowd at the other dock; Franklin was transferred to his berth, his body flat, his head resting on pillows. "Have a smoke," Louis said, holding out the pack. By the time the interviewers arrived, followed by a group of well-wishers who stood outside the car window and waved their greetings, the *New York World* correspondent was able to write, "Mr. Roosevelt was enjoying his cigarette and said he had a good appetite. Although unable to sit up, he says he is feeling more comfortable."

The first hurdle was over. "We've done it again," Louis crowed.

"Louis, *you've* done it again!" Franklin corrected him, as the train pulled out. They shook hands gleefully.

He remembered the first time Louis Howe had come to his rescue, in 1912, at the beginning of his campaign for re-election to the New York State Senate. He was flat on his back then, too, with an attack of typhoid fever which prevented him from making speeches practically from the outset. Louis had become interested in Franklin Roosevelt during the fight the fledgling State Senator had waged against Tammany Hall in his initial term, when he had refused to cast his vote for the nomination of "Blue-eyed Billy Sheehan" for U. S. Senator simply because Tammany leaders wanted Sheehan in. Roosevelt refused to be dictated to by party bosses, and all during the winter of 1911 he led a group of eighteen men who opposed the methods of Tammany. Louis Howe, as a newspaperman and seasoned politician, attended the meetings of the "reform" circle night after night in the smoke-filled library of the Roosevelts' house in Albany; and he was struck with the persistency, the dogged determination of the young State Senator, who was the first Democrat to be elected from Dutchess County in thirty-two years.

The campaign he had made in order to win over five-to-one odds spoke for itself, so far as Louis was concerned. Franklin had never been in politics (although he was active in Hyde Park and Dutchess County community affairs) until he was approached by three Democratic Committeemen to run for the office of State senator. The three—Judge John E. Mack, lawyer Tom Lynch, and Col. Thomas Newbold—all neighbors of his, "kidnaped" him one day in the summer of 1910 and took him out to a policemen's picnic. (It was "one of the first cases of deliberate kidnaping on record," he was to recall many years later. "On that joyous occasion of clams and sauerkraut and real beer, I made my first speech") They took him to other clambakes and picnics that month, and in the fall, just four weeks prior to election, he was nominated for State senator. In his acceptance, he made a bold statement: "As you know, I accept the nomination with absolute independence. I am pledged to no man, I am influenced by no specific interest, and so I shall remain."

He rented a bright red Maxwell from a country character by the name of Hawkey, and with him toured the county, making a whirlwind, crossroads campaign such as no Republican had made for three decades. Day after day, the bright red horseless carriage raced along the country roads at fifteen miles an hour; but when a farmer's wagon and team approached, the Democratic candidate not only slowed down but shut off the engine so the farmer's horses would not bolt. (This also gave him a good chance to talk to the farmer about his problems.) Once, when their automobile hit a dog, accidentally killing it, he and Hawkey hunted up the farmer in his field, told him what had happened, and offered to pay for the loss. He was so taken with their honesty that he began pouring out his troubles, principally about a standard-sized apple barrel, for which the Republicans in office had been promising legislation for some time; Roosevelt could lend a sympathetic ear because of his own farm at *Springwood*, and after some discussion, the man declared his support of the Democratic candidate. The uniform apple barrel became one of Franklin's strongest campaign issues because it was closely involved with the livelihood of most Dutchess County voters. Franklin made the most of it, and of the personal touch all through the campaign. He won many a Republican vote sitting in country stores listening to the farmers spout their cracker-barrel philosophy, though he couldn't stay long in one place. He covered the whole district and won the election by a margin of 1,140 votes. Afterwards he kept his promise and brought about the regulation apple barrel, along with other improvements for the farmer.

He received national attention in the party because of his opposition to Tammany Hall—("he bolted before his seat was warm," one commentator put it). As Chairman of the Forest, Fish and Game Committee he became interested in conservation, planting the seeds that were to bear fruit much later. He voted for women's suffrage at a time when it was considered "radical." And while there were those who considered young Roosevelt "arrogant" because of his somewhat lofty manner in the legislature, because of the proud upward toss of his head when he made some strong assertion, Louis Howe saw in him a bright, young, aggressive—and progressive—politician, whose charm, poise, and affabilty in personal contacts admirably equipped him for public office. How far he could go Louis only sensed at the time, but his instincts told him that Franklin Roosevelt had an indefinable quality, a kind of personal magnetism—as yet undeveloped, it was true—that could win people over and that was so essential to a public career.

Louis was glad to "come to the rescue" then, when Franklin asked him to take over the campaign at re-election time, at least until the attack of typhoid had passed. He went up to Dutchess County himself and put on an intensive campaign, mostly by means of the mails and all kinds of publicity, at which he was a master. He would come down to New York City, where Franklin and Eleanor were both confined by typhoid, bringing papers and reports, which were strewn all over Franklin's room by the time he left; and of course he smoked constantly, to which Eleanor objected strenuously. (She had not yet come to know Louis at that time, nor appreciate his worth as a campaign manager; the fact that he was winning votes for Franklin meant little or nothing in comparison with the upheaval the messy little man's visits caused in her household.) She was the first to recover, and felt that Franklin would have been well much sooner if it hadn't been for all the stale cigarette smoke in his bedroom during and even after Louis' visits. But the two only laughed at her and went on with their political strategy. And as a result of Louis Howe's unique campaign, Franklin was re-elected by a much more comfortable margin than before.

He had only served part of his second term, however; for it was in March that he was called to Washington to fill the administrative position of Assistant Secretary of the Navy under Josephus Daniels. (He had met Daniels at the national Democratic Convention which nominated Wilson for president. Franklin had helped to gather support for Wilson even though he could not vote for him, and Daniels had been impressed immediately with the young State Senator's charm and vigor. "It was love at first sight," he used to say, and after Franklin took office regarded him almost as another son.) In accepting the post, Franklin wrote joyfully: "It would please me better than anything in the world . . . All my life I have loved ships and have been a student of the Navy, and the assistant secretaryship is the one place, above all others, I would love to hold."

The youngest man ever to hold the assistant secretaryship in the history of the Navy, he was sworn in on March 17, 1913 (eight years to the day after he and Eleanor were married). "I am baptized, confirmed, sworn in, vaccinated—and somewhat at sea!" he wrote to his mother. "For over an hour I have been signing papers which had to be accepted on faith—but I hope luck will keep me out of jail. . . . I will have to work like a new turbine to master this job—but it will be done, even if it takes all summer."

One of the first things Franklin did was to ask Louis Howe to be his assistant in the Department. Louis, who had been given a leave of absence from his job as upstate political correspondent for the *New York Herald* to run Franklin's election campaign, now left his newspaper post altogether and came to Washington, bringing his wife and family.

With Howe to aid him, the thirty-one-year-old Assistant Secretary set about making a name for himself as an administrator, and he proved to be both vigorous and efficient. He started by making himself popular with the admirals and the seamen at the same time by consulting with the former on conditions in the Navy and giving attention to the latter—for one thing, he was shocked to find that a good many sailors could not swim, and saw to it that every enlisted man received swimming instruction.

Perhaps his greatest contribution to administration in the Navy was in the field of labor relations, the opportunity for which arose just a week after he took office. A delegation from the Brooklyn Navy Yard came to see him with complaints about arbitrary, unfair wage scales, informing him that he had statutory charge of all labor matters. (He had not known it before, but said at once, "That's fine.) He promised to look into the matter immediately, and three days later he received a signed order from Daniels putting wages under his jurisdiction alone, instead of the board of naval officers that had been taking the question of wages into its hands without consulting anyone. Then he set up what he later called "a perfectly practical example of collective bargaining" in all the naval yards. From that time on, there was not a single labor dispute in any of them during the seven and a half years he was in office; and work on ships increased in both efficiency and volume.

He felt that a big Navy was necessary to protect the country's coastline, and before the war in 1914 did all he could to increase the fleet and put it in full preparedness: he modernized antiquated shore bases and aroused more interest in the U. S. Navy than the country had shown for years. He did much of this on his own, for Daniels, while he admired his young Assistant and regarded him with paternal pride, was something of a pacifist himself and more inclined to let the status quo suffice. His slow-moving methods often irritated Roosevelt, who would cut through yards of red tape when he felt some project must be done quickly. (At one point during the war he was so enthusiastic in garnering supplies for the Navy that President Wilson had to rebuke him: "Mr. Secretary, it seems you have cornered the market on supplies. I'm sorry, but you will have to divide up with the Army.")

He loved the color and pageantry of the Navy, and thoroughly enjoyed his official inspection tours of bases and battleships. From the first he felt completely at ease in his naval duties, and was the perfect complement for Daniels, who preferred to stay at home and work from his desk. Poor Eleanor, who accompanied Franklin on some of the trips, was petrified for fear of not observing the proper protocol in such matters as boarding and leaving the ship, what to do while Franklin stood at salute, and other procedures, but he went blithely along, miraculously (it seemed to her) knowing the correct thing to do without any coaching. In Washington they entertained at official dinners or attended them nearly every night (with the exception of a single evening every two weeks when a group of close friends dined together informally). It was a life packed full of activity, and

Franklin thrived on it. His zeal often amused Daniels, who liked to tease him about it. One day they were gazing over at the White House from the balcony of the War and Navy Building while a photographer snapped their picture, and the dreamy smile on Franklin's face prompted Daniels to say, "I suppose you think you will be the next Roosevelt after T.R. to occupy that house?" His Assistant smiled more broadly, but said nothing.

With the entrance of the United States into the war, his life had become more strenuous with a thousand administrative details, and here Louis Howe was of invaluable help in matters of publicity and public relations, for which Franklin had little or no time. Louis helped in the handling of bids and contracts, also, and other toilsome tasks which were demanding but offered no glory. Franklin wanted to get into combat service, but was told by both Daniels and the President that it was far more important for him to stay at his post. He could not rest, however, until he managed to be sent to the front on a government mission in 1918, before the war ended; and when the armistice was signed, he had to go to Europe to oversee the selling of war matériel and the breakup of naval installations. Eleanor made the trip with him, and on the return voyage they sailed with Wilson aboard the *George Washington,* a ship Franklin had outfitted for the President when he went over to sign the peace treaty. Much of the last-minute work on the Covenant of the League of Nations was done on the desk Roosevelt had selected, and at the end of the voyage the President made him a present of it, a gift he treasured all his life. (During these years in the Navy Department he was able to acquire a great many items for his collection and he took advantage of every opportunity to pick up old prints and letters at fairly reasonable prices. One of his prize pieces was an excellent model of the battleship *Constitution.* His collection grew so large Eleanor thought the family would soon have to move out of the house to make room for it.)

There was no public figure he admired more than Woodrow

Wilson. At the opening of the 1920 Democratic convention in San Francisco, he created a sensation with a spontaneous burst of loyalty to the man who had founded the League of Nations. A huge portrait of Wilson was unveiled, producing a demonstration of wild cheers and applause, followed by an unexpected parade, as delegates from every state in the union except New York seized their standards and began marching around the hall. Roosevelt was at first mortified and then angry to see the Tammany man who held the New York banner remain stolidly in his seat while the procession grew longer and longer. He called out for New York to join the line, and somebody shouted that the Chairman of the State Committee had refused to allow it. The situation was so embarrassing to Franklin that he couldn't restrain himself from dashing up to the Chairman and demanding permission; and, as the demonstration showed no sign of abating, he received a halfhearted consent, which was all he needed. Vaulting over a row of empty chairs, he swooped down on the standard, and after a struggle, managed to wrest it away from the tight grasp of the bearer and march triumphantly toward the procession, holding it high! A joyful shout went up from Wilson men all over the hall, and in that instant he became the most popular figure at the convention; his show of spirit played no small part in his surprise nomination to the vice-presidency a few days later.

All that had taken place only a little over a year before—it was hard to believe. As the train rolled into New York, and the men came into the compartment to put him on the stretcher again, Franklin found himself eager to get to the hospital so he could start some kind of treatment which would put him back on his feet again.

There was a little knot of men waiting at the station to greet him when the stretcher came through the train window—the man who was to be his doctor, and who, by a happy coincidence, was an old schoolmate from Groton days, George Draper; the faithful Tom Lynch; and a lifelong friend, Livingston Davis.

He called to them all by nickname as heartily as he could—
"Livy," Tom, and "Dan," which for some reason had been the
doctor's name at school. "You're going to have a tough patient
on your hands," he warned the latter cheerily. He grasped Livy's
hand somewhat shakily, for his fingers did not have much
strength; and as the party moved off, he called, "Come along
in the elevator with us, Tom; I want to talk to you about the
New York Executive Committee; I've just accepted a place on
it."

But Lynch could not move; in the elevator everyone wondered
where he was, and Eleanor came hurrying back to find out what
had happened to him. She found him still standing in the same
spot on the platform.

"Tell Franklin I'll see him at the hospital," he said huskily,
turning his face away.

When he was finally established in the Presbyterian Hospital,
Franklin was tactfully prepared for a long stay by Dr. Draper,
who was able to strike exactly the right note of encouragement
and realism with his schoolmate-patient. Louis Howe decided
the time had come to give the newspapers some inkling of the
truth; he went so far as to mention in his story that Franklin
D. Roosevelt had contracted poliomyelitis and had lost the use
of his legs below the knees. But he emphasized that the patient
was recovering; and, in its story, the *New York Times* quoted
Dr. Draper's words of encouragement on examining Franklin,
which Louis was quick to include: "He will not be crippled. No
one need have any fear of permanent injury from this attack."

The article appeared on the front page of the September 16
issue, complete with headlines in boldface type; Franklin, listening to the account as Louis read it to him that morning, couldn't
resist sending a note to Adolph S. Ochs, the publisher, right
away:

While the doctors were unanimous in telling me that the

attack was very mild and that I was not going to suffer any
permanent effects from it, I had, of course the usual dark sus-
picion that they were just saying nice things to make me feel
good, but now that I have seen the same statement officially made
in the *New York Times* I feel immensely relieved because I know
it must be so.

I am feeling in the very best of spirits and have already been
allowed to take up part of my somewhat varied interests.

Between them, he and Louis, kept up the strategy of making
it appear that the worst was over and that Franklin's case had
not been severe. All of the press releases Louis sent out minimized
the degree of paralysis and magnified the prospects for a rapid,
complete recovery. He succeeded so well that letters began to
arrive indicating that people expected Franklin Roosevelt would
soon be back in the thick of things. One day, as he was going
through a batch of mail Louis had opened and had left for him
to read, Franklin found a memo from Herbert Pell of the Democratic Executive Committee asking him to attend the October
11 meeting, when important policies would be decided. Louis
had scribbled in the margin: "Mr. Pell had better wake up and
hear the birdies!" and Franklin himself knew that he had about
as much chance of going to the meeting as he did of going to
the moon. He had to admit that the accounts Louis had given
to the press were "a trifle optimistic."

Nevertheless, he stuck to his belief that the attack had been
"mild," for that description of it gave him confidence. "I'm
relying on you to get me out of here in a few weeks, Dan," he said
to the doctor, adding, as a concession to his badly-paralyzed legs,
"at least on crutches."

Dr. Draper smiled, promising to do his best. He was amazed
at his old schoolmate's magnificent bravado, at the combination
of humor and hopefulness in his attitude; because, after the first
few days, the doctor saw that Franklin Roosevelt was still a very
sick man. Moreover, he was severely crippled.

CHAPTER VI

The Battle for Health Begins

IT WAS LIKE BATTLING the windmills. The odds seemed so much against them, and yet Dr. Draper thought there might be a chance if he could maintain the balance between reality and the vision of recovery which his stricken friend saw ahead of him, no matter how far off in the distance . . .

One of the first things the doctor did, when he saw that Franklin's arm muscles were not much affected, was to order a strap put above the patient's head so he could pull himself up and turn over by himself. Franklin was delighted. What a relief not to have to lie flat on his back all the time or call for someone to turn him! He did not feel nearly as helpless with this rigging as he had before.

He was so pleased with any improvement, so grateful for any aid—and so intelligent about the use of endless hours in bed! Aside from going through the mail every morning, and dictating a few letters in answer, he had Missy bring in some three-by-five cards, and set about cataloguing his collection of American naval history—books, prints, letters—all the items he had acquired in the past ten years. He included the data found in library card catalogs, so that he would have an accurate record of his acquisitions. He wrote lying on his back, holding a thin pack of cards in one hand and wielding the pen with the other. His fingers became less shaky and his writing improved almost at once. And, as always, he spent some time every day over his stamp collection. For a patient as ill as he was to devise his own "physical therapy" was in itself a remarkable achievement.

However, what worried Dr. Draper was that the paralysis might be prevalent over a much greater portion of the muscles than they had suspected. Dr. Lovett, particularly, had been only moderately perturbed by the degree of paralysis. He even went so far as to predict in his letter to Dr. Draper that "it was a mild case within the range of possible complete recovery," and went on to say that the case "was evidently not of the severest type, that complete recovery or partial recovery to any point was possible, that disability was not to be feared, and that the only out about it was the long continued character of the treatment. It is dangerous to speak from impressions at the end of the second week, but my feeling about him was that he was probably going to be a case where the conservation of what muscular power he has may be very important, and it looked to me as if some of the important muscles might be on the edge where they could be influenced either way—toward recovery, or turn into completely paralyzed muscles." He added that he asked the Roosevelts to put themselves in Dr. Draper's hands and follow his advice.

Both Franklin and Eleanor had been more than ready to let George Draper lead the way toward the promised land of recovery, but there were many obstacles in the way. About ten days after he had taken over, the doctor wrote to his senior consultant in Boston:

Dear Dr. Lovett:
Just a line to report to you about Franklin R. I am much concerned at the very slow recovery both as regards the disappearance of *pain,* which is very generally present, and as to the recovery of even slight power to twitch the muscles. There

is marked falling away of the muscle masses on either side of the
spine in the lower lumbar region, likewise the buttocks. There
is marked weakness of the right triceps; and an unusual amount
of gross muscular twitching in the muscles of both forearms. He
co-ordinates on the fine motions of his hands very well now so
that he can sign his name and write a little better than before.

The lower extremities present a most depressing picture.
There is a little motion in the long extensors of the toes of each
foot, a little in the perinea of the right side, a little ability to
twitch the bellies of the gastrocnemii, but not really extend the
feet. There is little similar power in the left vastus, and on both
sides similar voluntary twitches of the hamstring masses can be
accomplished.

He is very cheerful and hopeful, and has made up his mind
that he is going to go out of the hospital in the course of two
or three weeks on crutches.

The doctor frowned, dreading to admit his greatest worry
about his friend's condition.

What I fear more than anything else is that we shall find a
much more extensive involvement of the great back muscles
than we have suspected and that when we attempt to sit him
up he will be faced with the frightfully depressing knowledge
that he cannot hold himself erect. It has occurred to me that
it might be possible for you to devise some kind of support for
him which we can put on while he is in bed, just preparatory
to getting him up in a chair for the first time, so that he will
not realize too suddenly that his back will not hold him.

I feel so strongly . . . that the psychological factor in his
management is paramount. He has such courage, such ambition,
and yet at the same time such an extraordinarily sensitive emotional mechanism that it will take all the skill which we can
muster to lead him successfully to a recognition of what he really
faces without crushing him.

My thought was that as soon as the tenderness has left completely so that you could move him about as you please . . .
you would come to New York to see him. At present I feel that

we should not get the greatest value from your presence because of the impossibility of manipulating him.

I have studiously refrained from examining his upper extremities because he believes them to be untouched by the disease. It is fortunate that one does not have much opportunity in the recumbent position in bed to call upon the deltoids or triceps— the biceps are fortunately pretty good so that he is able to pull himself up by the strap over his head and so help himself to turn in bed. This of course gives him a great sense of satisfaction.

In answering this letter, Dr. Lovett promised to come to New York whenever he was needed and suggested the use of strong saline baths as well as "electric light" for the paralysis. The patient himself was agreeable to any sort of treatment that would hasten his return to health. He quickly learned the medical name for all his affected muscles so he could discuss his case with the doctors. He even offered advice to the father of a ten-year-old boy in England, who wrote, after the press release, asking Roosevelt for suggestions to help cure his son, whose legs had been paralyzed by polio.

(He received all sorts of letters, many of them from other victims. One of them, written on September 20, included a picture card of its sender, a man about his age, sitting in a wheel chair, smiling happily; he offered good cheer and a blood transfusion if that should prove necessary. Touched, Franklin thanked him in reply, but said he was coming along very well. Another came from a "young girl only 87½ years old," who included some poems, and to her he said in answer: "If I could feel assured that time could treat me so lightly as to leave me at eighty-seven and a half years with all my vigor, powers and only a cane required, I would consider that my future was very bright indeed. There are not many people who can equal that record, even though they have been fortunate enough not to have been fellow-sufferers, with you and me, of infantile paralysis.")

Dr. Draper, Eleanor, and Louis Howe all encouraged him to

be as active as he could under the circumstances—in spite of the
fever, which still persisted at times, and the ever-present pain,
only partially dulled by opiates. The three, who were closest
to him during these weeks in the hospital, worked as a team,
each in his own sphere, but welded together as a harmonious
unit, to prevent him from slipping into the abyss of invalidism.
Franklin himself was captain, for without his objectivity and his
will to live there could have been no teamwork. His mother,
for all her outward cheerfulness, was inclined if not determined
to lead him toward the opposite goal of complete retirement and
semi-invalidism. Like Eleanor, she spent part of every day at
the hospital; but try as she might to maintain a bright, brave
face, the look of anguish came through, the tone of commiser-
ation crept into her voice. Her attitude annoyed her son, though
he didn't show his irritation and patiently explained to her that
it was better for him to stay in New York City when he left the
hospital than to go to Hyde Park as she kept insistently suggesting.

Eleanor finally saw to it that they were not alone in the room
too long; either she or Louis joined them, which, as a rule
brought about the elder Mrs. Roosevelt's abrupt departure, much
to everyone's relief. Franklin appreciated his mother's concern,
but not her fussing over his future course of action in regard
to his health. He—and the doctor—felt it wiser to solve one
problem at a time; the most immediate was for Franklin to
become well enough to leave so that he could begin leading a
more normal life.

He kept up a routine in order not to lose touch with the outside world. In the mornings after the doctor and nurses were
through with him, he would go over the mail that came to the
hospital and later would dictate a few answers to Missy, who
came for about an hour; if Louis brought any important letters
from the house, they would discuss them before sending a reply.
He usually worked on the card catalog for a little while before
lunch. The children (except James, who was at Groton) always

stopped in to see him on the way home from school—and that was the sunniest time of the day.

During visiting hours he frequently had company—old friends like "Livy" Davis and Lathrop Brown, Tom Lynch, Ed Rogers, Mary Newbold (now married), and Judge Mack from Hyde Park; his cousins Muriel and Warren Delano Robbins, and others from both the Delano and Roosevelt sides; and of course Uncle Fred and Aunt Kassie, who came from *Fairhaven* when they could, as well as other aunts and uncles; his half brother Rosy, who brought his family; and a few business acquaintances, like Black, who offered to hold Roosevelt's place in the insurance firm open till he was well enough to come back, no matter how long it took.

Franklin hailed his visitors warmly, raising his arm, palm up, in a typical gesture of welcome. "Come in, come in!" he would call out; and, although his face was often white and drawn, his voice was hearty. His friends and business associates who went to the hospital dreading the thought of seeing him flat on his back, who forced themselves to put on a "cheerful" face when they arrived, found that after a few minutes they felt much better; and, more often than not, would soon be laughing with him. With a wave of his hand or the upward turn of his head, he brushed aside any words of pity right from the start; and during the entire visit, he never complained, nor admitted his hard luck. Here was a patient who cheered up his visitors and sent them away in a happier mood than when they came. It was a cause for wonder. Often two or three of them would stand on the hospital steps, marveling at his manner in eager, awe-struck tones.

One afternoon his old "Chief," Josephus Daniels, came to call, his round, usually placid face full of concern for his former assistant. At the sight of Franklin's hollow cheeks and long, thin body under the covers, he could hardly speak.

"Come here, Chief," Roosevelt beckoned him to the bedside. Then, as Daniels bent over him, he drew back his fist and dealt a lightning blow at the jaw close to his. It sent his former chief reeling, open-mouthed and astonished.

Franklin was as tickled as a schoolboy over his prank. "You thought you were coming to see an invalid," he laughed, "but I can knock you out in any bout."

Ruefully rubbing his jaw, Daniels had to admit that he was taken by surprise, to say the least. A moment later, Franklin began talking about the old days in the Navy Department, and before they knew it, visiting hours were over.

Dr. Lovett came from Boston a number of times and, under his supervision, several back supports were tried while Franklin was still in bed. At first they raised him just slightly, to test the back muscles, which showed more strength than Dr. Draper had dared to hope; they held firm at higher and higher positions—he could sit up! Then came the great day when, with the help of the strap and a ring hung from the ceiling, he could pull himself up and, assisted by the doctor and a nurse, swing himself into a wheel chair. What a wonderful sensation just to be out of bed again!

"By golly, I feel like the King of England, sitting in state," he said gleefully to the doctor.

But he could not be out of bed for long. He was still too weak, and the puzzling fever kept recurring. Dr. Draper finally decided to let him leave the hospital on October 28, but was forced to put on Franklin's chart the cheerless words "not improving" under more than one heading. It was true, there had been some progress, but so slow that the doctor was worried and continued to give daily care.

The only one who did not appear to be worried was the patient himself. He could refer to his paralyzed limbs as "my somewhat rebellious legs" and to himself as a "prize patient" of the doctors, who "are much gratified with my progress toward recovery." He diligently went through arm exercises in bed every morning, with the help of Miss Rockey, who was still his nurse.

With the strap and ring (which he had put into his bedroom) he could soon swing himself into the wheel chair with very little assistance; and he figured out that if he had a simpler kind of chair, without the cumbersome arms, he could get in much more easily. A narrow chair, too, would be handier to get around in, through halls and doorways. Before long he was sketching ideas on a scrap of paper: a kitchen chair would do the trick— put it on a platform, with large-sized rollers underneath, and he'd have a real runabout! For a touch of convenience he added an ash tray on a swivel attached to the underside of the seat. He ordered one or two of these made up and found them so maneuverable he could scoot from one room to another fairly fast— and he did not feel nearly as much like an invalid.

All this did not happen at once. The ups and downs were maddening, particularly since there seemed to be no explanation for the latter. On November 19 Franklin had a definite relapse for several days; in addition to the high fever, he had pains in his eyes. What strange affliction this might be no one knew, and there was more than one anxious face until it cleared up.

The house on Sixty-fifth Street was crowded to overflowing. Franklin's room was on the third floor, back, where it was comparatively quiet. Miss Rockey, who came in every day, had to have a place to relax in the afternoon, when Eleanor relieved her. (Together they managed to lift Franklin when it was necessary, though his leaden body was difficult to move.) The nurse usually went into the large room on the third floor, front, which Louis Howe used at night during the week. (Most of the day he spent in Franklin's office, looking after business affairs, and weekends he spent with his family in Poughkeepsie.) Anna was given her choice between this room, which she would have to share with Miss Rockey in the afternoon and early evening, and a small one on the fourth floor, which she could have to herself; she chose the latter. Elliott had the room next to it. A connecting door on the fourth floor led into rooms in their grandmother's house next door, which were given to the two little boys and their nurse. Eleanor was left without a bedroom, but nobody seemed to realize it, least of all the lady herself. She slept on an extra bed in one of the little boys' rooms and dressed in Franklin's bathroom; she "was too busy to need a bedroom."

A crowded household, with a sick man at its center, could not fail to produce a certain amount of tension, created by a hundred minor irritations from one source or another. But in these early winter months they all tried to overlook it. Franklin was so happy to be out of the hospital and the children were so delighted to have him at home (not to mention his mother's joy at having him near her, more accesible to her advice) that none of them took notice of the strain.

After the eye trouble disappeared, Franklin seemed to make progress again. His confidence was enormous. The man in England wrote that his son was beginning to walk again, thanks to Roosevelt's advice; and Franklin answered at once to say that he was glad the boy was coming along so well, and that he, too, was "getting along very well, and expected to be walking on crutches in a very few weeks." He ended with the highly-colored prediction: "The doctors say that there is no question but that by spring I will be walking without any limp." It was only the eighth of December, and he felt so much better than he had in October that he did not consider his statement any exaggeration of the facts.

Christmas was only two and a half weeks away, and all of them were together in the twin houses on Sixty-fifth Street. That in itself was more than anyone had expected during the crucial weeks in the hospital in September. James came home for the holidays; a tree was set up and hung with ornaments, as usual. Franklin himself directed the trimming from a wheel chair, and he insisted on using real candles, according to tradition, fire hazard or no. (He had always been afraid of fires, from the time he had to help fight a fierce one in a barn during his boyhood, when he had seen horses burn and heard their whinnying screams of terror; some time later, *Algonac*, the old Delano home, had burned to the ground. Eleanor's aunt and two cousins had perished when their house went up in a flash fire.) Though his fear of fire amounted almost to a phobia, particularly now, when his helpless legs made it impossible for him to flee from the flames, he decided to put candles on the Christmas tree, and he set up an old-fashioned form of fire prevention. He tied a big sponge on the end of a cane and kept a bucket of water near the tree, so he could put out flying sparks or douse a burning candle if it lopped over. He himself clamped the holders on the lower branches with the same judicious eye for effect he had always employed, and the children called out criticism or approval of his placements; but James and Elliott had to do the higher branches—under his supervision. Eleanor watched the scene, delighted to see him take such an interest. And on Christmas Eve the whole family gathered around Franklin, just as they had always done, to hear him read Dickens' *Christmas Carol* in his silver-toned voice. It was always a treat, and none the less so now; his listeners forgot that he was in a wheel chair, forgot all but the magic of the story they knew by heart, but never failed to enjoy. If the final words, "God bless us every one," quivered softly in the firelit room, it did not seem strange, but rather a matching note for the mood of all.

The new year however, brought fresh calamity. Early in January Franklin's right knee buckled, and then the left, as the tendons behind them began to tighten; both legs bent double as they were drawn up beneath him. Dr. Draper was forced to put them in plaster casts as part of a remedy which caused his patient more excruciating pain than anything he had suffered before: every day for two weeks a little of the cast was chipped out at the back by driving a wedge in deeper each time, gradually stretching the muscles until the legs were released and straightened. That Franklin must be going through hell his doctor and everyone close to him knew, but he complained so little that he seemed to have superhuman powers of endurance. He was able to take great interest in his "torture chamber" and the workings of the wedge; his unending curiosity helped to pull him through the latest trial with the same strength he had shown in the earlier ones.

The agony was over at last, the casts were removed, and his legs, though still inert, were at least straight. By February Dr. Draper decided it was time for Franklin to be measured for braces. They were made up in Boston and arrived before the end of the month. Constructed of steel, the braces were heavy, weighing seven pounds apiece; and they stretched from his hips to his heels. Merely putting them on was an engineering problem involving Dan Draper, Miss Rockey, Eleanor, and himself; and then he felt so weighted down he did not see how he would be able to stand up. But he did, with the support of the doctor and nurse; first the braces had to be locked into position, so that his legs were held rigid in the steel; then he had to learn to push himself up from the chair by the power of his arm muscles alone (now he saw the benefit of the exercises he had been doing); then the doctor showed him how to maintain balance, for he no longer had the means of doing so, since he couldn't flex his toes. It was like being on stilts.

Once he was up, the doctor taught him to give a slight wriggle and then hold his body perfectly still, even stiff, from his shoulders to his ankles; finally he had to tip forward and upward slowly—very slowly, or he would tip too far and fall, as he did the first few tries. The biggest obstacle was his height. There was so much of him above the braces that had to be balanced! If he had been about five feet tall, the doctor said, he wouldn't have had any trouble. As it was, he couldn't gauge the forward angle he had to strike and, after a second, he swayed and went down. The doctor had to catch him, and they would start in again from the beginning. It was a tedious process, but eventually he could stand!

He was learning the value of working for and achieving "small goals" on the way to larger ones. The next was to "walk" with crutches, and this again seemed an interminable process. Although both the doctor and his charge showed infinite patience, the odds at times seemed unbearable. To begin with, the braces had to be sent back for adjustment a number of times; this was usually the case, Dan Draper said; medical appliances never fit the first time. Even after adjustment, the braces were heavy and cumbersome; Franklin felt uneasy in them, not really sure they would hold him. The crutches were very difficult as well; like sharp slats under his armpits, they were apt to cause sores unless his weight was distributed evenly on his wrists, hands, and shoulders. And it was so hard to learn how to set them down in such a way that they would not slip and send him crashing to the floor! Time after time the doctor had to catch him. When at last he was able to take a few steps, he was not really walking, but simply maneuvering his body forward with his hips. However, he was sure he would improve with practice and was determined to learn to use the crutches when no one was standing by to help him. If he fell, he would pick himself up by grabbing onto a chair, take hold of the crutches, and try again.

The winter dragged along, borne by alternate waves of hope and despair. The overcrowded house, the unspoken struggle between his mother and the rest of them, particularly Eleanor, for supremacy in determining his future course of action, began to tell on everyone's nerves. Only the two younger boys seemed oblivious to the repressed hostility that surcharged the air of outward cheerfulness. As Franklin's general health improved, he spent part of every day downstairs, and he would get down on the floor of the library with the boys just as he used to, wrestling and roughhousing with them as if nothing was wrong with him. They were apt to forget completely about his legs, and there was danger of injury to the muscles from a fast-moving foot or the accidental jab of an elbow as they tumbled about him. His mother deplored his playing with the boys like this, since she felt that Franklin should have it "absolutely quiet," but he only laughed at her and said he would rather risk a few broken bones than his children's companionship. So that they would know what he was up against, he taught the boys the names of the muscles he was concentrating on, and they would memorize them; calling off the medical term as he pointed to each pair, all the way up to "gluteus maximus."

At other times, the noise of the children got on his nerves, particularly during meals, when he wanted to discuss business with Louis, and Anna and Elliot would get into a high-pitched argument. Anna was his favorite, but he would be so annoyed that he would order her sharply to be still. She was old enough to sense the anxiety over her father, and had been undergoing a strain herself in adjusting to a new school in New York, although she had not told anybody. As a result, a scene usually followed, which ended in a burst of tears from Anna, who would leave the table and run sobbing up to her little room on the fourth floor.

As often as not, her grandmother would go up to comfort her, and on one of these occasions, she learned that Anna was dissatisfied with her cubbyhole of a bedroom. Sara Roosevelt, who was none too kindly disposed toward Louis Howe and felt that if it were not for that "ugly little man's influence" Franklin would be much more likely to retire to Hyde Park, seized on Anna's discontent to further her own plans. With a few well-chosen words, as she sat stroking Anna's long golden hair, sympathizing with her, she convinced her that it was unfair for a fifteen-year-old girl to be stuck away in a tiny fourth-floor room while Louis Howe was given a large room with bath on the third floor.

This was all Anna needed. None of the children cared much for Louis, who never paid them any attention, and whose droll humor, acrid wit, and political discussions were way over their heads. They were all happy on Sunday mornings, not only because there was usually a large, leisurely breakfast, but because they knew Louis would not be there to frown disapprovingly if any of them distracted their father's interest. Forgetting that she had once been offered the larger room but had turned it down because she could not have it to herself all the time, Anna went to her mother one day in March and requested in no uncertain terms that she and Louis change rooms. Eleanor, worried at the moment about the braces, wondering whether Franklin should go to Boston and have them fitted directly on him, had no time to delve into her daughter's problems; she knew nothing of the situation at Miss Chapin's school, where Anna felt completely out of place. The most she could see was that adolescent girls were certainly difficult to understand and that Anna was being especially trying. She dismissed the subject curtly by telling Anna she should have made up her mind in the beginning about the third-floor room—it was too late now.

Poor Anna went off nursing her grievance, sure that her mother did not care in the least what happened to her.

Around the middle of April, Anna was in the library one evening, putting up an armload of books Franklin had taken from the shelves. (He had a kind of pincers on a stick so he could reach for them from the wheel chair.) He had had a miserable day of unsuccessful attempts to use the crutches and the tender spot under each arm bothered him, but, as usual, he had not given any indication of his distress. When Anna accidentally dropped the whole load of books and they went spilling onto the floor, the clatter jarred his nerves out of all proportion to the actual sound.

"Sis, if you can't do a thing right, don't do it at all!" he snapped at her.

Astonished, hurt, and aggrieved at what seemed to her most unjust severity on his part, she flung at him, "Well, I was only trying to *help*, Father!" Then, overcome by the thought of her father's tragic condition and her own misery, she began to weep wildly and rushed from the library, leaving the books scattered on the floor.

Eleanor, coming in a little later, started picking them up automatically and putting them into place. Franklin, watching

her, asked what on earth was the matter with Anna that made
her so touchy of late.

His wife shrugged. "I guess she's on edge, too," she smiled.
"She's at that difficult age." Casually she mentioned the matter
of the rooms.

"Where did she get that idea?" he demanded.

She shrugged again. "I would guess from your mother."

Franklin's face darkened, his jaw tightened. "Mama is carrying her dislike of Louis altogether too far, and I'm going to tell
her so."

"Now, Franklin, I'm sure your illness has been a terrific strain
on Mama; she only wants what she thinks is best for you,"
Eleanor placated him, adding out of honesty, "even though we
don't agree with her . . ."

"You're darn right we don't!" he said emphatically. "If I
didn't have my finger in a few pies, political or otherwise, she'd
have a much sicker 'boy' to worry about, and she may as well
get used to the idea that I'm not going to be an invalid!" His
mood changed abruptly with his determination. "You've been
under a tougher strain than anyone, Babs. It's a wonder you
haven't broken down."

She smiled, unable to tell him all she had been through, because she had never stopped to analyze it herself. She only knew
that she "had a very bad tendency to shut up like a clam when
things were going badly," particularly where her children were
concerned, since she wanted to protect them. They and everyone
else mistook her outward calm (of which she had a great deal,
combined with common sense) for inner serenity, which no
person could maintain in a prolonged period of stress like this.

Franklin was able to slough off his anger quickly; when Anna
came back downstairs for dinner he received her with open arms
and a plea for forgiveness; he told her a fable to make her laugh
and at the same time understand that she had nothing to com-
plain about.

For the time being, things were smoothed over, but the petty irritations continued; the hidden struggle against the elder Mrs. Roosevelt still seethed. It never occurred to Eleanor to take Anna into her confidence "and consult with her about our difficulties or tell her just what her father was going through in getting his nerves back in condition," she admitted long afterwards. If she had, she might have saved them both much unhappiness.

The whole situation became so electric that even a tight shell like Eleanor Roosevelt's had to crack. It was still April, a rainy afternoon, and she was on the sitting-room sofa, reading to the two youngest boys. Suddenly, without warning, her voice broke, and she found herself sobbing. She "could not think why," but she was sobbing as if she were lost and no one could find her. She could not stop. The two little boys stared at her in silent wonder, but she could not control herself. She sobbed and sobbed. Elliott, coming home from school, took one look at his mother and fled. Louis Howe came in and tried his best to find out why she was crying, but she could not tell him, neither could she stop. He wisely left her alone; the two little boys finally went off to bed, and she sat on the sofa by herself and cried her heart out. Worn out at last, she found an empty room in her mother-in-law's house, locked the door, and bathed her face in cold water. It was the only time in her life that she ever gave way to what she herself called "an emotional jag," and from then on she seemed to "have got rid of nerves and uncontrollable tears."

Her psychological storm, moreover, cleared the air generally. Anna, finding that her mother could also go to pieces, felt closer to her and began to confide in her; the school troubles came out, and the tantrums diminished. Franklin eventually had it out with his mother and told her in no uncertain terms that, although he expected to go to Hyde Park for a period of convalescence during the summer, he had no intention of retiring there for the rest of his life. She was momentarily satisfied with the assurance that he would come to *Springwood* to regain his health, and left shortly afterward to put the house in order.

Dan Draper urged Franklin to take an active interest in business or politics, even if it tired him, so that he would lead a more normal life; if he concentrated solely on physical fitness, he would find it more difficult to accept the discouraging slowness and the setbacks that the doctor knew must occur. It was necessary to keep a balance, and an overemphasis on the physical might do more harm than good. Louis Howe jumped at his advice—they must get Franklin out of armchair politics, which was all right up to this point, but the time had come for real participation again. Eleanor did not see how this could be done, but Louis had the answer: *she* must go into politics. Franklin would have to take part, if only in self-defense.

Eleanor had no idea how she would go about it, but Franklin was so eager for her to try that she began making contacts at once. Before they left for Hyde Park, she had attended a luncheon of the Women's Trade Union League and become an associate member; she had also presided at a luncheon to raise funds for the women's division of the Democratic State Committee, although she had not the "faintest idea" what to say or a glimmering of the work the organization did. Franklin had to fill her in; he also wrote a letter of advice to Caroline O'Day, head of the women's division, concerning the coming campaign. It was not much, but it was a beginning.

During May he made arrangements for various kinds of apparatus to be set up in Hyde Park to aid his recovery. He had begun taking gentle exercises for his legs, and to continue these he had his bedroom at Hyde Park outfitted like a physical therapy gymnasium. Above the bed was a contraption like a trapeze with pulleys so his legs could be pulled up and down slowly. He also had an exercise board put in, a traction frame, and a special mechanism which enabled him to hoist himself out of bed alone and into a wheel chair at the side, if somebody held the chair steady.

On May 23 he received a letter from a victim in Waterloo, Iowa, who said she had been stricken with polio at about the same time he was, and she described a treatment from which she derived great improvement: parallel bars had been set up in her brother's yard and, by hanging on to them, she had been walking, a little longer each day. He had heard of the method before, and the woman's testimony made him eager to try it. Although the doctor thought it might be too strenuous for him, he had a set of bars put up on the south lawn; they were ten feet long, fixed in a round base; the lower bars were waist-high, the upper ones came to about his shoulder. Both doctors had recommended swimming if possible, in water at least seventy degrees, so he arranged to use Vincent Astor's indoor, heated pool until he had a small one built near the house. His mother ordered an electric tricycle from Europe, but this proved to be utterly impractical.

When everything was ready, he was driven to Hyde Park by car, but before he started on a strict routine, he went to Boston to be measured for braces which he hoped would be more comfortable. Dr. Lovett suggested that he also be fitted for a "corset," which might help him to walk, as it would hold him more erect. He was willing to try anything; swimming, which Lovett emphasized again, had much more appeal, but if a corset would improve his walking, he would wear one. He confided to Mrs. Charles Hamlin, a river-family friend who had come to the doctor's office while he was there, that although the movement and feeling in his hips were normal, he had less and less the farther down he went, and only about fifteen per cent of normal control over his feet and toes. But he hastened to add that he was waking them up and on his way toward being able to "double-quick it" around Potomac Park again (as he had done with a group of men in Washington, where the Hamlins had lived while he was in the Navy Department). His friend recorded in her diary that he looked tired but seemed cheerful, confident that "he was gaining very surely."

Back at Hyde Park, he entered on a rigorous schedule to make a reality of his boasts. So successful had he and Louis Howe been in their correspondence with key political figures that late in May the *Chicago Tribune* carried an item about his being considered for governor by the New York Democratic Committee; he had to get himself in condition! He found that sunshine and fresh air were of the greatest benefit generally, so he spent as much time out-of-doors as possible.

His principal exercise was with the parallel bars on the south lawn. Every day, by putting most of his weight on his shoulders and arms, he would drag himself back and forth, back and forth, the length of the bars, hoping to strengthen the muscles of his now painfully thin legs. It was strenuous, uphill effort, and to ease the strain he would keep up a sprightly conversation with the members of his family, Missy LeHand, or Louis, who were on hand to keep him company. Sometimes John Mack, Henry Morgenthau, Jr., and his wife, Elinor (who had a farm nearby and had become close friends of the Roosevelts), the Newbolds, and other neighbors would come over, and he would tell them to join the family circle while he continued his arduous exercise. At the risk of damaging his muscles, he kept on. One day, missing the bar as he started to grab hold of it in his inching along, he slipped; several small ligaments were torn, and until they slowly, painfully healed, he had to give up the bar exercises. As soon as the setback was over, he started in again, doggedly.

Even more grueling was the daily workout with the crutches, which Dr. Draper had prescribed to give him greater facility in using them. He suggested that Franklin try walking on his crutches a little farther each day along the graveled road that led from the turn-around in front of the house to the brownstone gateposts a quarter of a mile away at Route 9. Bordered by a double row of magnificent maple trees, the driveway was one of his favorite, familiar spots at *Springwood* (how many hundreds of times had he spun up and down it on his bicycle!) and now he determined to make it on crutches. The first time, flanked by his mother's chauffeur, Louis Depew, on one side and the house man, Robert McGaughey, on the other to prevent the crutches from slipping when he set them down, and accompanied by Eleanor, his mother, and Louis, who watched him fearfully, he was able to pass only a few of the maple trees when he had to stop, leaning on the shoulder rests. "Don't expect to get far today," he panted. "But I'll reach the gateposts by September!"

The next day he was able to get farther, slowly, laboriously slamming down the tip of one crutch, twisting his body forward with his hips, and slamming down the other, his braced legs bearing almost none of his weight. He would strain every muscle in his body with every "step." The sweat would roll off of his face and down his neck; and often, before he had gone very far, the back of his shirt would be wringing wet. Sometimes his cousins, Laura Delano and Margaret Suckley, who came to visit him, thought he would surely collapse; but he kept on, laughing and chatting, commenting on the trees. ("You know that row of wonderful maples east of Rosy's," he might say, "runs from the top of Teller's Hill and probably as far as the Rogers' farm —those trees were planted by a blind man in 1740 or so." And he would recall the story of John Crook's son, who lost his eyesight in an accident, but in his love for the country put in the row of maples, many of which were still standing, nearly two hundred years later. And for every one that had fallen or been struck by lightning, another had been planted. "There is nothing quite like it anywhere in America," he said with satisfaction.) He had a store of legends about Dutchess County, which he enjoyed telling as he moved painfully, perspiringly along, as if his mammoth struggle were a mere pleasure walk. And indeed it was a joy to him just to be making the effort, because he had come so close to complete oblivion and because he had deep faith in his power to recover.

He did manage to cover more than half the distance, but he never quite made it to the gateposts, before, in sheer exhaustion, he would have to give over the crutches and get into the wheel chair, which was pushed along by somebody accompanying him. He would be wheeled back to the house for a rest. In New York he had had to be carried up and down the stairs, but he hated the feeling of helplessness it gave him to be carried.

He taught himself to crawl, placing most of his weight on his hands and dragging his body behind him. To go upstairs he sat on the tread and hitched himself up backwards a step at a time, hauling his body up by the sheer power of his arms. At Hyde Park he had a hand-drawn elevator—like an outsized dumbwaiter—installed in the back hall. It was big enough to hold his wheel chair, and in it he pulled himself up and down several times a day. Later, ramps were built over the stairs. From his bedroom window he could look out on a magnificent view of the Hudson River Valley; he was doubly glad now that they had remodeled the whole house in 1915, when he had designed this wing and one on the other side, as well as the wide front portico with its tall columns instead of the narrow porches all around.

No matter how much rest he had to take, he was back on the driveway the next day, optimistically striving to reach the gateposts. His legs didn't improve much in strength, but his arms and shoulders began the development which later made them enormously powerful; and he was learning to handle the crutches with much greater ease. In July he wrote to a friend who had sent best wishes in regard to the fall nomination: "Though I am very much better and improving every day I am still forced to get about on crutches and could not possibly run a campaign this fall. There is no possibility of my running for the governorship this year," he added, leaving the opportunity open, of course, for the future.

Nearly every afternoon the whole family, including Missy,

Louis, and any guests who happened to be around, went down to the pond in the woods below the house to swim that summer, before Vincent Astor offered his pool. It was a lovely glade, and here Franklin took the sun and swam. He would sit on the side of the dam and let his legs dangle in the water, and then he would slide in.

Swimming was easy after the other exercises; his legs actually moved without having to be pulled with every ounce of energy he could muster. In the water they were light instead of leaden. He splashed delightedly with the children, and saw to it that Franklin, Jr., and John learned to swim under the instruction of Mr. Depew, who was there principally to haul him out when he began to feel chilly. One thing he had to avoid was chill. Remembering the Bay of Fundy, he once hollered to the driver, "Water got me into this fix, and water has to get me out again!"

The words were more prophetic than he could have dreamed at the time.*

* Another version is: "The water put me where I am and the water has to bring me back!"

CHAPTER VII

The *Weona* and the *Larooco*

NOT ALL HIS HOURS, of course, were spent in strict exercise or complete rest. He often relaxed by taking a tour of the grounds in his wheel chair, pushed by Robert McGaughey, who knew the route that Roosevelt liked best to take, one which led to his half brother Rosy's, the *Red House*. A path was put down between the two houses so that his chair could be pushed along more easily to the dirt road that joined them. He knew every tree on the grounds and kept a sharp eye open for signs of decay or disease. At Rosy's he would discuss conservation of the trees, farm problems, and family gossip; on the way back, he inspected the farm and livestock; he liked to run the farm on a business basis, although his mother thought it should be maintained merely for the family's convenience. (Rosy, who had worn a long beard for many years, looked and acted like a gentleman farmer; Franklin could not imagine himself in such a role, whether he was crippled or not.)

Occasionally they all went on informal picnics beside a brook called Val-Kill, and it was during one of these that he got the idea for building a small pool of their own right there. He laid out plans for it at once, sketching them on the scratch pad he usually carried in one of his pockets. He also designed a cottage, which they called *Val-Kill Cottage*. (Eleanor and the children,

looking over his shoulder, offered various suggestions for both
pool and cottage, and his friend, Henry Toombs, who was a
professional, became the official architect; but the site, and the
general design of both came from Franklin.)

He and Louis Howe spent many hours on the east porch, making model boats to sail across the Hudson, a hobby he had
started when James and Elliott were small, and which they all
had enjoyed since. The year before, in June 1921, Elliott's
"yacht," *Resolute,* had made a record crossing by covering a mile
in fourteen and a half minutes. Now Roosevelt set out to
better that record by experimenting with different kinds of wood
and spar metals. "I'll beat all my rivals yet!" he boasted when
they were all (even the youngest boys) hard at it early in the
summer; but the boys only grinned at him. Elliott's challenge
was "Prove it!" and his father did. The boys' interest waned
or varied; they went on a camping trip with their mother, for
one thing. But the two men and a neighbor made twenty-seven
ship models among them. (Sometimes Franklin worked by himself, sitting in an easy chair on the front portico; if he dropped
a tool and it rolled too far away from the chair, he would have
to wait till somebody came out and it could be picked up before
he continued.) Louis had a favorite name for his boats—*Horse's
Neck*—and made a whole series of them.

They held races from the Rosedale Boathouse, each model
followed by a rowboat. Franklin would get in the stern of their
boat, while Louis, who was light, would be in the bow, and
Mr. Depew would be at the oars. (Once in a while Roosevelt
would sail his own models from the railroad siding below the
house.) Eventually they established semiannual races—in the
spring for the "Roosevelt Cup" and in the fall for the "Hyde
Park Cup."

As with any subject he took up, he went at building the
models with scientific absorption, not satisfied until he had solved
the riddle of producing the maximum speed in small craft. Later
he wrote in detail:

My first interest in building small boats came through my older children and I built 1 or 2 in the beginning that were fairly accurate models of the *Resolute* and the *Reliance*. I then became interested in the question, "How fast can a small boat be made to sail?" I discarded the so-called rules of the model yacht enthusiasts affecting displacement, depth of keel, sail area, etc., and devoted myself to the problem of how to make the fastest possible small boat of a given size. I easily adopted a standard of 38″ over-all length, and have tried almost every kind of experiment from the English cutter to the skimming dish, and even double-keeled boats and catamarans.

. . . the first boats I made were real models, complete down to the last detail. Now, however, in order to get the necessary lightness of construction, I use balsa wood for the hull, balsa wood or oiled silk for the deck and aluminum for the spars . . .

The first year the boats took nearly sixteen minutes to cross the Hudson, a distance of ⅝ of a mile. Since then some of them have done it in 10 minutes and 15 seconds. This is not bad for a tiny craft only 38″ long. The maximum sail area was reached this year in a boat which successfully carried a mast 6 feet long. You can imagine that the sport produces not only a vast amount of discussion from all who take part in it as to the respective merits of the various types of boats, but produces also keen rivalry in the mechanical skill and appliances for the saving of weight, new forms of rigging, etc.

It goes without saying that all the children of the neighborhood are tremendously interested, though I am not sure that their interest is any greater than that of the older generation.

He might have added "if as great." He took much pleasure before his illness, in making things with his large but sensitive hands, and now he had the time to devote to it. He became something of an amateur carpenter and turned out several pieces of furniture, including a bookcase of mahogany-stained cherry-wood for his mother. At night he spent hours sorting and pasting stamps without using tongs, a practice most philatelists would have frowned on, but he never tore, smeared, or wrinkled the stamps.

He read often in bed—biography, history, or detective stories—
and he talked about writing books or articles, but never seemed
to get around to it: his history of the Navy came to be a family
joke at which he himself could laugh. In September, when he
was invited to collaborate on an article about international
affairs, he dictated to Missy a humorous, self-perceptive answer:

In regard to my own actual pen-to-paper possibilities I am
always in the delightful frame of mind of wanting to say "Yes" to
anything in the way of writing, be it a magazine article or a 12-
volume history of the Navy—

Missy started to smile, and he added,

always provided that the writing is to be done next week or the
week after. (Miss LeHand who is taking this is nodding her head
and saying "Too true—too true!")

Then there is another complication—i.e., I am carefully trying
to stay out of print on controversial subjects, and by all that is
holy if I got started on any kind of article on international
matters my remarks would most assuredly be controversial.

He finally did write an article on relations between the United
States and Japan, which was published in *Asia;* and he began
promoting the League of Nations once more, publicizing the
Woodrow Wilson Foundation, which he had established just
before he was taken ill. As a starter, he posed for a photograph
with Franklin, Jr., and John in the library of the Hyde Park
house, showing him as he presented them with membership
certificates to the Foundation. The boys wore their sailor suits,
and he had an arm around each of them as they stood by his
chair looking over the certificates, which bore Wilson's picture
at the top. It was good publicity for Franklin as well as the
Foundation; the ravages which suffering had left in his face—
deep lines between his brows and dark patches under his eyes—
were scarcely noticeable, and his expression was one of complete
serenity.

He was indeed quite happy with the progress he had made
during the summer, although by no means satisfied that this was

the best he could expect of his still "rebellious" legs. He planned to go to Boston again before returning to New York for the autumn because the braces needed further adjustment ("The left toe catches in or rubs along the ground," he wrote to Dr. Lovett on September 22); but the sun and water had done him so much good that he hoped to continue the treatment somehow. (If nothing else, he would buy a sun lamp, as one of his fellow victims had suggested in a letter.)

Politically, he succeeded in getting Al Smith nominated for a second term as governor of New York, principally through his advice to the Democratic nominating committee and an open letter to the newspapers calling on Smith to run. (He had become acquainted with "Al" when the latter was in the New York Assembly at the same time Franklin was State senator.) He and Louis planned these moves as they whittled and carved the balsa wood for the model boats, and worked them out later on with Judge Mack, Tom Lynch, and Henry Morgenthau Jr. He could not go to the nominating convention, but Eleanor went with Elinor Morgenthau—it was the first time women were permitted to take part in a state convention. When Smith was nominated over Hearst (who, Louis Howe reported, received "only five handclaps and about fifty hisses"), the two elated women (delegates) led the Dutchess County delegates three times around the hall in a cheering procession. Roosevelt chuckled at the picture as Howe described it; shy, retiring Eleanor was fast becoming a "lady politician," as Smith dubbed the two friends. "I am really sorry that you could not be there," he wrote to Franklin; "but take care of yourself—there is another day coming."

They were back in the house on Sixty-fifth Street before the end of September, and in October Franklin decided to try going to his insurance office at 120 Broadway for a few hours every day. (His own law offices—Marvin, Emmet, and Roosevelt, a firm he had formed with two friends in 1920, after the vice-presidential campaign—were downtown in a building that had a flight of stone steps in front; but there was only a single step at the

Broadway entrance, which he thought he could manage.) It was with some trepidation that he made the attempt that morning around the middle of October. A few people going past stopped to watch as he got out of the car, but he hardly noticed them.

He had mastered the technique of hauling himself from an automobile when he went to Hyde Park, but it would always require a good deal of concentration. He had to make sure his braces were locked in place, grab hold of the "jump-seat" and pull himself forward, project his stiff legs from the car, and push them in front of him. Then, clinging to the "jump-seat" and leaning on the armrest, he hoisted himself up and out of the car and shifted his weight to the driver, who stood at the door to help him, holding the crutches. Once these were under his arms, he relaxed, smiled almost triumphantly at a pretty young girl turning her head around as she went past, and made his slow path across the pavement, up the low step, and, even more slowly, across the marble-floored lobby to the elevator.

He had to watch out for the floor; it was polished and slippery.

A few mornings later, just after he had made it through the entrance, one of the rubber-tipped crutches failed to hold on the shiny surface, and he went crashing down! There was nothing to do but get himself up again; his driver wasn't strong enough to raise him. Roosevelt looked around at the people who had stopped when he fell, watching him sympathetically, but with the shyness of strangers, too reserved to offer help. Fixing on a young man with stocky shoulders, he called lightheartedly, as if this were nothing very unusual, "How about giving us a hand, young fellow?" The boy was glad to help; he and the driver lifted Franklin to his feet, from which point, with a nod and friendly smile at the tenants he knew by sight, he continued on his tedious way, aware of the eyes that followed him to the elevator, but not abashed by them. Left crutch, right foot; right crutch, left foot. . . .

Riding up to their floor, a small, dapper-looking man who had witnessed the incident and was impressed with the remarkable spirit Roosevelt had shown, introduced himself as a next-door neighbor in the building—he was a lawyer, Basil O'Connor. It was the beginning of an association that grew into a partnership which, in turn, became a lifelong friendship.

In spite of this unnerving incident, Franklin continued to come into the office for several hours a day. He would see Louis Howe and other close associates at home until ten-thirty, when he would leave for 120 Broadway. He always had lunch at his desk around one-thirty, sometimes with colleagues, who found him excellent company; he never referred to his illness nor complained about the way he was feeling, even when his legs bothered him, as they frequently did, because he was inclined to overtax them. He worked until four-thirty, when he went home for tea and exercises before dinner. After his fall, he sometimes let himself be wheeled into the building quickly, but he preferred trying to accustom himself to the crutches, with which he could at least approximate walking. He even wore the corset, to hold him erect, although he wrote to Dr. Lovett in November: "The corset I am getting on well with as far as walking goes, and in this I think it is a distinct help. It almost cuts me in two, however, when I sit down. I am more glad than ever that I do not belong to the other sex!"

When the November winds grew sharp and the rain pelted against the New York pavements, he had to skip his daily jaunt to the office because he didn't want to risk catching cold or falling. He missed the sun and the swimming exercises. He felt that he was losing some of the ground he had gained during the summer; and, although he felt much healthier and probably could have stood the weather better, he was not going to be cooped up another winter the way he had been a year before, until everyone in the house, including himself now and then, was ready to fly off the handle at the slightest upset.

He said nothing of the latter to anyone, but he began thinking of a trip to a warm climate—Florida perhaps—where he could

continue bathing in sun and water. As always, his mind turned
to boats, and he decided to investigate houseboats as a possibility.

"What I am looking for is a boat that is fairly low in the
water," he wrote to an agency late in November, "so that I can
easily drop overboard and crawl back on deck. Also, if possible,
a boat whose cabin is not down a ladder . . . I do not care a rap
about a luxurious craft . . ."

It was not until the end of January that he heard of a boat
which sounded feasible—the *Weona II,* owned by W. J. Henry
of St. Augustine, Florida. After some correspondence, he hired
the houseboat from February 16 to April 1. He was to take over
on the sixteenth, but before then a few slight changes had to be
made in the boat so that it would be functional for him. He
thought "a couple of rope-ends suspended in several places above
the steps," by which he could pull himself up and let himself
down, would be all he needed to navigate the steps—much better
than a chair with a wide board against the tread, suggested by
Captain Henry, owner of the boat. In his letter, Franklin wanted
to know the exact number of steps (and their dimensions) on
the ladder from the saloon to the deckhouse, and also whether
there were any steps from the low afterdeck down into the cabin.
These were considerations he never would have dreamed he
would be making in the days when he sailed the *Half Moon* or
her successors along the Atlantic Coast, but he did so now with
interest and care and without any audible sighs for his past
agility. (His uncle Fred's advice to look forward and not backward had been, all along, more of a corroboration of his own
attitude than a piece of counsel.)

When the alterations had been made, Franklin and Eleanor,
accompanied by Louis Howe and Esther Lape (the last was a
lawyer Eleanor had come to know well in her political work),
went to Fort Myers on the train, and from there embarked on
the *Weona II* for a cruise to Miami and the Florida Keys.

As soon as Franklin felt the warm sunshine and sea breezes he
began to take up the outdoor exercises again, practicing with

the crutches on deck and "walking" as he hung onto a rectangle of railings he had put in on board. They all tried fishing, and his luck was best. To Eleanor, life on a houseboat seemed rather confined and, at night, when they anchored in the dark, tropical waters of the Keys, it "all seemed eerie and menacing"; but as long as Franklin was improving, she was more than willing to put up with the strangeness, the inconveniences, and the nightmare of shopping for provisions in noisy Miami. In the evenings, they had a good deal of discussion about the Bok Peace Plan Awards, of which Esther had just been put in charge. Franklin had long been thinking of ways to remedy the shortcomings of the League of Nations, and now decided to try his hand at devising a peace plan to enter in the Bok Foundation awards. He and Esther had many conversations about it as they rested on deck or lounged on some beach where they docked. (The sun-warmed sand felt good as he piled it over his pipestem legs; he had strained some ligaments when he slipped going down the ladder on board, and after that spent more time lounging in the sand.)

His first three companions had to get back to their duties at home, but four others (two of Roosevelt's business associates and their wives) were taking their places; so Eleanor, Esther, and Louis got ready to leave just as the two couples arrived "in store clothes"—Franklin's term for anything more formal than fishing togs and a floppy old sun hat or a bathing suit.

As the cruise entered its second lap, Franklin decided a log should be kept, as on any good ship. One of the first entries began: "All up betimes (whenever that may be)." And the next day, when they headed up Little Shark River: "Three o'clock, all started trolling up the fascinating winding river, stared at curiously by bold pelicans and shy herons." A few days later, when a ten-pound red grouper had been the lone catch, he entered: "For lack of fish (trolling upstream in a small boat) the party tried to console themselves with spying out sweet bay leaves, red orchids [half-hidden in the grey veils of hanging moss] and at least 8 varieties of winged fowls in the air—blue and white heron, Florida duck, ibis, aigrette, water turkey, kingfisher, and swallow-tail kite." In March they were at anchor in Tussock Key, a deserted spot, where he referred to the "early morning bathers, *au naturelle*," and at night to the "marvelous political talky-talk" that went on till all hours. On days when the party made a good catch, they ate fish for breakfast, lunch, and dinner; on other days they had to resort to cans most of the time.

In safe waters (where the current was not too strong and they did not have to beat off the sharks), he swam and picnicked on the beach with his guests, who came in "shifts" to keep him company; he sun-bathed and crawled around in the sand. Always, always he worked to strengthen his legs. The muscles were flabby as dough—what was left of them. One of the doctors had said that forty per cent of the weight lost by polio patients was dropped by damaged muscles, and it was very difficult to bring that weight back to normal, because those muscles had to be exercised so slowly, at first only by gentle massage, then by mechanical exercise, like stretching, done with the help of the therapist's skillful hands. (In cases like his, where the nerve injury was severe, it was a long time before a patient regained control over the movement of those muscles, and frequently it was only partial; sometimes control never returned, but this possibility he never countenanced.) Braces gave support to paralyzed legs, but nothing more, so far as he could tell in the length of time he had worn them. His calves still looked skeletal, thin as the steering post of a car; his thighs were not much bigger around than a milk bottle; his buttocks had withered considerably.

The undamaged muscles of a polio victim, however, doubled and sometimes tripled in strength, because they were constantly in use. Franklin's shoulders and arm muscles grew apace, but the legs lagged stubbornly behind; yet he kept just as stubbornly working with them. And when the cruise was over in April, he wrote Dr. Lovett that he was "convinced there is a vast improvement in the legs muscles. While on the houseboat," he continued, "I worked out a number of mechanical problems," and went on to describe the equipment he had put on the boat.

There were signs of spring in New York when he returned: patches of green lit up Madison Square Park, he noticed on the morning ride to the office, and the pigeons were nesting along the ledges of the building at 120 Broadway. He was less self-conscious about using the crutches than he had been in October, not only because he could manage them better, but because his generally improved health gave him a feeling of greater confidence. He and Basil O'Connor were becoming good friends, and before long were consulting each other on law cases.

It was too early to make the move to Hyde Park for the summer, so he concentrated on finishing the first draft of a peace plan which he had begun on board the houseboat. Eleanor had been asked to serve as one of the judges in the Bok Foundation, so he probably would not submit his plan if she accepted the post; but he wanted to put his ideas down on paper while they were uppermost in his mind, and he wanted to have a permanent record of them for possible use in later years. The defects of the League of Nations, which were becoming more apparent as the months went by, especially after the United States refused to join, distressed Roosevelt deeply, and he determined to design a project which could be more easily carried out.

He started an active reorganization of the Boy Scout movement in New York State and kept accepting posts in other groups until Louis said he would soon be connected with every club in New York City. Both of them kept a constant finger on the political pulse.

Toward the end of May the whole family gathered at Hyde Park again; James and Elliott, who were both at Groton (the latter under loud protest) came as soon as school was out. Louis, Missy, and various guests from time to time made up the household over which Sara Roosevelt reigned like a queen. She was happiest when all her "children" (she considered Franklin's five

more as her own than as grandchildren) were under the maternal
roof, where she could direct their lives according to her dictates—
at least in her own mind—and Franklin let her remain under
the delusion as long as her regulations were more or less to his
liking. Upon occasion he could be as stubborn as she, and he
usually won out. But, for the most part, he was too busy concentrating on his recovery to bother opposing her on what seemed
to him minor matters compared to the major issue he had won—
his refusal to retire.

He entered on a strict routine, just as he had the summer
before. In the morning he did the exercises and then went out
to the parallel bars, wearing only one brace now. He found that
his right leg was stronger than his left and, in order to strengthen
it more, he thought it would be better not to rely on the brace
when he was using the iron bars to support most of his weight
as he dragged along. Up and down, up and down the length
of them he went, trying various other exercises as well, each
time working longer than he had the previous summer. He felt
more and more that braces did nothing to further his recovery,
if they did not actually hinder it. "A leg in a brace does not have
a chance for muscle development," he wrote to a friend. "This
muscle development must come through exercise when the brace
is not on—such as swimming, etc."

That year, instead of attempting to reach the gateposts on
his crutches, which Dan Draper decided might prove a strain on
his heart, he tried a mild form of horseback riding. At around
one o'clock every day he would "ride" for an hour, which meant
nothing more than having Anna lead a gentle pony around the
grounds while her father, mounted on its back with the help of
two men, tried to increase his sense of balance by remaining
astride. He and Anna both enjoyed this period when they could
have a visit together, free of the many outside interests besides
the other physical therapy which absorbed most of Franklin's
hours. In the afternoon they all swam and sun-bathed, as before.

He wrote an account of the way he was spending the summer

to Mrs. Lake, one of the nurses he had had, and he ended with the comment: "I am convinced that the muscles are vastly better than when I last saw you." He repeated his conviction that sun "helps tremendously" and confided to her that he was taking a few osteopathic treatments; but he told her to keep it confidential, as he did not want Dr. Lovett to know, since the doctor objected to osteopathy.

He found a delightful means of exercising when he was sitting in the old double-swing down in the apple orchard one afternoon, and he wrote about it to a fellow-patient he had become acquainted with in Dr. Lovett's office—a Mr. Abram Elkus from Indiana, who wrote suggesting a rowing machine, adding a question about the national Democratic situation. Roosevelt answered that Dr. Lovett had said he was not ready for a rowing machine yet, but he went on: "I have tried an old-fashioned double-swing. I sit in one seat, put my feet in the other seat and push down and pull up with my legs, thereby making the swing go forward and backward. It seems to develop my knee muscles in a splendid way."

Then, after mentioning a possible cruise in Buzzard's Bay aboard the boat of a Harvard classmate, John Lawrence (when he expected the salt water and the pulling of himself about the docks to be "excellent for muscles"), he turned to politics: "I am having an amusing and strenuous time over local politics in the Hudson River Valley. We are doing some fine organizing work—especially with the aid of the ladies, and as you have probably read, we are trying to get John E. Mack nominated for the Court of Appeals.

"I have heard little since I saw you in regard to the national situation. I cannot help feeling that Harding's unfortunate taking off * has helped rather than hurt the Democratic Party. Coolidge, as you know, is not a world-beater, but in his past career he has been clever enough to take advantage of situations after the other fellow has done all the work. Witness the Boston

* Harding died earlier in 1923.

Police strike, where Andrew Peters practically settled things before Coolidge made any move. It looks now to me as if he would be nominated next year. He will be considered, of course, a conservative, and that means we must nominate a Progressive without fail.

"Personally, I cannot see the strength of Underwood or Ralston. I wish that Al Smith would express some views on national questions. He is not yet regarded as a truly national figure. It goes without saying that I should of course be delighted if he could be nominated, but honestly I feel that the odds are against it at the present time."

He and Louis, along with members of the Democratic State Executive Committee, had discussed the possibility of Governor Smith as a presidential candidate for some time, but this was the first he had mentioned it to anyone outside the close political circle around him, and he wondered whether he was perhaps a little previous. This man, an acquaintance in the Middle West, might be a good sounding board. Franklin knew that the question of religion would play a part in the campaign if Al Smith ran, but he also felt strongly that it should not be a consideration in a country that was supposed to be a democracy. His position was that if Al Smith merited the nomination on the basis of his record, he should get it; and he—Franklin—would stick to his belief no matter what opposition he might encounter. He had said at the time he was battling Tammany Hall, "I love a good fight!" And he would always feel that way. The same instinct for battle gave him the spirit to combat his paralysis, but he never would let this personal bout take over. His first interest and love in the outside world was politics, and no matter what else was bothering him or taking his time (like the physical therapy), politics would always come before.

He had a quiet time to think and to work with Louis before he set off for Buzzard's Bay. His mother decided that James and Anna were of an age when they "should" see Europe, so she whisked them off. Eleanor was taking the two youngest boys,

Henry Roosevelt (her nephew), and young George Draper (the doctor's son) on a camping trip through eastern Canada and northern Maine to Lubec, from which point they were to take off for a couple of weeks at Campobello. (It was quite an undertaking, but she would have the able assistance of Marion Dickerman, a friend she had found in her political work, with whom she was planning to start a small factory for hand-finished furniture.) Elliott was going with Franklin on John Lawrence's boat.

Franklin considered sailing up to Campobello to meet the "gypsy" party, but he felt he had too much work to do at Hyde Park getting his legs into shape (he was only going to Buzzard's Bay for a short time), and he had no desire to return to Campobello. Not yet. "You go, Babs," he said. "The rest of the family might as well have the pleasure of the place." He smiled. "I'll wait till I can run up the cliff road from Welchpool Harbor to the house again!" He knew how frustrating it would be to see his beloved Campobello from a wheel chair; the agony he had gone through there in his illness did not bother him as much as the thought of not being able to enter into all the sports— to play two rounds of golf on the course he had laid out and plunge into the icy Bay of Fundy afterwards. Now the thought of putting one toe in that chilly water made him shudder!

The cruise with John Lawrence (a good part of the time they stayed in port, living on the boat) proved so pleasant that the two old friends decided to spend some time on a houseboat together in the winter. Franklin's enthusiasm for the *Weona* trip was infectious. By October they were beginning to talk about buying a houseboat! The project would require some figuring. Franklin's illness had already cost thousands of dollars, and the cash outlay for a boat would be hard to manage just now. They could not expect to find what they wanted for under five thousand dollars, and it seemed a lot to pay for something he would use only a few months of the year. Lawrence had heard of a boat they could buy for a little under four thousand, but it would take nearly another thousand to fix it up. The children's education was no small expense each year, and while his mother would have taken it over gladly, Franklin wanted to be as independent as he could under the circumstances.

He and Eleanor discussed the matter pro and con until far into the night, until he finally decided wearily, "Well, I might as well write Johnny to go ahead; at least that way I won't be a burden to anyone!" The bitterness in his voice was a shock to his wife: they had all tried so hard to overlook his handicap; the two youngest boys certainly seemed scarcely aware that their father had been ill, or was in any way different from the father they had always known. (Or if they noticed the change, they were young enough to accept it easily.) Franklin himself had taken the lead in making light of his disability with a quip or a joke. Until this moment she had never realized the extent of his gallantry, but she never forgot it—and she never again heard him make a "bitter remark" about his paralysis.

Eventually word came that the houseboat under consideration was purchased and repaired. (In his letter, Lawrence included a political postscript: "Has Cal Coolidge interfered with your plans, or my likelihood of being the next Secretary of the Navy?") The next question was the name of the boat, which must be a combination of Roosevelt and Lawrence, they agreed. At first they thought of *Larose* or *Rosela,* but in the end they hit upon *Larooco,* which included the abbreviation "Co." And John pointed out that "the double O and seven letters have usually been typical of good luck in yachts." The *Larooca* was an old scow to say the least, and so needed a sign of good fortune in its name.

On his own boat a more elaborate log must be kept. Louis Howe designed the cover for it, painting a water color of "the Patron Saints of All True Fisherfolk" (i.e., liars), St. Ananias and St. Sapphira, to whom the logbook was dedicated. Together, he and Franklin drafted a set of "Rules For Log-Book Scribes."

I

This log-book must be kept entirely accurate and truthful. In putting down weights and measures of fish, however, the following rules may be used:

Weights: 2 ozs. make 1 log-book 1b.
5 oz. make "a large fish."
2 "large fish"—"a record day's catch."

Measures: 2 inches make 1 log-book foot.
2 log-book feet make "big as a whale."

Anything above whale size may be described as an "Ichyosaurus."

Note: In describing fish that got away, all these measurements may be doubled;—it is also permitted, when over 30 seconds are required to pull in a fish, to say, "After half an hour's hard fighting . . ."

II

The poetically inclined are warned that *Larooco* does not rhyme with "Morocco." Also the combinations, "knows-I-felt" to rhyme with Roosevelt & "saw hence" to rhyme with Lawrence, are not permitted.

III

Verbatim reports of the private conversations of the chief engineer with his carburetor must be represented only thus: xx!!—??—xx—!"

An additional note ruled that "all references to 'community life' must be written in code."

With this set of accommodating rules, the *Larooco* started merrily on its first cruise. Its crew consisted of Captain and Mrs. Robert J. Morris, who served as skipper and housekeeper-cook, and the engineer. Missy LeHand came along, as before, to take care of correspondence, and the list of guests ranged from relatives to diplomats and politicians—Ex-Governor James Cox of

Ohio, William Jennings Bryan, and a number of Dutchess
County Democrats—Tom Lynch, Henry Morgenthau, Jr., and
J. C. Penney were among the companions on the cruises. Franklin made most of the entries himself in his long, slanted hand-
writing, with its generous flourishes and dashes. The opening
entry was dated "Sunday, February 3, 1924: Gave all hands
the opportunity to go to church. No takers. Hence left dock
at 11:30 A.M., proceeding down St. John's River about 18 miles,
thence south into canal. Very narrow channel and little water.
Most of the way a straight cut through young pine lands. Moored
to old piling at 5:30 P.M., 2 or 3 miles short of the toll chain.
Pondered deeply over interior decorations (of boat—not myself)
—green or light blue—or both." Later he recorded that he had
painted three quarters of a chair a "booful blue," and the Sunday
edition of the *Miami Herald* showed him hard at work in his
straight wheel chair, paintbrush in hand, a broad smile on his
face. Louis, who never missed an opportunity for publicity, saw
to it that the papers pictured a Roosevelt well on his way toward
becoming robust and active again. One of the doctors he had
consulted in the summer had written to him: "There is one
thing about this infantile paralysis—you will get progressively
better year by year until you die"; to which he had replied,
"That is mighty encouraging!" And he seemed to be proving the
prediction.

What was more, he made a kind of ritual out of feeling better,
not only year by year, but day by day. He taught himself to go
to sleep immediately at night, shutting off the complex currents
of the day as if by a light switch, and to wake up with the immediate thought that he was feeling better than he had the day
before. In France, a doctor named Emile Coué had been ac-
corded world-wide fame for his psychological approach toward
achieving a healthy life, the simple formula for which was the
repetition of the words: "Day by day in every way I'm feeling
better and better." Franklin had discovered such a formula for
himself, but it did not require the mechanical repetition of a
few words. His was an attitude of mind that sprung from greater

depths and needed no Mumbo Jumbo to make it effective. His was an unexpressed thought that was sounded within him each day like the reassuring peal of morning bells, and it sang out more strongly with each succeeding day as he went through his exercises and practiced with the crutches. He offered to send a record of his own private treatment to the worthy Coué, but so far had had no response.

His third notation in the log began briskly (February 5): "Bought 23-ft. sea-skiff (Dory-type), 7 ft. beam, 2 cycle Bridgeport engine. Tried her out in St. Augustine Bay for about an hour, then bought her from Mr. George Washington Corbett for $375. At six Maunsell Crosby came on board, just in from New York." (Crosby was a Rhinebeck neighbor Sara Roosevelt had suggested, an amateur ornithologist who proved to be an excellent companion.) But the entry ended solemnly: "Yesterday when approaching the town, we saw the flags at half-mast—President Wilson died Sunday morning. Our own ensign will remain at half-mast for thirty days." Nowhere was the loss to the world more keenly felt than on that Florida houseboat.

After two weeks of erratic but delightful cruising, the temperamental *Larooco* came into port at Palm Beach but tarried no more than half a day. That night (Sunday, Februray 17) Franklin scribbled in the log: "In the morning M.S.C. and I went ashore and motored all over Palm Beach for about an hour; not having been here since 1904, I found the growth of mushroom millionaire houses luxuriant. The women we saw went well with the place, and we desired to meet them no more than we wished to remain in the harbor an hour more than necessary. Up anchor at 1, and with starboard engine running well and port engine coughing spasmodically, we got down to the south end of Lake Worth and anchored for the night." They rose early to catch sight of any birds that might emerge from the moss-covered trees along the shore, or the waterfowl parading on the beach. Maunsell's knowledge of birds was a constant joy (his full name,

Maunsell Schiefflin Crosby, was well known among naturalists, as he had been on many expeditions for the American Museum of Natural History): by the second day of his visit he had identified "33 different kinds of birds," according to the log. On February 18 Franklin noted: "Maunsell has identified *98* different kinds of birds." He could not help ribbing his friend with a dreamed-up species: "the pink Bazoo," which Crosby acknowledged with a gracious grin. He was a delightful companion, and in one of the letters to the elder Mrs. Roosevelt about the cruise Franklin thanked her for having suggested their neighbor. He continued: "The *Larooco* is impossible to steer in a wind as she is shallow and high and has not enough power." The *Blue Laroo,* as she was dubbed, was to give them plenty of engine trouble, but to Franklin it only made the cruise more interesting.

On Sunday, "2/24/24," the log read: "M.S.C. left for home at 10 P.M. He saw 99 different bird species on the trip. We shall miss him much." A week later the mail brought a long nonsense rhyme, *Those Laroo Blues,* which rivaled even Edward Lear and was sent "with profuse apologies to everybody concerned" from M.S.C. It began:

> *The* Blue Laroo *had a doughty crew*
> *When she sailed for My-am-eye.*
> *Her mast was tall, but her draught was small,*
> *Though her cargo was gin and rye.*

In numerous stanzas the eccentricities were described in detail, and "Part 2" opened:

> *Oh, day after day, in the self-same way,*
> *She turned and she swerved and she blew.*
> *There was never a ship that could spin and slip*
> *Like the Beautiful* Blue Laroo.
>
> *Oh, I'd like to sail on the back of a whale*
> *Or ride on a dangerous gnu,*

> *But never again will I go amain*
> *On the beautiful* Blue Laroo.

Delighted, Franklin sent back a piece of doggerel about the *Blue Laroo* rising up to meet the "pink Bazoo." He could be as outrageous in his humor as anyone else! (One night he referred in the log to "the usual game of Ma and Pa Cheesy.")

But if clowning provided entertainment and relaxation, it by no means filled the hours outside of the daily routine of physical therapy. He began a project he had long threatened, a history of the United States. Armed with an oversize (8½" x 14") pad of yellow lined paper and a number of books he had been consulting, he set about writing an introduction that would present his point of view in regard to history, which included the social significance of events as well as the record of them. He would analyze the conditions which brought about the discovery of America, rather than present a mere statement of the facts. Once started, he wrote a couple of hours every day, sometimes on deck, with the pad resting on his knees. He revised as he went along, leaving smudgy inkblots between the lines, or putting in marginal arrows here and there to indicate which sentences should be linked together.

Only two guests came aboard after Maunsell left—Eleanor Henessey, a friend of Missy's, who stayed only a week; and Livingston Davis, who arrived while the *Larooco* was tied up in Tavernier Creek; he "looks like a sick child," Franklin recorded, "and is recuperating from shingles, boils, bunions, and a cold in the head."

The sixth of April, Sunday, he spent "a quiet morning answering lots of mail and exercising with canes and crutches." In the afternoon he and Missy went fishing and "had a very exciting time." He hooked a tarpon, but after an eight-minute struggle "the hook pulled out! He looked like a fish of about 30 pounds." A few minutes later Franklin landed a "fine Kingfish, about 12 pounds," and Missy got a grouper, "next a very big 7 lb. snapper." Missy, for all her fragile appearance, had a sturdy hand with a rod and reel; its firmness often netted her a catch when another female would have settled for a strike.

Missy was one of those rare people who could be both active and quiet, efficient and understanding, serious and humorous. She went about fishing, swimming, shopping for supplies, and playing rummy or pachisi with the same subtle energy she applied in taking dictation or at her typewriter. More than once on this cruise she had seen her "boss" put down by a depression so severe that it would be noon before he could pull out of it and face his guests with the lighthearted manner at which they marveled. Yet she never pried, nor attempted superficially to "cheer him up," but stood calmly by till he was ready. She never spoke of these spells, because she knew he would come out of them, and he always did.

Franklin had hoped that some of the "chicks" could come down during their spring vacations; he had received a telegram saying that Anna probably could not make it, but that Elliott would. In the end neither of them did, and now the cruise was almost over. The *Larooco* left the Keys on April 10, heading for Miami. The log entry on Sunday, April 13, read: "Capt. and Mrs. Morris, M.A.L. and I went to Bear's Cut for a picnic lunch and final swim. At sundown *Larooco* went out of commission and at 10:30 P.M. ½ owner F.D.R. left for New York. *Larooco* goes to yard tomorrow and will be cared for by Atlantic Boat Works. So ends Cruise no. 1."

From New York on April 29, F.D.R. wrote to the other half owner, John Lawrence (who was unable to make use of his share at any time): "I can only say as a general proposition that the cruise was perfectly delightful. *Larooco* is the most comfortable and livable boat in Florida. We had engine trouble, lots of it, but we knew we were going to have engine trouble before we left."

He felt refreshed, stronger, though far from as mobile as he wished to be. But mobile or not, he was ready for political action.

CHAPTER VIII

Miracle Weapon—Warm Springs

TWO DAYS LATER, on May 1, he accepted the post of manager for Al Smith in the preconvention campaign that Louis and a few others had organized to promote the Governor's nomination for president. Both Eleanor and Franklin had announced their support of Smith publicly in February, just before the cruise; the name of Roosevelt was nationally known and would insure the vote of the Wilson Democrats; at the same time, some of Smith's advisers observed, a man who had to direct the campaign from a wheel chair wouldn't hamper their activities and they could do things pretty much as they pleased; Franklin Roosevelt was the ideal choice.

They reckoned without his spirit and enthusiasm: once he had decided that he could take a month off from his physical rehabilitation without losing the ground he had gained so far, he threw himself into the political campaign, assuming full charge with a vigor that brooked no opposition from ambitious office-seekers or politicians. The little staff around him worked loyally and hard. Eleanor made speeches before women's clubs, parent-teacher groups, and state-wide conferences. (Louis went along with her the first few times and sat in the back to criticize so he could help her. Afterwards he pointed out that she giggled in several instances when there was nothing to laugh at, and she realized that she had been covering up her nervousness. To break her of the habit, Louis mimicked her and it sounded so inane she went through the rest of the campaign without a flutter. His advice was short and pointed: "Have something you want to say, say it, and sit down.")

Roosevelt showed such command in his management that Al Smith, who had been searching for someone to give the nominating address, came to him late in May with the request that "Frank" should be the one to place his name before the delegates. Now that he was back in the political fray, Franklin found the offer too tempting to resist, though how he would manage to get up to the podium he was not sure.

During the first week in June the family moved to Hyde Park as usual, where he continued his activities. One sunny afternoon his neighbor and tenant farmer, Moses Smith, who had dropped by for a chat, found him sitting on a blanket at the side of the road, a pad of paper in his lap.

"What do you think I'm doing?" Franklin called out as he came up, "—writing my nominating speech for Al Smith!"

He found it exhilarating. He had been watching the Governor's progressive program from the sidelines; from time to time Eleanor brought people to visit him: women like Maude Schwartz, Rose Schneiderman, and others she had met at the Trade Union League; Lillian D. Wald, Marion Dickerman, and Nancy Cook; Mrs. Carrie Chapman Catt and Mary Simkovitch (the social worker who, with her husband, founded Greenwich House in New York City). Because he had to sit and listen, because he still felt the tremendous curiosity he had always shown toward life in general, and because he had an innate love of people, he listened intently to the stories he heard. He learned a great deal about the co-operative movement from Maude Schwartz—about its success in England, its failure to get a foothold in America; he learned much more about the struggle of the needleworkers from Rose Schneiderman in an hour or two than he had in the three years he had been State senator, when he had been only half-aware of the difficulties under which they and other workers labored. He realized that it was as arduous for them to take one step forward as it was for him. Al Smith, born on the lower East Side in New York, had been slowly instituting a few reforms, and Franklin, impressed with the improvements he had made so far on the state level, thought that the Governor should have the chance to try out his ideas on a national level. If his delivery of the nominating speech would help, Franklin was ready (not to say eager) to accommodate, but both he and Louis were well aware that a thousand arrangements had to be made before he could do it.

He began by practicing a new way of propelling himself—using only one crutch, shoved under his right arm. He found that if he had a strong arm to grip with his left hand, he could swing on his arms and shoulders and bring his body and braced legs forward by sheer strength. He always made sure the braces were locked, for without the rigid steel he could not stay upright. He tried out the method with Louis Depew, taking the gravel path in front of the house; but when James, now sixteen and six feet tall, came home from school for summer vacation, he took the chauffeur's place, holding his lean, muscular arm for his father's support.

Together they practiced every day, until James had learned to synchronize his pace with his father's tortuous movements so that they went forward at the same time; he learned to replace his look of anxiety with an easy smile the way his "Pa" did, so that they appeared almost to be strolling along the gravel path. They talked about the convention and when, one morning, Franklin asked, "Jimmy, would you care to come along and lend me your arm?" his son was so elated he could hardly maintain a slackened gait. He was to be his Father's page!

Near the end of June the whole family went into New York for convention week. Franklin was a member of the New York State delegation and announced his intention of attending all the sessions on the floor at Madison Square Garden with his fellow delegates. Louis arranged to have a chair with arms set in for him, but otherwise he wanted no concession to his handicap. Above all, he was not going to appear in a wheel chair.

Eleanor was in charge of the committee presenting the resolutions on legislation for women to the Resolutions Committee and had to be at her post outside the door where the important meetings went on, waiting to get her resolutions in, and waiting again to find out what was happening to them. It was Jimmy's job (using the crutch-and-arm method they had developed) to get Franklin into the great hall early, so that the floor would not be too clogged for passage. A heat wave marked the opening of the convention and lasted till the dragged-out sessions drew to a close, but it was a minor consideration compared to the supreme effort it took for Franklin merely to get seated. When he and Jimmy reached the chair, they stood beside it a few seconds, Jimmy supporting him and taking his crutch. Then he grasped the arms of the chair and slowly lowered himself into the seat. (They had practiced this at home for a few days before the convention until he had perfected the technique.)

From the first it went smoothly, and he was usually settled by the time his fellow delegates came in. The galleries, however, had a good view of the arduous procedure, and after two or three sessions, he was welcomed by a round of applause as he made his way on Jimmy's arm to his place in the hall. He was able to relax once he was seated, and he began to enjoy himself immediately: there was nothing quite like the national convention, for all its noise and confusion! Even when the clamor of demonstrations started, and delegates rose wildly to parade, he was unperturbed (though Jimmy's face showed plainly that he was afraid his father might get hurt). It was good to be back in the midst of the hullabaloo, handicap or no.

He decided, furthermore, that when the time came for the nominating address he would go to the rostrum alone—it would be better that way.

The day of his speech there was quite a family gathering in the anteroom off the platform: Eleanor, knitting furiously to preserve her customary calm (she had knitted all during the convention, and Will Rogers, sidling up to the box one day, queried, "Knitting in the names of the future victims of the guillotine?"); his mother, wearing a pleased, expectant smile, even though she disapproved of "that vulgar Al Smith with his brown derby and his everlasting cigar"; Anna, excited for the first time during the convention; Elliott; and Jimmy, ready with his arm to escort his father to the rear of the platform. (And, of course, Missy and Louis were there, the latter fuming with apprehension and chain cigarettes.) It was unbearably hot and stifling in the little room.

At last the signal came, and they started toward the platform, Jimmy carrying the second crutch. Franklin felt confident, yet keyed to a high pitch inside; though he hardly realized it, the perspiration was pouring from his brow and his grasp on Jimmy's arm was like a vise. Just as they reached the spot back of the speaker's box, a sudden thought struck him: what if it wasn't strong enough to hold him?

"Shake the rostrum!" he let out a loud whisper at Joseph Guffey, the national committeeman from Pennsylvania, who was seated near there. He had to call out twice before the bewildered Guffey realized that he wanted to make sure it would bear his weight. At a nod from the committeeman, he took the other crutch from a now-shaking Jimmy and swung forward with high courage. He couldn't lift his arms, so he lifted his head way up and back, greeting the throng in front of him with a broad smile; when he got to the podium, his salute was returned with a roar of cheers above the heartfelt applause.

He began to speak, acquiring more and more confidence as he progressed toward the actual nomination: "He has a power to strike at error and wrongdoing that makes his adversaries quail before him. He has a personality that carries to every hearer not only the sincerity but the righteousness of what he says. He is the 'Happy Warrior' of the political battlefield. . . ."

He could hardly make the candidate's name heard over the tumultuous acclamation, which began before he had finished the sentence (with its felicitous phrase that was to become one of the most famous in the history of political speechmaking), and ended one hour and thirteen minutes later! He received what was probably the longest demonstration the Garden had ever witnessed.

The day after the balloting began, a columnist in the *Herald Tribune* wrote: "From the time Roosevelt made his speech in nomination of Smith, which was the one great speech of the convention, he has been easily the foremost figure on floor or platform. That is not because of his name. There are many Roosevelts. It is because, without the slightest intention or desire to do anything of the sort, he has done for himself what he could not do for his candidate.

"Believing Roosevelt to be out of reach, the delegates cast a lingering look at him over their shoulders and renewed the search for somebody who could be nominated . . . But always back to Roosevelt their gaze would go, and more than once it was found expedient to hush a little delegation which was talking about sending up his name, lest unforeseen results might happen . . ."

Six days later, while the balloting dragged on and Smith still had not received the nomination, the *Evening World* remarked: "No matter whether Governor Smith wins or loses, Franklin D. Roosevelt stands out as the real hero of the Democratic convention of 1924.

"Adversity has lifted him above the bickering, the religious bigotry, conflicting personal ambitions and petty sectional prejudices. It has made him the one leader commanding the respect and admiration from all sections of the land . . . Roosevelt might be a pathetic, tragic figure but for the fine courage that flashes in his smile. It holds observers enchained. . . ."

Al Smith did not win the nomination that year, but Franklin, reading the accounts with the rest of the family, felt well satisfied with his own political comeback. However, he was not at all satisfied with his physical comeback: his legs must become much stronger, his "walking" much smoother, before he would attend another convention. He was of course getting "better and better every day," but the process was too slow. He must find some way to speed it up.

He went back to Hyde Park for the remainder of the summer to resume the exercises and swimming; he made arrangements for the building of their own pool and for the cottage beside it that was to house the furniture factory as well as living quarters for Nancy Cook and Marion Dickerman, Eleanor's two partners. (This project, patterned after a similar one in Vermont, was to give employment to farmers around Dutchess County during the off season when the crops were harvested and there was little to do on the farm. Franklin was enormously interested in helping the farmers, especially the young hands, who were apt to drift to the cities for factory jobs when there was not enough work or profit in tilling the soil.)

He continued to see various friends as he walked forth and back along the parallel bars, and one of those who visited him was George Foster Peabody, a wealthy New York banker. Peabody told him of a pool at Warm Springs, Georgia, whose waters had brought about an almost complete cure of a local boy who had been stricken by infantile paralysis three years before and was unable to walk at the time he started bathing in the warm water. It was known to have marvelous properties, Peabody said. He talked so much about the place (on which he had an option) that Franklin decided to investigate its possibilities in the fall, before he went down to Florida to get the *Larooco* out of dry dock.

Early in September he was writing to John Lawrence about the plans for the second cruise. He hoped John would be able to join them for part of it at least. Then, since he had made a couple of speeches for John W. Davis, the candidate the Democrats had finally chosen, he added a political postscript concerning the third-party (Farm-Labor) candidate's chances: "A political flea in your ear for what it is worth—The La Follette vote even through the East is much larger than any of us have any idea of. Of course this may change before the election, but my personal opinion is that if the election were held tomorrow neither Coolidge nor Davis would obtain a majority in the electoral college, and the election would be thrown in the House. This of course is highly confidential—don't use my name."

The following month he and Eleanor took the train for Warm Springs. When the engine stopped at the sleepy little station, badly in need of paint, half obscured by scrub pine, the prospects for a health resort in the neighborhood did not seem too promising, but Franklin, coming out to the back platform on his crutches, was cheery and optimistic.

"Any room out there for me?" he called good-naturedly to the little group waiting to meet him, including Tom Loyless, the lessee-manager of Warm Springs, Mrs. Loyless, and Roy, a strapping young Negro assigned to help in the cottage the Roosevelts were going to use. Roy's strong arms were needed at once as Franklin had to be carried off the train. "Now sideways down the steps," he advised Roy, who picked him up easily.

On the drive out to the resort, the scenery improved; he noticed especially one "beautiful stand of pine." Eleanor, characteristically, noticed the poverty and neglect of much of the land, the miserable little shacks of the Negroes. The resort itself, though they had been prepared by Tom Loyless on the way, was even more dreary and unpromising than the station. A shabby old hotel, perched precariously on the hillside, adorned with the clapboard cupolas and frilled porches of the nineties, the Meriwether Inn offered far from a merry welcome to their eyes as the car turned in the main driveway; Franklin labeled it at a glance a "first-class fire-trap." Luckily the Roosevelts were going to stay at the cottage of some local people, the Harts. Their place, next door to the Loyless', was one of a handful of cottages scattered around the area near the pool, which made up the "resort."

Originally a fashionable "watering-place" before Civil War

days, Warm Springs had long since fallen into disrepair and was a far cry from others of its kind, like White Sulphur Springs or the Spa at Nauheim, Germany, where Franklin had gone with his parents as a boy. Meriwether Inn had been rebuilt around the turn of the century and had enjoyed a brief period of popularity, but with the advent of the automobile, people from Columbus and other neighboring towns went farther afield to find a cool spot in the summer. Warm Springs soon became neglected, the inn sagged, the grounds were overgrown; in 1919, when Tom Loyless had taken over the managership on an annual lease basis, the resort was all but a ruin. He had been struggling since then to put the place back on its feet.

The second summer he was there, he told Franklin and Eleanor, the Joseph family had built a cottage on the slope and their son, Louis, who was recuperating from infantile paralysis, came to the pool to swim every day. By the end of the summer the boy showed enough improvement to arouse medical interest from his physician, Dr. Johnson, and to give Loyless the idea of promoting Warm Springs as a health resort. By the end of three summers, when Louis Joseph was walking without crutches, everyone was proclaiming a miracle. According to legend, the mineral waters had long been noted for certain restorative powers. The Creek Indians brought their wounded warriors to the springs for healing, and they so revered the spot that anyone traveling to the "warm waters" was granted safe conduct; no tribal warfare could take place on the hallowed ground. In the early days of the resort, the waters were featured as "a specific for all cutaneous diseases, and one of the best remedies for chronic rheumatism, chronic diseases of the liver, kidney, and bladder." But the Joseph boy's results went beyond all claims that had ever before been made.

The particular quality of the water, its buoyancy, which enabled people to stay in two hours and longer without feeling tired, came from its high mineral content. The geological explanation of Warm Springs was that the rain, falling on Pine

Mountain five miles away, "runs down 3,800 feet to a deep pocket of rock, where it is warmed by the inner earth, and then returned to the surface at a temperature of 88 degrees F., and at a rate of 800 gallons per minute." (Engineers estimated that it would take twenty tons of coal every twenty-four hours to duplicate this feat of nature.) The heated water gushed out at the base of a hill and flowed into a cistern under the cement floor of the pool.

If it were not for the huge rectangular pool, 50 by 150 feet, full of the warm mineral water, there would have been little incentive to spend even a night at Warm Springs. But as soon as Franklin had his first dip—he sat on the brink beforehand, dangling his feet in the "marvelous" eighty-eight-degree water, which immediately started his toes tingling with "more life than he'd felt in them since August 1921"—he knew he was going to stay at the run-down little resort until he had given it a thorough try.

He had a swimming partner that first morning—Louis Joseph, the young boy who had shown such phenomenal improvement in the three summers he had been using the pool. When Franklin saw him approaching the porch of the cottage, walking slowly with a cane, he commented—accurately—"Abdominal and low-back weakness." He added rather incredulously, "No braces?"

The boy shook his head, smiling. "Not any more."

The two swam in the pool for more than an hour; it was very easy to swim or to float or to kick their withered legs in water like this. Exuberant, Franklin slyly grabbed Louis and ducked him and roared with laughter as the boy came up sputtering. After more than an hour, they climbed out and lay in the sun for another hour. He was highly enthusiastic about the possibility of a cure. Dr. Johnson came by to meet Franklin and give him some advice from the experience with Louis' case.

His friendliness and ebullience were like a ray of sunshine in the gloomy resort. Shabby though it was, he could see the whole area developed, cleaned up, landscaped, shining—a haven for people like himself, searching for a way back to health. His letters told the story. At the end of the day he arrived, he wrote to *Hyde Park:*

Dearest Mama,

We are here safely and I think Eleanor has written you this morning. I spent over an hour in the pool this A.M. and it is really wonderful and will I think do great good, though the doctor says it takes three weeks to show the effects.

Everyone is most kind and this afternoon Mr. Loyless has taken us for a trip through the surrounding country—many peach orchards but also a good deal of neglect and poverty.

The cottage is delightful and very comfortable and with Roy and Mary, the cook bequeathed to us by the Harts, who own the cottage, we shall be most comfortable. The Loyless family are next door.

It is too bad that Eleanor has to leave so soon, but she and I both feel it is important for her not to be away the end of the campaign as long as I have to be myself.

I will write you again soon and in the meantime you can be sure that I am really taking all the precautions of a *cure* and getting every minute's worth out of it.

A great deal of love, and kiss the chicks.

Your devoted son,
FDR

Missy came down when Eleanor left, and a week later he sent his wife further account of his progress:

Dearest E,

It is just a week since you left, but the time has passed almost without our realizing it, as the life is just the same day after day and there is no variety to give landmarks. The mornings are as you know wholly taken up with the pool and four of the afternoons we have sat out on the lawn or as Roy calls it the "yard," and I have worked at stamps or cheques or accounts or have played rummy with Missy. The other three afternoons we have gone motoring with Mrs. Loyless and have seen the country pretty thoroughly. I like him ever so much and she is nice but not broad in her interests, but she chatters away to Missy on the back seat and I hear an occasional yes or no from Missy to prove she is not sleeping.

The legs are really improving a great deal. The walking and general exercising in the water is fine and I have worked out some special exercises also. This is really a discovery of a place and there is no doubt that I've got to do it some more.

Various people came over Sunday. The Harts to stay with the Hudsons a block away, and today the pool was very gay, at least twenty people.

Thank Louis for the papers and tell him I hear nothing of interest.

I have a hunch that Davis' strength is really improving, but I still think the election will go into the house. Anyway, I am philosophic enough to think that even if Coolidge is elected we shall be so darned sick of conservatism of the old money-controlled crowd in four years that we will get a real progressive landslide in 1928.

Much love, take care of yourself.

Your devoted
FDR

Just before his trial stay ended, he sent a final impression to his mother: "The heavenly weather here continues, we have not had a single rainy day since coming, and I spend my full two hours at the pool every morning. Every other afternoon I have been driving with the Loyless's and have got to know both the surrounding country and most of the neighbors. On Wednesday the people of Warm Springs are giving me a supper and reception in the Town Hall and on Friday evening, our last day, I am to go to Manchester, 5 miles an hour for another supper and speech. I think every organization and town in Georgia has asked me to some kind of party, and Missy spends most of her time keeping up a huge and constant local correspondence.

"*When I get back I am going to have a long talk with Mr.*

George Foster Peabody who is really the controlling interest in
the property. I feel that a great 'cure' for infantile paralysis and
kindred diseases could well be established here."

In addition to his belief that Warm Springs was a discovery
of a place, he made a personal discovery concerning his response
to the water, which elated him so that he could not breathe a
word of it except in a single letter to Peabody. On about the
second or third morning in the pool, he found that he could
stand longer, could put at least "five more pounds on his knees"
than ever before. He worked out exercises with Dr. Johnson to
develop the power to put weight on his legs so that they would
hold him. By the end of his visit, he had raised it to ten pounds
and had a greater degree of movement in his right leg than
he had developed so far.

Before he left, an Atlanta paper asked for a feature story,
showing FDR at Warm Springs, swimming in the pool and
sun-bathing beside it—wearing his floppy old white hat. In posing for the picture outside the pool, he hid his legs, "so as not
to frighten people." He appeared relaxed and comfortable, reading the newspaper. The story, entitled, "Swimming Back to
Health," was picked up by a syndicate, and before long, Warm
Springs had received national publicity.

Franklin was somewhat annoyed at the article, because it gave
the impression that the water was an outright *cure,* and he
thought it was too early to make any claims, yet his hopes for
his own recovery were soaring and his intuition told him that
the place was *right.* His visionary outlook saw it transformed
into a beautiful thriving resort for all those afflicted with paralysis
of some kind. He and Tom Loyless began making plans to
renovate the old spa. Tom, who was not well, also believed
in its possibilities to the extent that he pledged himself heart
and soul, beyond his strength, to the task of building it up.

Aside from his wish to be in New York for the election,
Franklin found that the Georgia air grew sharp in the late
autumn. While the water in the pool might be warm, the

weather was too cold to permit more than a dip without getting chilled, and it was impossible to sun-bathe after November 1. Leaving Tom with instructions to have the cabins moved around to make the little "watering-place" more attractive as a starter, Franklin and Missy took the train north in time to cast their votes for Davis, who would need all he could get.

The surprising outcome was that the tight-lipped Coolidge walked away with the election, and La Follette carried only one state in the electoral college—his own, Wisconsin.

In the few weeks that were left of the old year, Franklin went to his office, looked after his business interests—he had made a whole series of investments since his illness, none of which was very successful, and some incredibly outlandish, about which Louis Howe loved to needle him—and took care of his organizational duties in the Woodrow Wilson Foundation and the Boy Scouts. He had a ramp built over the steps leading to the Sixty-fifth Street house, so that he could get up to the door by himself, using crutches on the ramp, then handing them to the chauffeur and pulling himself by the railing up to the door. (Shortly after he had mastered the technique, he told one of the secretaries with whom he had been working at the Foundation to wait in the car when they reached the house so that he could show her what he had just learned to do.)

Around the first of January, he entered into a law partnership with Basil O'Connor in the building at 120 Broadway. One of the first things he did was to persuade his new partner to promise to come to Georgia for the purpose of looking over the property at Warm Springs the following April.

In the meantime, he went to Florida for a second cruise aboard the *Larooco*. He had had the battered houseboat "re-engined with two Regal motors," the steering wheel shifted from fore cabin to top deck, and a new electric-light-generating motor installed. The yard, however, had taken poor care of her; furniture and other articles were stolen. He wrote Tom Loyless from Miami that he was having a "busy, pleasant time inspecting engines, replacing stolen articles (at the yard's expense) for deck and cabin." Missy LeHand and his chauffeur, "Monty" Snyder (who was later to go with him to the White House), had come down with him, and Maunsell Crosby was joining them in a few days (despite his declaration "never again to go amain").

The second day aboard, while they were still tied up at Miami shopping for supplies, Franklin invited the Executive Council of the American Federation of Labor, "with wives, etc., thirty in all," to come on board, when he "had an interesting talk with William Green, the President, and other leaders," as he wrote in the log. He felt that despite the election of the conservative Coolidge—or perhaps because of it—the country was going to be ready for progressivism before the next presidential election; and he was not going to miss an opportunity to help the trend along. He wanted Green and other labor leaders to know that Democratic Party—at least that segment of it influenced by F.D.R. and other party leaders—stood in support of trade unionism.

Leaving word for Maunsell to join them at Tavernier, they got under way on February 7 and proceeded down Biscayne Bay, arriving at Tavernier at one-fifteen P.M. two days later; "F.D.R. steered most of the way." He had shifted the wheel to the top deck so it would be easier for him to take over, and he was delighted to be back at the helm, even on a tub like *Larooco,* and sitting on a deck chair. He loved to feel the wheel under his fingers, to navigate the boat through the narrow creeks as he used to navigate the *Half Moon* through the Lubec Narrows off Maine. In the afternoon they had a good swim, and he could see that his leg strokes were much stronger as a result of the three weeks at Warm Springs. Much as he enjoyed the cruises on *Larooco,* he was eager for the time to pass so he could continue the treatment at his "discovery" place.

Then, on February 11, when he and Missy were returning from a fishing bout in the launch, a heavy squall blew up, pounding them with wind and rain. As they came alongside the houseboat, Missy climbed on board safely, but "F.D.R. fell on floor of pounding launch and tore knee ligaments"! It made him a little sick to think of a setback just now, but his only comment in the log was, "Had to be passed in through galley window. Heavy wind and rain all night, but anchors held." In the morning, he was afraid his leg might be broken, so they got under way at ten and headed back for Miami and a doctor. He "came on board and diagnosed only torn and pulled ligaments and strapped leg up. Tried in vain to locate Maunsell Crosby but he had evidently left for Tavernier to find us." (Crosby arrived at one A.M., having gone to Tavernier and come back.)

It was a nuisance to be laid up for several days while his knee slowly mended, but he was relieved to know that no bones were broken; he was finally able to get "a stiff brace on leg and was carried on deck." He fervently hoped there would be no more accidents.

Tom Lynch came down to do some fishing and political planning.

Other guests arrived, business associates of Franklin and members of their families. Franklin, the genial host at the wheel, became the "Admiral." From February 24 to March 24, various members of the party took turns writing the daily log; that night one item in it read: "Our dear Admiral gave a most graphic and amusing account of his political career from the beginning." Another item on the twenty-sixth referred to the Admiral "in a frivolous mood" . . . "planning to cheat the U. S. Government" on his income tax, but they all knew better than to take it seriously. When the houseboat moored close to the Navy yard on the Gulf of Mexico, the Admiral received an invitation from Captain Stearns in charge of the base to moor the *Larooco* at the Navy docks. The next day they all visited the yard and went swimming with the Captain and his family off the family dock. If Franklin suffered any nostalgia for the days when he tramped through a Navy yard from one end to the other on inspection tours, he gave no indication of it. He had always enjoyed the

Naval atmosphere, rich in ceremony, and he still enjoyed it. At Boca Chica Key they found a nice beach for bathing, when Missy and the Admiral "desported" themselves. There was "grog" at sunset, poker parties at night and, when a "blow" kept them houseboat-bound for a couple of days, there was a "great business of stamp-cataloguing" by all as well as the Admiral.

The entry for Sunday, March 8, was made by Julian Goldman, who noted Eleanor's arrival for a visit marking the Roosevelts' twentieth wedding anniversary, with an appropriate adjective: "Could we commence the Sabbath in any better way than to proceed to the station to greet the Heavenly Mrs. Roosevelt . . ."

Henry Morgenthau, Jr., and his wife arrived in the middle of the week for the same event, and Louis Howe showed up "only four hours late" on March 15. After much conversation, he was finally bathed in the ocean under protest and, because of his dour expression, christened "Little Sunshine." That night he found a hot-water bottle filled with cold water, a pair of bathing slippers, and "a slightly damp sponge" in his bed. As the "Admiral's" propensity for practical jokes was well known, Louis had no need to ask who had been the inspiration for this one.

The weather turned so warm that several members of the party, following Eleanor's lead, had their cots brought up on deck and slept out there, "armed with citronella." They were anchored off Boca Chica again on March 17, another hot day. Appropriately, there was a discussion about "what the 1st chapter of *The Green Hat* is really about," and in the evening "much festivity due to the fact that it is the 20th anniversary of the FDR's." A special green paper tablecloth covered the ship's board, and there were place cards and "refreshments." After a number of toasts to the happy couple, Henry Morgenthau made a moving speech, followed by a formal presentation to the "Honorable FDR" of a pair of linen panties! On this note of hilarity, the company retired.

The tone of pure recreation was maintained throughout the second cruise, which Franklin regarded only as an interlude until he resumed the therapy at Warm Springs. He made no attempt to work on the history again, or on a novel dealing with the story of John Paul Jones, which he had barely begun and was always threatening to complete. He had been married for almost a generation—two of his children were practically grown up; Anna was going to Cornell in the fall to study agriculture—and he had to learn to walk all over again. He was not going to waste any time bemoaning the fact, but at the same time his eagerness to get on with his recovery put out of his mind the temper required to pore over books and struggle with words. He wanted—and needed—relaxation on these cruises, and that was furnished in plenty.

The day after the anniversary celebration the log recorded "heavy gloom at the departure of ER and Missy." But the following week James came down from Groton to spend Easter vacation aboard the *Larooco*. Franklin took over the log again: it was good to have one of his sons aboard. The first day they fished with Henry Morgenthau and "J.R. got a Mackerel." After the Morgenthaus left, they spent a few more days fishing off the Keys "and then headed North on the homeward journey." They ran into rough weather, when Franklin noted slyly one morning, "Sea too much for JR's breakfast." It would make a funny family story when they got back. As they neared Miami, the weather turned much colder; Jimmy had a "cold swim" at Bear's Cut, but Franklin would not risk getting chilled; he would wait till he reached Warm Springs.

The next to the last entry read, "Tuesday, March 31, 1925.

"Miami. Packing and having hair cut in morning. At 1 James and I, in Scott Watkins' (Capt. Charlie's son) car went to Fort Lauderdale and made arrangement at Pilkington's Yacht Basin to take care of *Larooco* during the summer. After our return we went down to Cocoanut Grove and spent 1½ hours with Mr. and Mrs. William Jennings Bryan."

And on April 1: "Placed *Larooco* out of commission at 6 P.M.

and took train for Warm Springs, Georgia. Here ends a very delightful 2nd Cruise of the Good Ship *Larooco*.

At the little resort, they found, to Franklin's amazement, that some dozen fellow victims of infantile paralysis had managed, one way or another, to get to Warm Springs after reading of its health-giving properties in the story about Franklin that the syndicate had picked up. People who had been suffering silently, hiding themselves away in back rooms as Roosevelt might have hidden himself at *Hyde Park,* came out of their retirement to search for health in this obscure, neglected little "watering-place." As he gazed at their faces, so full of a hope which rose above shyness and timidity, he realized that he must somehow help these people who had come so far, expecting so much. He began by teaching them, in a very practical way, how to exercise in the warm water, as Dr. Lovett had taught him: there was Fred Botts, the very thin young man from Pennsylvania, whose legs were more spindly than Franklin's, and the two fat ladies, doubly grotesque because of their size. With his great optimism, Franklin did it cheerily, unaffectedly, as if they were working out a problem together. They were in the same predicament, just as they were in the same pool, and they must all help to find the way out. He called the emaciated young man "the skeleton from Pennsylvania" and taught him to swim, stretching his legs way out and pumping them up and down; he also showed him how to kick to keep afloat.

"Just hang onto the side of the pool and concentrate on kicking while I move your legs," he said, as he continued to pump the thin legs up and down. They were at the shallow end of the pool, and Franklin was sitting on the bottom, water up to his neck, working steadily. "Move along with me," he directed, "and before you know it, you'll be moving by yourself—that's the beauty of this water!"

At the first sign of motion from Fred, he let go of the young man's legs. "That's it!" he called out enthusiastically. "Now you've got the idea—keep at it," he encouraged. The process took a number of sessions—and several warnings from Dr. Johnson not to "over-do"—but eventually Franklin taught Fred Botts to swim.

He taught the others to play around in the water and to exercise in it. One day he tried teaching the two fat ladies to do an ingenious one he had invented, "the elevating exercise in the medium of water," he called it. The trick required standing in the water, putting as much weight on the muscles as they could tolerate. As he showed the two oversized ladies how to do it, amidst their giggles and squeals, the lesson took on the aspect of hilarious fun. He recorded later: "One of these ladies found great difficulty in getting both feet down to the bottom of the pool. Well, I would take one large knee and I would force this large knee down, then I would say, 'Have you got it?' and she would say, 'Yes,' and I would say, 'Hold it, hold it.' Then I would reach up and get hold of the other knee very quickly and start to put it down and then number-one knee would pop up. This used to go on for half an hour at a time." The scene resembled a Mack Sennett comedy except for the seriousness of the underlying purpose, which prompted him to keep trying. "Before I left," his account ended, "I could get both those knees down at the same time."

One problem he had to solve was the attitude of the regular guests at Meriwether Inn, who began to show up for the spring season soon after he arrived. Not that there were a great many of them, but they had been coming to Warm Springs for some years and the revenue that Tom Loyless collected from his hotel guests helped to make the payments on the mortgage. They felt that "their" resort had been invaded by a lot of polio "patients," whose appearance, with crutches, wheel chairs, braces, and other medical appliances was distasteful to the regular guests, not to say distressing, because they were afraid of "catching" the dread disease. They shunned the newcomers in the pool, staying as far away as they could from "those people," who seemed to be having such a good time, despite their handicaps.

The ignorance, selfishness and prejudice of such an attitude made Franklin's blood boil, but he could not very well "educate" the paying guests, nor could he suggest that Tom ask them to leave. (Poor Tom was ailing rapidly; Franklin was shocked when he saw how altered the manager's appearance was in the few months since they had met in the fall. Tom, a former newspaper editor, was still doing a column for the *Macon Daily Telegraph,* but it was such a drain on him to get it out that he asked Franklin to take over for him. Delighted at becoming a newspaper columnist, Franklin dictated a number of short pieces on a variety of subjects to Missy and found it a great lark. He touched on all his favorite issues: the need for a new foreign policy, tolerance toward immigrants, conservation, civil service reform, government efficiency, and other topics he could use to spread the beliefs of the Democratic Party as he saw them. While he went about writing the columns as if for recreation, he kept a political eye open for possible syndication of his work; but he received no offers, although one or two of the columns were printed in the *Atlanta Journal.*)

The hotel guests complained, too, at the sight of the paralytics in the dining room. Only a few patients had rooms at the hotel; most of them stayed at a boardinghouse in the village or at the home of Dr. Kitchen, a local physician, who, like Dr. Johnson, had begun to take great interest in the springs since the "cure" of Louis Joseph. The patients were brought out to the resort every day by car and, as there was no place to go for meals but the Meriwether Inn, they had to eat in the hotel dining room. Franklin quickly found two solutions: he suggested that Tom fix up the basement as a dining room for the paralytics—"no steps to climb"—and he had a small pool dug for his "gang," connected with the large pool but about thirty feet away and shut away under a shed. Eventually, he meant to buy the Warm Springs property if he could, but for the present he was determined that these fellow victims have the same chance as he to benefit from the waters which had put new life into his wasted legs.

Under Franklin's direction games were organized in the pool—bars and rings were set up; water polo and water basketball, of his own devising, were enjoyed with shouts of laughter. Exercises were supervised by Dr. Johnson and "Dr." Roosevelt, who together drew up a large, if crude, muscle chart, so that patients could see exactly which muscles were being exercised and the amount of improvement that was made.

After an hour or more exercises and games, Franklin would call out, "All right now, everybody stay in the sun for an hour!" And they would all lounge around outside the pool and let the sun bake into their muscles and bones. As they rested, they would compare notes, talking over various ways toward rehabilitation. The others looked to "Dr. Roosevelt" as their leader (not to say savior, in some cases) and he would occasionally give them advice, based on his own experience. "You've got to *know* you're going to improve," he told them, leaning back, his quill cigarette holder fixed at a forty-five-degree angle between his lips. "Keep yourselves mentally alert; don't lose contact with the things you enjoyed before infantile paralysis."

People in the village and the surrounding country continued to be friendly. Neighbors brought in gifts of flowers (sometimes in vases or bowls that Eleanor, who drove down with Louis and Anna toward the end of April, thought must surely be family heirlooms), fried chicken, or a load of wood for the fireplace. The Hart's cottage became a kind of headquarters for the Warm Springs Development Association that sprang into being, figuratively if not literally. Franklin drew up plans for a new pool for the patients, for simple little cottages, including one for himself, near the Hart's. On little scraps of paper he would rough out an idea whenever it struck him; his friend Henry Toombs would know what the sketches meant when he showed them to the architect in Hyde Park. He was so involved in the resort, and his general condition so improved, that he decided to stay till the middle of May, as he wrote to James and to his half brother Rosy. He also sent a letter to John Lawrence, comparing the benefits of the houseboat with those he had experienced so far at Warm Springs.

"The two months in Florida this year and last did me an undoubted amount of good," he began tactfully, since without John he could not have bought *Larooco*, "yet I realize that on a houseboat it is very difficult to get the kind of exercise I need, i.e., swimming in warm water. The sharks made it impossible to play around in deep water for any length of time, and the sand beaches are few and far between, and even on them I get sunlight chiefly, but very little swimming. There is now no question that this Warm Springs pool does my legs more good than anything else. Last autumn I added at least ten pounds to the weight I could put on my knees, and already this spring I think I have gained another ten pounds. I am able to be in and out of the water here for at least two hours every day. Therefore, from the sole consideration of getting my legs back I must contemplate next winter giving up the Florida trip and coming here instead. This would have been impossible up to now as there were no heating facilities for the cottages or bathhouses, and these are needed in February and March. Now, however, they are putting in heat, and next winter I will be able to come here instead of going to Florida." He added a little political gossip, and Missy typed the letter, sending it off right away.

In his answer on May 14, Lawrence was perfectly agreeable with Franklin's plans, and told his old friend to sell or charter the houseboat, whichever would be simpler. He ended with a rather remarkable paragraph: "I am delighted to hear you are getting better, and also that you are trying to save the Democratic Party from wine, women and Hollering, principally the latter, I believe. Go to it. We shall need a sound party to keep the Republicans in line, and don't forget that I am looking forward to being one of the 10,000 Secretaries of the Navy that you have pledged *8 years from now,** when you have the honor of calling the White House your own, and swimming in the fountain."

Franklin chuckled when he read the prediction, and Louis' only comment was that it was a bit previous. He was still confident that his Franklin would be president, but he had tagged the date as 1936. He did not think Roosevelt would be strong enough, either physically or politically, before then. Louis showed as much pleasure as it was possible for him to exhibit in his skeptical way over Franklin's improvement and the general plan for developing Warm Springs as a haven for paralysis victims; beneath his cynicism a soft heart beat with sympathy for the suffering of his fellow men, but there were few who knew the true Louis. Franklin was one of them.

The little man was almost as eager as his protégé for Franklin's complete recovery. Now he told the Roosevelts of a Dr. William McDonald, who had become a specialist in treating cases of infantile paralysis and had set up a practice in his house at Marion, Massachusetts, where he worked with cases individually, handling only a few. He had been very successful in the use of a "walking board" he had devised. Louis and his family were going to Horseneck Beach at Westport Point, not far from Marion, for a month in the summer; it was Louis' idea that Franklin should visit them at the beach and investigate the possibilities of Dr. McDonald's method at the same time.

The idea of the "walking board" appealed to Franklin's imagination. He was susceptible to any and all suggestions that might lead to full recovery and, although he was convinced of the value of Warm Springs, his hopes soared at the thought of finding a faster route than any he had discovered so far. At least he could investigate this Dr. McDonald and his new method. A "walking board"—it sounded more thrilling than a flying machine!

* That would be exactly 1933, the year F.D.R. took office.

CHAPTER IX

Skirmish in Massachusetts

HE LEFT WARM SPRINGS late in May, with a promise to Tom Loyless and the little "gang" that he would be back in the fall to "supervise" the improvements being made at the resort. He divided his time between Hyde Park and New York for a month, taking care of business matters in New York and supervising the building of the pool and cottage at Val-Kill. Some time in the two months before he went to Massachusetts he let himself be "bled" by Dan Draper for an experiment the doctor was conducting in a search for a serum that might be injected to prevent residual paralysis in polio cases. Franklin went up to Presbyterian Hospital one day and let his old friend take 500 cc of blood from his veins to inject into the bloodstreams of two children stricken with the disease—one of them Perry Osborne, the son of a mutual friend of theirs.

James and Elliott were on a western trip by themselves, the first time they had been off on their own; and Anna was in Geneva, New York, taking a course in agriculture to prepare for her entrance into Cornell. The two youngest boys and Eleanor were at Campobello for the summer. He wrote letters to all of them since he could not see them, but he gave little hint of his loneliness, except to say to Anna, "I wish I could get out to

Geneva to play around with you for a few days. By Golly, if
I have to call you up next Saturday for failure to hear a line I
will jolly well reverse the charges!" Then he related all he was
doing and ended, "I am busy as a one-armed paper hanger with
the itch!" He added a characteristic postscript: "Will you please
sign the enclosed on page 2 and 3 and get it sworn to before
a Notary Public in Geneva, returning it to me. The Notary will
charge you 25¢ which I will reimburse you when next we become acquainted with each other."

In a note from Campobello, Eleanor told him that "everyone
asked after" him. She went on: "I adored being here, and the
quiet is heavenly but even though I know you couldn't enjoy it
I can't help wishing all the time you could be here. If you and
the boys have a schooner next summer you might cruise up and
just stay on the boat and be here for a little while."

He did not know when, if ever, he would return to Campobello. It was true that he often longed to be back on the cool,
green island, especially now, when "Babs" and the little boys
were there; and on certain days, when the wind blew off the
ocean making the air over New York pure and clean, he remembered Campobello so vividly it was as if he were actually trans-
ported there for a moment; he could smell the spray and see
the rocky cliffs. But until he could go on one of those wild
"cliff walks," on which he used to lead the whole family a merry
chase, he did not care to return.

He had to get hold of some ready cash, for one thing, just
now. The new treatment would probably be very expensive and
the return on his investments was just about enough to cover
running expenses. He decided to hold an auction of a large portion of his naval collection—lots of prints and books, maybe even
one or two of the models. He hated to think of parting with
them (he had the true collector's instinct for hanging on to his
acquisitions), but his recovery came before anything else. With
Louis' help, the auction was arranged and held, and Franklin

realized better than a thousand dollars to go toward rebuilding his still badly paralyzed legs.

Around the fourth of August, he and Louis drove up to Massachusetts. He described the scene to his mother in a letter the day before:

> The car will as usual be crowded (He had brought Roy and another boy up with him from Warm Springs), Louis and I on the back seat with various packages tucked around and under us, and several score suitcases, braces, crutches, canes, sandwiches thrown in for good measure. However, it saves $11 for each person to travel thus to the beach! I will try to go to see McDonald Thursday or Friday, depending on the tide, as I have to go from cottage to road after half ebb tide and get back before half flood.

The interview with Dr. McDonald, who proved to be pleasant and understanding as well as scientific, was so heartening that Franklin sent a long telegram to Eleanor at Campobello and wrote a letter to his mother about "the grand plan of going to Dr. McDonald next Monday for a month. He is very encouraging and will take me in hand at once, though he had made up his mind to take no more cases this year. His work is evidently very strenuous for the patient, so I shall devote myself to it wholly. I hope to get a wee cottage two doors from him and to move in with Roy and Ricketts." He suggested that his mother visit the Delanos in Fairhaven, not far from Marion, and drive over to see him at "work." He and Louis were going to see about the cottage that evening.

Sara's answer was as excited as his note: "I was very glad to get your letter of Tuesday, and all my thoughts are in Marion, and tomorrow I can think of you there and beginning the treatment. I feel so hopeful and confident! Once able to move about with crutches and without braces, strength will come and now for the first time in more than a year I feel that *work* is to be done for *you,* my dearest . . ."

Luck was with them in finding a cottage, which belonged to Edward Hamlin, brother of Charles Hamlin, who, with his wife, Bertie, Franklin's old friend, was living in nearby Mattapoisett for the summer. Bertie, who had acquired a name for herself in the field of magazine articles, was interested in McDonald's method and wanted to do a piece concerning its recuperative value for polio patients in general and Franklin in particular. Since he wanted visitors and had always enjoyed her company, Franklin urged her to come over as often as she wished.

He sent an account of his routine to his mother:

I am safely installed and the work is underway. Got here with Louis on Monday at 2. Dr. McDonald came at four and gave me the complete muscle tests. Yesterday I swam for 1½ hours in the morning, had the exercises with the Dr. at 4, and then tried the walking board for ½ hour. He seems pleased with the general lineup and I feel with him that things have now got to the point with the muscles in general where there is something to work on and I can go right after it. Braces are of course laid aside, he is hot against them, and confirms what I have told you for two years and you would not believe.

The swimming work is just what I did at Warm Springs, only the water being much colder I cannot stay so long . . .

When you get to Fairhaven, I think I can come over to lunch on Sunday and stay all afternoon and perhaps for dinner, too, as Sunday apparently is an off day.

Why don't you come back with me and spend Sunday night? I am on a diet also and hope to get off 10 lbs . . .

Three other cases here—one little Edward Parish—all showing remarkable improvement.

Mr. Edward Hamlin (who has given me this perfectly sweet little cottage) is three doors away. Miss Harriet Hamlin next door and the Doc. three doors at the end of the street.

Missy has just arrived and will be here off and on. Louis comes back tomorrow to report on the host of things he had to do for me in New York as of course this change of plans made all sorts of complications with my work and various activities.

The month he had intended to stay lengthened into three as the treatment thrived and his progress increased. The walking board was not so different from his parallel bars at *Hyde Park;* the "board" was a rectangular wooden platform with a wooden railing on all sides, by which he held himself up; and in a hand-over-hand movement that the doctor showed him, he made his way around and around the platform, pulling his legs— without braces—after him. However, it was easier to have a wider area in which to walk, instead of merely going back and forth as he had along the bars, and Dr. McDonald worked so closely with him, showed him how to handle himself with such care and detail that the process seemed easier; he was able to put more weight on his knees without having them buckle under him.

In his enthusiasm he overdid it, and one of his knees locked during October. Bertie Hamlin, who had been coming as often as she promised, arrived with her husband one day after it happened and was amazed to find him in the best of spirits. She wrote later in an article for the *Boston Globe* * that "he was carrying on a rigid program to improve the situation. He made endless rounds for two or three hours a day, holding onto the wooden railing . . . Several of his friends were sitting around and he talked and laughed cheerfully as he circled the platform, holding himself up by the railing and dragging his almost useless legs after him."

The exercises were equally as rigorous. Franklin wrote to Dan Draper toward the end of September, describing the method in medical terms: "Where Lovett gave a single direct pulling exercise for the quadriceps in the direction of gravity, McDonald exercises the quadriceps with and against gravity, direct motion singly, in pairs, alternately, reciprocally and also with a rotary motion, singly, in pairs, alternately and reciprocally."

His mother and many of the Delano clan came from Fairhaven to see him—Aunt Kassie, her daughters and their husbands, Uncle Frederic, and various cousins. Louis brought some polit-

---

* Also in *The New Republic,* April 1946, after F.D.R.'s death.

ical associates up from New York, and there was much campaign talk for the next year's elections. It was Franklin's theory, as he had said the previous fall, that the people would be ready for a progressive Congress after two years of "Cal" Coolidge's conservatism, and it was up to the Democratic Party to see that progressive candidates were nominated. He had been wrong in his prediction of the La Follette vote, but many leaders in both parties had been misled into believing that the third-party vote would be stronger than it was. Now Roosevelt stuck to his conviction that the Democrats, if they put up the right candidates, could take over the Congress in 1926. All this was hashed out as he groped his way about the walking board or went through the exercises.

Eleanor and the two little boys stopped overnight on their way back from Campobello; and when James and Elliott came home from their western jaunt, they stayed two nights with him before going back to Groton. (Elliott, as usual, objected strenuously to returning to Groton; this year he had fallen in love with the west, and it was all Franklin could do to convince him that he must continue his schooling.) Later, in November, Eleanor joined him again for a longer visit.

This time they were able to go for a tour of Cape Cod to see some of the old houses there and at Plymouth. Dr. McDonald was laid up for several days, as he had strained his heart carrying one of his patients, Janet Wright, into the stadium at the Brown-Yale game. (While the patients were in treatment, living at Marion, they led a kind of community life. The doctor and his wife frequently came in for a game of bridge with Franklin and whoever happened to be there for a fourth.) Though he had no treatment for the week that Dr. McDonald had to rest, Franklin did the walking regularly and felt that his muscles continued to improve. It was a great relief to him not to have to wear the heavy braces all the time, though without them he was still unable to stand or hold himself straight for more than a few minutes. It was the doctor's theory that the patient should have as much freedom of motion as it was possible for him to experience, and to this end he taught his patients various ways to move about.

During Eleanor's visit, Bertie and Charles Hamlin invited her and Franklin to come for dinner at their home in Mattapoisett. Franklin, brimming with high spirits over his latest accomplishment, left his braces in the cottage and his crutches in the car and had Roy and Ricketts, the two men who had been tending him, transfer him from the car into the Hamlins' house and to a seat at the dining-room table. He did not like to be carried as a rule (and Louis Howe had laid down the law against his ever being carried in public), but the Hamlins were old friends and there were no guests outside of the family.

"Don't come back till nine-thirty," he told the men when he was settled.

His hostess was somewhat surprised, as she was sure they would be through with dinner before then, but she said nothing; they could always sit around the dining-room table till the men got back.

Franklin entertained them with anecdotes about Warm Springs and the treatment here in Marion—incidents which struck him funny, like teaching the fat ladies to stand in the pool, or some attempt he had made in working with Dr. McDonald that was an utter fiasco the first time, and which he made sound hilarious.

When dinner was over, he pushed back his chair and said without any preamble, "See me get into the next room." Before they quite realized what was happening, he had dropped down on the floor and went into the living room on his hands and knees; there he got up into another chair by himself and was calmly awaiting the rest of them when they came in. He explained that Dr. McDonald taught all his patients this way of helping themselves so they would have greater freedom to move about if necessary—especially for safety reasons. He had taught himself to *crawl*, hauling his body along by the power of his hands, as he did to go upstairs the first winter, but this was so much faster.

"You know my fear of fire—I'm very happy to have this means of making a getaway in case of danger . . . Or boredom from some of Eleanor's friends," he added with a wicked grin.

Charles Hamlin, overcome by his high courage, by the obvious pleasure "that superb young fellow" took in being able to perform such a simple act, coughed suspiciously and on the excuse of hearing the phone went into the den for a few minutes. Eleanor, however, following Franklin's line, related in an injured tone the way he had more than once avoided visitors during the warm weather. When he came home from swimming and saw her sitting on the porch with someone he found a bore, he had the driver go right past the house and he would not come back until the guest, tired of waiting to see him, had given up and left. Eleanor, who had seen him go past, was mentally tapping her foot the whole time. (Franklin chuckled with glee as she finished the story, but she insisted that it was not amusing.)

For all of his lighthearted attitude, he was in dead earnest about learning to walk, if possible, before he left Marion. He was so wrapped up in the treatment that he had not even taken a few days off to go to Hyde Park to vote, but had cast an absentee ballot. He had written to a friend earlier in his stay, "This time I think I have hit it! Dr. McDonald has gone one step further than the others, and his exercises are doing such wonders that I expect within another 10 days to be able to stand up without braces. What I did before in the way of swimming at Warm Springs was all to the good, but now I begin to see actual daylight ahead." And his optimism continued as he advanced further along in the course McDonald laid out for his patients. The other three were youngsters in their teens and were probably more pliable than Franklin—Janet Wright made a complete recovery through the treatment—but none of them was more zealous than he, nor as faithful in carrying out the program. In general, the doctor devoted certain hours during the day to each of his patients individually, but at times they worked together, and Franklin, with his love for the young, had soon made friends with all three of his "fellow victims."

"Tomorrow night the two little infantile paralysis girls dine here," he wrote to his mother late in November. "The walking," he informed her, "progresses slowly but definitely."

For the latter part of his stay he scarcely wore both braces any more; as a rule he needed only the left one. With that and the crutches he could now move with a fair amount of "speed" and much more easily than before. The doctor had him try using canes instead of crutches, a few steps at a time, steadying him with only slight support. Each day he went a little farther, and a little farther . . .

Then came the day in December, just before he was preparing to leave Marion, when he walked all the way from the house to the edge of the wharf—nearly a block—wearing only one brace and using one cane! Dr. McDonald and Roy accompanied him but hardly touched him at any time. He stood on the pier and cried out joyfully, "I can walk! I can walk!" He was nearly overwhelmed by his emotion—and exhaustion, which set in as soon as he stopped walking; his knees were shaking, his body trembling. To go back, he put one arm around Roy and one around the doctor—he was taller than either of them—but before they started, Mrs. McDonald, who had come down to the pier, wanted to snap a picture of the three as a record of his achievement. He posed gladly, his exultant smile a radiant reflection of his deep feeling.

He was not to show greater progress under McDonald's treatment. Although he returned to Marion the following summer full of hope, he never learned to walk entirely without braces and he could never go far wearing only one. Yet he considered his improvement tremendous and he never gave up the struggle for recovery nor relinquished his fighting spirit. Not that he fought consciously, or realized fully that he was waging a war against the disease of infantile paralysis. His work with the other patients at Warm Springs had sprung out of a spontaneous reaction to give help where help was sought and badly needed; and this response of his would eventually become a "crusade," but at the moment he was not aware of its enormous potential. It did not occur to him that there was anything unusual in the intensity and the scientific approach of his attack on his own affliction and on poliomyelitis in general. When he heard from Dr. Draper that the serum for which he had donated a pint of blood had been highly successful for little Perry Osborne, he wrote back: "It gave me a real thrill and at the same time made me feel like a hero decorated for valor in a battle in which he did not take part!"

CHAPTER X

The "Spirit of Warm Springs"

BEFORE HE LEFT Warm Springs in April, Franklin had written his friend Livy Davis about the "clinic" he was operating in and out of the pool and outlined his other activities with his usual zest: "In addition to all this, I am consulting architect and landscape engineer for the Warm Springs Co.—am giving free advice on the moving of buildings, the building of roads, setting out of trees and remodelling the hotel. We, i.e., the Company plus F.D.R., are working out a new water system, new sewage plan, fishing pond, and tomorrow we hold an organization meeting to start the Pine Mountain Club which will run the dance hall, tea room, picnic grounds, golf course and other forms of indoor and outdoor sports. I sometimes wish I could find some spot on the globe where it was not essential and necessary for me to start something new—a sand bar in the ocean might answer, but I would probably start building a sea wall around it and digging for pirate treasure in the middle."

He was eager to get on with the development of the resort— or, more accurately, its metamorphosis into an informal, non-institutional rehabilitation center, where paralysis victims could come as they might go to a pleasure resort and at the same time take advantage of the opportunity to rebuild their bodies in the health-giving waters of the springs. He was very definite about the kind of place he wanted Warm Springs to be, but there were obstacles in the way, the principal one being that George Foster Peabody still owned the controlling interest in the property. At this point Franklin was not at all sure he could take over the mortgages, but it might be the only way.

By the time he left Marion, it was almost Christmas, so he went to *Hyde Park* for the holidays, always, of course, carrying on his political activities. At Louis' instigation, letters were sent to Democratic leaders all over the country in an effort to unify and strengthen the organization on a firm liberal platform, and answers from influential men in every state had been pouring in for some time. Unlike Smith, who concentrated on his local area, Franklin wanted to increase his own national following, which had budded in the 1920 campaign, and which, according to Louis, could be made to blossom by remote-control political hydration, as it were. (Indeed, one of the planks in the platform was "wet," as opposed to the "dry" influence that had put Prohibition into effect in 1920.)

He continued to use his enforced retirement as a means of talking with people from all walks and strata of life. He had the time to listen and he was eager to hear what they had to say. The last week in November his friend Bertie Hamlin had come over to Marion for tea one afternoon and found him saying good-by to a young man who was leaving to catch the Fall River night boat to New York. "After he had gone Franklin told me that he was an East Side Jew—a tailor—from New York," she recorded in her diary later that night. "He had come over on the boat the previous night, and had been over once before to spend the day. Franklin said he had a chance in this way to learn a great deal about conditions in the young man's life—his clubs and other organizations—at first hand. He felt he got to the bottom of situations that could and should be remedied—the scandalous housing conditions—labor—schools—churches and the family life. He said the patience of people under unbearable tenement living

—the lack of decent provisions for sanitary purposes—sometimes one water faucet for a whole house—and that in some cases the properties were owned by wealthy people who left the care to agents who had no interest but to extract the rent."

As he broadened his own outlook, he tried to broaden the official outlook of his party. He wanted to see Jeffersonian democracy in practice and felt that it could be applied in 1925 as well as in the days of the founding fathers. In his recent reading, he had been much impressed with Claude Bowers' *Jefferson and Hamilton,* which he reviewed for the *New York World* in December. He was more of an orator than a writer, but his expressed convictions in a review of this sort helped to spread the doctrine of liberalism as being the core of the Democratic Party—and to publicize the name of F.D.R.

During December and January he tried to sell or rent the *Larooco* so that he could use the cash for some of the immediate improvements at Warm Springs, but when he could find no "takers" for the houseboat, he decided to make use of her for one more winter. He and Eleanor went down to Fort Lauderdale on the first of February, shortly after which *Larooco* went into commission on her third (and last) cruise. Maunsell Crosby, the amiable ornithologist who had become a permanent fixture— and a fast friend—was again aboard. His birthday, February 14, was celebrated by "cake with candles" and "valentines for all hands," according to the log; but outside of that and the visit of Sir Oswald and Lady Cynthia Mosley, who came for a few days' fishing, this cruise was less of a pastime and more of a marking time, as far as Franklin was concerned, till he could get on with the plans for Warm Springs.

Tom Lynch came down to plot political strategy for Dutchess County, and February 24 contained a most important entry in the log: "A quiet day—Charles S. Peabody and William Hart [the man in whose cottage Franklin had stayed at Warm Springs] arrived, and we began talking over the possible purchase of Georgia Warm Springs from George Foster Peabody and his nephew." They stayed only three days, but a great deal was accomplished in that short time.* In a letter to his mother on March 7, Franklin, after commenting on the sudden death of one of his favorite *Fairhaven* aunts * and listing the latest arrivals (among them John Lawrence, who finally came to take a look at the boat in which he had half ownership), stated, almost casually:

"I had a nice visit from Chas. Peabody, and it looks at if I had bought Warm Springs. If so, I want you to take a great interest in it, for I feel you can help me with many suggestions and the place properly run will not only do a great deal of good but will prove financially successful." He added, "I go there March 27 and hope to find it warm enough to use the outdoor pool." He hoped his mother would see how much the place meant to him, and it was for her benefit that he included the possibilities for financial success, since she was afraid he was going to "bankrupt" himself by the venture.

The March 15 entry read: "William Hart comes from Columbus, Ga., and J.S.L. left for the North at 11 A.M. Hart and I discussed plans for Warm Springs all day and evening."

At eleven the next morning Hart left for Georgia with a promise to start the wheels moving in the renovation of Warm Springs. Poor Tom Loyless, who had undergone an exploratory operation which resulted in the discovery of cancer, was on the point of death, and it was up to Roosevelt, Hart, and a few others to carry out Tom's dream of turning Warm Springs into a curative center.

Elliott came aboard the next day, "looking rather pale." The guests had all gone (Maunsell's departure Franklin noted, as

---

* He wired the ailing Tom Loyless: "We will see our dream carried out."
* This was Aunt Annie Hitch, well-known "practical philanthropist," who had often sent boxes of goodies when he was at Groton. Now he wrote: ". . . it is as dear Aunt Annie would have wished it, active up to the last. "You know what a shock it is to me for in so many ways Aunt Annie and I were sympathetic, *and her passing is as I would have mine be*. She was so keen about everything and with it had such a twinkle in her eye that it is no wonder people in every walk of life in Newburgh loved her."

before, "much to our regret"); even Missy had left; so, outside of the crew, he and Elliott had the houseboat to themselves. As on James's visit the previous year, he devoted his time and energy to his son's vacation and went in for unusually strenuous fishing. He wanted his boys to know that just as he could still match—and sometimes best—them in wrestling, he could still take an active part in other sports, so long as he did not have to stand on his feet. His swimming was getting better all the time, and from the waist up he was becoming so strong that he could easily tussle with a large catch. Part of the time they spent "trying to harpoon whip-rays."

He made Elliott, who was probably the most "difficult" of the children, feel that they were shipmates together, and so far gained his son's confidence that Elliott unburdened himself in regard to Groton and his resentment of the strict discipline at the school. Franklin was interested in his attitude as compared with his own toward the rigorous rules laid down by Dr. Peabody. He did not succeed in instilling in Elliott the reverence he had always felt toward the Rector, but at least he understood his son's turmoil a little better; and without sounding too much like a father, he tried to get Elliott to see that life would be easier at Groton if he just applied himself a little more in his studies.

Of course Elliott, like James, came in for his share of teasing during the cruise. One item in the log read: "Elliott and I went in for a swim in the Bath Tub" (a shallow pool they had found near Tavernier) "and his 'tan' came off under the application of soap!" The next day they were "off early for a day on the reef . . . An onshore breeze made it a bit choppy and Elliott was about to succumb when a 12 lb. grouper struck his hook. For a minute it was a grave question as to whether grouper would come in or breakfast go out. Grouper came in, and Elliott beat Jimmy's record by retaining his insides."

On Monday, March 22, Elliott was the hero of the day's entry, which began, "Last night we caught the record fish of all time!

Elliott had put out a shark hook baited with half a ladyfish and about 8 o'clock we noticed the line was out in the middle of the creek." It took the combined efforts of the fishermen, captain, and crew to haul in "a perfectly enormous Jewfish," over seven feet long, five feet around, and weighing between 450 and 500 pounds. The account ended, "We borrowed a Kodak and films at Key Largo, and took many photos of him."

It was a grand finale to Elliott's vacation and *Larooco's* last cruise. Four days later the log read: "Spent the day peacefully near the 'ole swimming hole' on the South side of Bear Cut. Completed packing up various things to be sent to Warm Springs, as Johnny Lawrence and I have decided to offer good old *Larooco* for sale, and we have a superfluous quantity of china, linen, etc." And the last entry, on March 27, noted briefly: "Completed all final arrangements and said farewell to the good old boat. Elliott and I left on the evening train for Warm Springs."

At the little resort a group of patients who had come down early greeted him eagerly, with a sigh of relief. Tom Loyless had died the week before (Roosevelt had sent Mrs. Loyless a letter of sympathy from the *Larooco* on the receipt of a wire from her) and, although Hart had been doing his best to start negotiations for the continuance of the building program, things were pretty much at a standstill; two of the patients were installed in "The Wreck," a cottage that had been halfway repaired the year before, and others were at boardinghouses in the village. They were bathing in the patients' pool, but without exercises or organization.

Franklin's first move was to get the treatments under way again. A table was installed in the pool, twelve inches below the surface so patients could stretch out and perform exercises under water. He saw to it that the inn was opened, so patients would have a place to stay. At his suggestion, ramps were put over the steps leading to the porch, so that wheel chairs and crutches could easily mount them. Now that he was going to own the ramshackle hotel, he would admit all the polios who wanted to stay there; if "able-bodied" people did not like it, they could go elsewhere. His only stipulation was that handicapped guests be placed on the first floor, so that in case of fire it would not be too difficult to get them out. (As soon as he was financially able to do so, he would tear down the old tinderbox.)

Peabody's nephew Charles came down with Basil O'Connor to make the final negotiations, and on April 29 (1926) the signature of Franklin D. Roosevelt was put on an agreement to purchase the entire property of Warm Springs, including the pools, the inn, cottages, and twelve hundred acres of land for $200,000. It was the greatest gamble he had ever taken, and yet he had never felt so sure of success in any venture before.

He and Eleanor had talked over the deal from every aspect, and for once his wife was dubious about the outcome. The figure was nearly two thirds of his fortune, and she was afraid the risk was too great. The children were of an age when they would soon be in college all at once—Anna was already at Cornell—and if the venture failed, their education might suffer. To this Franklin had countered, "Ma will always see the children through." Furthermore, he did not see any reason to contemplate failure before the project had been given a fair trail. They had also discussed the part Eleanor should play in the development of Warm Springs; she had assumed the assistant-principalship of the Todhunter School, started by her friends Nancy Cook and Marion Dickerman, and it was finally decided that she should continue her position: Franklin would not be in Georgia all the time anyway in view of his political career, which they both agreed came first in importance from a long-range point of view.

Eleanor was still skeptical about the enterprise when Franklin wrote her that he had signed the papers, and she could not help expressing her feelings in a letter written on May 4: "I know you love creative work," she assured him; "my only feeling is that Georgia is somewhat distant for you to keep in touch with what is really a big undertaking. One cannot, it seems to me, have *vital* interests in widely divided places, but that may be because I'm old and rather overwhelmed by what there is to do in one place and it wearies me to think of even undertaking to make new ties. Don't be discouraged by me; I have great confidence in your extraordinary interest and enthusiasm. It is just that I couldn't do it . . ."

The only piece of advice Franklin took from her letter was that he was not in the least discouraged by her skepticism—or his mother's, or Basil O'Connor's. He sat in his wheel chair on the porch of the Harts' cottage, held conferences, and gave orders to connect the two little treatment pools and start a new larger one. He sent for Dr. Leroy Hubbard (whose work he had had O'Connor investigate), orthopedic surgeon of the New York State Department of Health, who had gained a reputation through his nine years of experience in the convalescent care of infantile paralysis. The doctor could not come immediately, but sent his assistant, Miss Helena T. Mahoney, a trained physiotherapist, to start work in the treatment pool with true scientific approach. Together they would conduct the first medical experiment at Warm Springs during the summer.

Franklin was bubbling with plans; he hired a young man named Curtis, who had studied hotel management at Cornell, to run the Meriwether Inn. He had workers start whitewashing the cottages that were there, and began making plans for new ones. At the pool, his "gang" found him more brimming with vitality than he had been before, if that was possible. He directed the games as before, but was even more inventive. When he was in the pool, he could walk around in four feet of water as if he "had nothing the matter" with his legs, and it was hard to believe that there was anything wrong with him; his laughter rang out above the rest; he encouraged them all. Yet when they saw him coming to the bathhouse in his straight little wheel chair or making his way, still at a pitifully slow rate, on the crutches (occasionally he would teeter and struggle to keep from falling even now), they knew his problems were as difficult as theirs—

and worse than some who came for help. They were inspired to follow his lead, to progress as he progressed. Each week brought new patients and he welcomed them all, no matter how much or how little money they had. He had told Tom Loyless more than once the year before to "send the bill" to him when some paralytic was faced with having to leave for lack of funds, and he was going to continue the policy somehow.

Even though he knew Dr. Hubbard was a reputable physician, he wanted the endorsement of other medical men and sent letters to a number of them, describing the place and the experiment he intended to make. Before he had a chance to receive replies, he heard that the American Orthopedic Association was holding its annual conference in Atlanta. It was a golden opportunity!

"Take a letter," he said to Missy. He dictated an immediate request for an appearance at the conference, to ask for "technical guidance and help." A reply came almost by return mail: as a layman he would not be allowed to appear at the conference. Undismayed, he called Atlanta and talked to the first doctor who answered from the conference headquarters, but he was still coldly, definitely refused an audience. By now his instinct for battle was thoroughly aroused. He told Roy to bring the car around, and three hours later arrived in Atlanta, where he headed straight for the convention. If he could not appear officially, he could lobby for his experiment, his "dream"; he had had plenty of experience at that, and his persuasive powers were great. He had brought along his small "kitchen" wheel chair, and in this he rolled up and down the corridors of the convention hall, buttonholing the doctors, telling his story, enlisting support. At first they regarded him suspiciously, but if they stopped to listen to him they were won over by the way he gave his account of the curative effects of the wonderful waters at Warm Springs.

In the end he succeeded in winning the Association's unofficial approval of an experimental period, presided over by an investigating committee of three orthopedic surgeons who would receive reports from the physician in charge (Dr. Hubbard). If they were satisfied from the reports that the water and the treatment at Warm Springs was beneficial in enough cases during the months from June to December, the Association would give not only its approval, but its active support, by recommendation of Warm Springs as a therapeutic center.

It was a challenge, and one that Franklin, driving back with Roy after the flush of victory had subsided, felt was an indispensable goal, one that must be achieved before they could think of expanding or publicizing the place to any extent. He knew the name of Warm Springs must become widely known before it could be expected to function as a successful center, but it must have the right kind of publicity, based on sound fact, not on cheap sensationalism or gross exaggerations.

Within a few days the physiotherapist, Miss Mahoney, arrived, and the trial balloon treatment period was set in motion. A stocky, square-shouldered woman, whose face and manner showed a sturdiness equal to her physical make-up, "Mahoney" (as she was soon called by everyone, including Franklin, who was an inveterate user of first names) looked over the situation with a practiced eye and began making notes of essential improvements that had to be made right away: things to be done in the patients' cottages before they would be safe for paralytics burdened with braces and crutches; iron bars put along the sides of the treatment pool, in addition to other equipment; two rings suspended from crossbeams above the pool. (The latter was Franklin's idea; rings could be a source of fun as well as exercise, and he insisted on as much play as work in the rehabilitation program.) Then they would have to find some way of transporting the patients who were housed in the cottage colony, which was up on the slope, down to the treatment pool.

In the next day or two Franklin got hold of an old jalopy, in the village, which was used as a bus. Every day, with Mahoney at the wheel, it would come jolting down the slope in the morn-

ing sunlight, packed with patients, headed for the pool. At the
same time, while he was in the village, Franklin bought a Model-
T Ford touring car and had it fixed up at the blacksmith shop
so that he could drive it by hand—his inventiveness had devised
a system, which he worked out with the local blacksmith: slim
rods were welded to the foot pedals and brought up to a hinge
behind the dashboard; two holes bored in the dashboard allowed
the rods to come through, where the tips were fitted with wooden
knobs, which Franklin called "spools." The knobs were hand
controls for the foot pedals and, by pulling them out and pushing them in, he could start and stop the car as well as any man
with normally mobile legs. (His later cars were fitted with
variations of the same device, and the last one, which carried
the license plate "FDR-1, 1945," included an extended hand
brake rising from the floor board to the left of the wheel.) When
his "spools" worked, he was overjoyed with the sense of freedom
it gave him to be able to scoot around the countryside by himself
when he felt like it—to investigate the winding mountain roads,
stopping to talk to farmers (he had made friends with the man
who ran a farm on the top of Pine Mountain), discussing the
crops with an eye to developing the land as he had done in
Dutchess County. Leaning his arms on the wheel, he would
chat in a leisurely way, as if he had nothing else to do. His
bouncing flivver was soon a familiar sight along the back roads
of red clay, and no native needed a second invitation when he
would grind to a halt, fling open the door, and call, "Hop in!"

Dr. Hubbard came down by the end of May, but before then
Mahoney had set up a schedule for the experiment. After she
had loaded the "bus"—with the aid of strong young men from
the village, whom they hired to help lift patients, push wheel
chairs, etc., and whom Franklin dubbed "pushboys"—and they
were all, including those from the inn, gathered at the pool,
exercises began. Most of the patients had to be helped into their
suits and lifted into the pool. The physiotherapist joined them,
standing in water up to her waist at the treatment table, and

took them, one by one, giving each special exercises and muscle massages beneath the surface of the water. (Using the muscle chart Franklin and Dr. Johnson had drawn up, muscle testing was given to each patient and, on the rating, an individual course of exercises was set up.) For over an hour she worked with the patients, her strong hands and the warm, mineral-laden water enabling them to stir their stubborn limbs into action, however limited at first.

Franklin usually arrived at the pool after the treatment was under way since he spent a good part of the morning driving about in his flivver, supervising the building of roads, the construction of several new cottages (one for himself), the enlargement of a golf course he would never be able to use, and the transplanting of trees (for the "campus" he envisioned around the resort). He was constantly making notes on little scraps of paper—plans for new improvements. He would be hailed with delight by all the bathers in reply to the loud honking from the Ford as he drove up.

In the pool, he worked hard on his own exercises with Mahoney when his turn came, and occasionally made suggestions for the treatment of some particular patient. When the exercise period was over and Mahoney climbed out of the pool (admonishing them not to play so long that they wore themselves out), Franklin took over to direct the games. He conducted swimming races, organized teams for water basketball, and created an atmosphere that was more like a high-school gymnasium pool than a "hydrotherapeutic center," as Warm Springs was later designated by the American Orthopedic Association. The games were followed by a sun bath, then a rest period for the others, while Franklin went off in his Model-T again—he had too many affairs to look after to think of resting. When Dr. Hubbard came, a "walking period" was added to the day, again at Roosevelt's suggestion; patients could use the hotel porch for the present. Then he would put in a sidewalk, with rails and parallel bars. "Walking practice" became a regular feature of the therapy.

And, of course, there must be parties—bridge in the evening: Franklin often "made a fourth" at some table in the shabby old parlor of the hotel, though he claimed his game was miserable. (Occasionally there were poker parties, when six or eight men sat around the table in his cottage or the Harts' or the Rogers' —one of the patients who had bought a year-round cottage. Franklin, who had sharp poker sense, enjoyed these games and usually won.) And picnics: he made himself vice-president in charge of picnics and saw to it that everyone came along. He discovered a shelf of rock, called "Dowdell's Knob," overlooking the valley, and decided it would be a perfect spot for barbecues. The "Knob" became the scene for many a roast or fish fry, when, with full stomachs, they sat around the dying fire and told stories and sang—and forgot for a while the ache of braces and the fact that most of them, including himself, would have to be helped or carried by the "pushboys" back to the odd collection of cars that had brought them up the mountain road.

Two of the patients who came that spring were the daughters of wealthy fathers, and both men showed an interest in contributing to the development of Warm Springs. Franklin was not at a loss to cite various projects—a new central building (*not* a hospital, he insisted), a glass-enclosed pool for wintertime use —and his mind immediately leaped to the idea of enlisting the financial help of masses of people from all over the country— large contributions and small ones. With his friend Henry Toombs he laid out plans for a whole section of good-looking year-round cottages to be built up on the slope and sold to people who had a "polio" child or who merely wanted to live in the country. They might sell some of the property by the lot, which would help to develop the place; he was ready to sketch out a general scheme for the whole twelve hundred acres over the next twenty years, and he was undaunted when the somewhat pessimistic architect pointed out that Franklin did not even know if he would be in business the following summer. Toombs's realism only won him the title, "Henry the Tomb," from the irrepressible Roosevelt, who had supreme confidence that things would work out as he said.

He was not afraid to try.

Dr. Hubbard voiced grave doubts about the efficacy of underwater treatment in the beginning: it had never been tried before. They had no proof of its success—to which Franklin replied that they therefore had no proof of its failure. They must give the method a thorough trial.

His secret was that although he was the fountainhead from whom ideas gushed forth as abundantly as the springs poured from Pine Mountain, he included them all—patients, professional staff, pushboys, and other hired help—in the undertaking; it seemed more of a co-operative movement than private enterprise, and in many ways it was. Most important of all, he gave the patients the feeling that this was their project, that they must work as hard as he to make it a success. The "skeleton from Pennsylvania," Fred Botts, became, as a result of his experience as one of the earliest patients, an official "welcome man" for new arrivals, making them feel at home. Other adult patients, who had been stricken as Franklin was, at the peak of a career, were consulted on the advisability of various improvements, given the job of keeping track of any problems that came up while he was in New York, with suggestions for possible solutions. The children loved him for his laughter, his warmth and affection; because he would take the time to joke with them, to pick a bouquet of flowers and pin them on a little girl "because she was beautiful," or teach some little boy himself how to swim. He imbued them all with enough confidence to be able to face the regular summer guests (who began to appear around the middle of June) so that they as patients felt exclusive rather than excluded. They could laugh off the impolite stares and ignorant complaints. They were "in the know"; the regular guests were the outsiders.

By the end of June the experiment was well under way, and it looked as though the results were going to be good. Muscle tests of the twenty-three patients, including himself, showed more firmness in damaged tissues, greater mobility. He had said, "I'll find my improvement with the others; I'm not a man to accomplish much of anything alone," and he applied this attitude toward every aspect of the work at Warm Springs. He had committed himself to go to Marion again for the summer, and there was political work to be done before the fall elections, but he was loath to leave just when things were humming. However, he knew his "gang" was in capable hands and that they would continue to progress; he was counting on it.

Mahoney, working with him on the treatment table a few days before he left, asked him how much improvement he expected. He realized that it was unusual for him to be experiencing any improvement at all this long after the illness—usually patients did not respond to aftercare that took place more than a year from the time they were stricken—but he was not satisfied, not yet. It required only a moment to evaluate his hopes realistically, in the light of Dr. Hubbard's findings. Then he said, "I'll walk without crutches. I'll walk into a room without scaring everybody half to death." He hesitated, thinking of the nominating speech at Madison Square Garden. "I'll stand easily enough in front of people so that they'll forget I'm a cripple." The resoluteness in his voice left little doubt that somehow he would achieve his goal.

CHAPTER XI

The Battle Continues

EARLY IN JULY, before he went to Marion, Franklin became president of the Georgia Warm Springs Foundation, Incorporated, a temporary arrangement set up by Basil O'Connor to put the enterprise on a corporate basis so that they could proceed with the development in a businesslike way until a permanent, nonprofit organization could be formed. O'Connor was secretary and treasurer and Louis Howe one of the directors. Two thousand shares of common stock valued at $50,000, were issued to Roosevelt—at O'Connor's insistence—so that he would have a chance of regaining part of his investment. Franklin was equally insistent on giving the stock back to the corporation later on, but for the present he agreed to accept it.

He had rented a house in Marion big enough to accommodate the whole family—or as many of them who wanted to come there. His mother chose to open her house at Campobello, where the two older boys joined her later in the summer. Franklin, hard at work on his walking exercises with Dr. McDonald, wrote her on August 10: "Your letter makes me very homesick for Campo!" But he would not relieve his nostalgia until his legs were much stronger, and the memory of his illness much weaker. Not that he brooded on his long siege with infantile paralysis—he was

161

far too busy—but his self-perception told him that the sight of the island would call up the active vacations of former years, and the shades of departed joys would make him mournful. He was not one to spend time grieving.

Moreover, he was too occupied with the coming congressional election to experience more than momentary yearning for a lost playground. The house in Marion was something of a summer political headquarters for the New York State Democratic Committee. Al Smith had asked F.D.R. to act as temporary chairman of the state convention in September and to make the keynote address. Franklin was delighted; it would be a splendid opportunity to take a crack at the Republican Party and the frigid Cal Coolidge. "Look out for the fireworks!" he warned, and went to work on his speech.

There were rumors that he himself might be drafted, not for the governorship, but for U. S. Senator; he wanted neither one, but Louis, hearing definite details of the scheme, was afraid he might be tempted. "I have been warned of a plan to get you up to make a speech and then demand you to accept the nomination by a stampeded convention with everybody yelling 'We want Franklin!' " he hurried to advise, continuing with typical Howe humor: "This is of course a possibility, but I hope your spine is still sufficiently strong to assure them that you are still nigh to death's door for the next two years. Please try to look pallid and worn and weary when you address the convention so it will not be too exceedingly difficult to get by with the statement that your health will not permit you to run for anything for two years more."

Reading his letter, Franklin chuckled. His legs might be useless spindles, but from the waist up his appearance was anything but worn and weary; it was, on the contrary, hale and hearty. The exercise, the outdoor life he had managed to lead winter and summer since his illness, had given him a robustness that belied any claims of invalidism. There was a vitality, a glow of good health about him that inspired the other patients in Marion, as at Warm Springs, to increase their efforts, to work as tirelessly as he on the walking board, and to believe that recovery, if not full, then in large measure, was possible.

He went on preparing his speech, and the ringing tone of his voice at the convention was hardly that of a man "nigh to death's door." Still using one crutch and a cane, he was received with cheers as he approached the rostrum; and, at his smiling confidence, the cheers were doubled. In fine form, he lit into the myth of "Coolidge prosperity," charging the President with failure to help the farmers or end the coal strike that had deprived so many families of heat the previous winter. "The people of the East have well learned, through months of struggle to get coal for their furnaces and stoves, the hard meaning of the (Republican) slogan 'Keep cool with Coolidge,'" he jibed, with a foretaste of the sort of political thrust which made his speeches famous and which brought him the cheers of the convention and more. He spoke into a radio microphone, which sent his voice out to a wider audience than he had ever reached. It was probably one of the first political speeches to be broadcast, and the results proved that his propensity for trying new media (just as he was willing to try new methods for a cure) was one of his greatest political assets.

He knew in advance that he would not be drafted, for Tammany Hall had set up its slate some time earlier—Robert F. Wagner for senator and Al Smith for governor—but his speech, which made headlines the next day, won him greater following among voters outside of New York and made fast his position as one of the leaders of the Democratic Party.

Right after the convention he left for Warm Springs, accompanied by his mother and Missy. He had persuaded his mother to come to Georgia for a couple of weeks with the aim of arousing her interest in the project to the extent where she would invest some of her capital in its future. He felt that if she got a first-hand view of the work that was being done already, she would surely be convinced, as he was, that the place had great possibilities.

They found "Henry the Tomb" supervising several construction jobs, one of them Franklin's cottage, on which work was finally under way. Franklin hoped his mother would build one of those he and Henry had planned in the spring; if she did not live there, it would be a good piece of "income property" for her. The elder Mrs. Roosevelt would not commit herself until she had observed the therapy, as well as the surroundings in which it took place. (One could practically hear her sniff at the sight of the Meriwether Inn, and the work being done to change the physical aspect of the resort seemed in its initial stages haphazard, clumsy, all but impossible.) They found twenty-three patients still taking the treatment, some of them new in the past five weeks, some of them carry-overs from the spring who had remained all summer and would stay until the cold weather drove them away.

Franklin was greeted with shouts of joy at the pool; now that he was back, everything would be all right. The troublemaking tourists were beginning to leave anyway, but he was there to champion the patients, if necessary, before the summer guests were all gone. He was glad to be back; there was something intangible here for him that was missing in the treatment at Marion, for all of Dr. McDonald's close care. He asked if they had been "good boys and girls while Papa was away" and was answered by a chorus of laughing voices all at once. In the water, Mahoney, working at his leg muscles, decided to give him another test and found that he had gained in strength. He acknowledged that the summer had done him good, but the cold water at Marion was of small benefit compared to Warm Springs; he was full of renewed vigor—the special toe-tingling variety he found here—after one session in the pool. His mother sat by the side and watched—Franklin on the treatment table, Franklin with the other patients, conducting the games, leading the laughter . . .

Sara Roosevelt could be generous to a fault where her immediate family was concerned—she had made Anna, who had been married in April, a present of $2,000—but where the spending became a business venture, her Victorian conservatism took over and she was not ready to agree to any investment without a good deal of consideration. The "experiment" was most interesting; she was sure many patients might benefit from the treatment.

However, she left without actually agreeing to any of the propositions Franklin suggested, and she implied that he would do well not to let his enthusiasm run away with him or he might be penniless in a very short time. With a rush of words, he wrote her on October 13: "I miss you a lot and I don't have to tell you how I loved to have you here, and I know you were really interested in seeing what I think is a very practical good to which this place can be put and you needn't worry about my losing a fortune in it, for every step is being planned either to pay for itself or to make a profit on."

He might be a political power, a leader of men and benefactor to those less fortunate than he, but at times like this he was still the "good boy," cajoling his mother. The next week he sent her a birthday present, for which he fabricated an elaborate story to tease her and perhaps poke fun at her cautious attitude: "It came via a Scotch sailor who is beating his way from New Orleans to Baltimore and it was probably stolen or undoubtedly it was smuggled in. . . . I think it a really fine specimen, and it is of the rather rare variety which has different shades as you view it from different sides! It came over in the ship with the sailor who swears he got it in the Mediterranean, would not be more definite. Now aren't you intrigued!" He finished with the scarcely subtle information: "My house is started and they have dug the cellar and are beginning the foundations."

In the end, his mother consented to underwrite the construction of one of the year-round homes which Franklin had blue-printed for the slope, but she spent little time there and it was rented on an annual basis. Outside of this endowment, she steered clear of her son's wild dreams for Warm Springs, although in theory she approved of his aims and once or twice tried to raise money for the Foundation.

On November 8 he left for New York, where Louis was drumming his fingers until Franklin's return. The election had proven his 1924 prediction correct as to the "public reaction to the old money-controlled crowd": the Republican majority had been wiped out in the Senate, and in the House only thirty-five were left. There was little doubt that the letter campaign staged by the Roosevelt-Howe forces was in large measure responsible for the Democratic victory in Congress. Elated, Franklin planned to stop in Washington his way back to Warm Springs in February, and wrote to his Uncle Fred, who was there: "I wish much that I could stay with you. However, I have to give the annual dinner to the 1920 newspaper boys * and also have to see crowds of senators and congressmen, and it is really much easier for all concerned for me to go to the same hotel that I spent one night at last year—I think it is the Continental—near the station."

Late in February he and Eleanor arrived at the resort with Missy and Mahoney (who had come to *Hyde Park* in December when the weather in Georgia was too chilly to continue the therapy and the little colony disbanded; Franklin had not wanted to lose any of the ground he had gained during the summer, so during December and January she had continued to give him the exercises on a board laid across two sawhorses). During January he had received word from the American Orthopedic Association that, on the basis of Dr. Hubbard's report, which showed improvement in every one of the twenty-three patients who had received treatment at varying periods of five to seventeen weeks from June till December, the investigating committee

---

* This was the "Cufflinks Club," which received its title from the gold cuff links F.D.R. gave his staff and press men after the 1920 campaign. Among the members, who stayed together for twenty years, were Marvin McIntyre and Steve Early. Louis Howe always planned the clever entertainment at these dinners, including costumed skits, which he wrote.

of the Association had approved the work done by the doctor and was recommending "the establishment of a permanent hydrotherapeutic center at Warm Springs." One of the most important obstacles was overcome.

As soon as the news of official endorsement came, Basil O'Connor had the papers drawn up to make the Warm Springs Foundation a nonstock, nonprofit, permanent institution, while the temporary corporation they had formed earlier became the Meriwether Reserve, a subsidiary organization, which would take care of the handling of the hotel, the public pool, and the golf course. The Foundation qualified under the State Board of Charities, which would permit the acceptance of grants or gifts; its Board of Trustees, to which names could always be added, included, besides Roosevelt and O'Connor, George Foster Peabody, Herbert N. Straus, Louis McH. Howe, Dr. Leroy Hubbard, and the two businessmen whose daughters were patients.

One of the latter, Margaret Pope, had brought with her this time her own physiotherapist, Alice Lou Plastridge. After a week of observing the underwater treatments, she decided to accept the position of assistant physiotherapist at Warm Springs, which Franklin offered her when he saw her giving Mahoney a hand with the patients in the pool. New people were arriving daily, some with special problems, and they all required more help than those who were returning for the second or third time. Mahoney needed an assistant, and Alice Lou Plastridge, who was gentler by nature, not quite so "strict" with the patients, would be a good foil for her.

The promising state of affairs sent Franklin's spirits to the skies. As if his investment were not large enough already, he had recently bought 1,750 acres of land on Pine Mountain (including the farm belonging to the friend he had made on his jaunts in the Ford, Ed Doyle, who was going to work the whole tract). He sent an exuberant report to his mother: "We are safely installed in the *old* cottage, not unpacked as we hope to move into the *new* cottage by early next week. The new cottage

is *too* sweet, really very good in every way, the woodwork covering all walls and ceilings a great success. . . . Of course I am
taking a good deal of stuff out of the hotel, but there is much
to buy and today Eleanor and Missy have gone to Atlanta to
buy a stove and a refrigerator and they get back about six.

"This morning I have driven with Mr. Curtis and Miss Mahoney over the 'Pine Mountain Scenic Highway'—five miles long,
out to the 'Knob,' marvellous views all the way and cost me
only $1,050! I've been in the pool each day and done all the
exercises and stretching and am feeling finely. The weather is
warm and bright, the peach blossoms coming out, everything is
nearly a month early . . . I am going ahead with the big work
of preparing for 50 patients and hope Major Proctor [of the
Harvard Infantile Paralysis Commission] will soon raise some
money—the golf course comes along well and is going to be very
good."

(Though he never mentioned the game nor the longing he
felt to be out on the fairway himself once again, making a long,
swinging drive with his brassie, he took great interest in plotting
the course and found spots where he would be able to ride
alongside in the Ford, kibitzing the plays of able-bodied guests.)

Throughout the winter, he worked on the development of
Warm Springs as he worked on the development of his legs. A
Dodge replaced the old jalopy as patients' bus to the pool. Two
more treatment tables were added, and a bevy of girls from the
physical education department of nearby Peabody College came
to assist the two physiotherapists. A full-time swimming in-
structor was hired. Edsel Ford spent a week visiting the Piersons,
son-in-law and daughter of an associate of his who had sung the
praises of Warm Springs because of the improvement his daughter had shown. Ford was so impressed with the work and the
spirit of Warm Springs that he offered to donate money for any
project Roosevelt selected. Franklin immediately suggested the
glass-enclosed pool, and later received a check for $25,000 for its
construction from Ford.

The "new" cottage became familiar; it was built for his convenience with a door at the back leading into the long living room on one side, so that he could go in and out on his crutches easily by himself. He wanted to have as much independence as possible. (He still could not dress without assistance, and would never be able to put on his trousers by himself.) Once he knew the number of paces it took to cross the living room, he began experimenting on his own. He had a few ideas about learning to stand at his public appearances and, without telling Mahoney or the doctor, proceeded to work them out in private. If he could stand with his back pressed lightly against a wall for support, he could talk to committeemen or have his photo snapped and not have to depend on the third crutch of public sympathy, which he abhorred, for his political success. He began by getting to the wall, turning himself slowly around, inch by inch, until he could lean his back and shoulders against the wall, taking some of his weight off the crutches. He stood like this for a few minutes until he felt balanced. Then he hesitantly set the right crutch away from his body and let it slide to the floor. So far, so good. . . . He began putting the left one from under his arm, but there was too much weight on his weak left foot: he went sliding down to the floor with the crutch!

Pushing both crutches before him, he crawled to the nearest chair, hauled himself up into it, and started all over again, making a mental note to lean harder against the wall when he let go of the second crutch this time. If he still failed, he would keep on trying . . .

He did not have much time to himself with his various activities, but he made the most of short intervals of practice. One day, after he had finished dictating and Missy had left to type the letters, he got up on his crutches, reached the wall, turned himself around, leaned long enough till he felt really steady, set away the right crutch, set away the left crutch, leaning slightly harder against the wall, steady, steady . . .

"Is anybody home?" he heard someone call from the front

porch. It was his neighbor. If he could just hold his balance,
stay up . . .

"Come in, Leighton." His voice was strained, almost fearful
with suppressed excitement. "In *here*," he called as the screen
door opened. His neighbor's expression changed from one of
anxiety to happy relief as he stepped inside and saw the tall
man balanced against the wall, without crutches, smiling, and
heard the booming words, *"I'm standing alone!"*

To publicize the Foundation, Franklin had a small booklet
printed, containing a short history of Warm Springs and describing the work being done there in aftercare treatment of poliomyelitis patients; only one paragraph was devoted to his
discovery of the springs as a health restorative for paralytics and
his subsequent purchase of the property. His mother objected
strenuously because he had made no mention of other places
that had helped him, like Dr. Lovett's clinic in Boston, and
particularly Dr. McDonald's private therapy center in Marion,
where, in her opinion, her son had received the first *"real"* improvement. She had heard that the doctor was hurt at the
omission, and she thought Franklin in "any subsequent circulars"
should give credit to the other doctors who helped him; she even
gave him a little gratuitous advice on the wording he might use.

His reply was characteristic of his dealings with his mother
when she pushed him too far and his annoyance overcame his
filial devotion; his tone was the same as he had used in telling
her five years before that he would not retire to *Hyde Park* as
an invalid: "Of course I can't be responsible for *all* the silly and
untrue stories which gossip spreads," he informed her severely.
"No circular about Warm Springs, no statement or authorized
account has spoken about Warm Springs as being the only place
which has helped one . . . If Dr. McDonald is hurt I am sorry,
but he has no cause to be. I am not giving to the public any
history of my own case—if I did I should include Dr. Lovett,

Mrs. Lake, etc., etc. Why Dr. McDonald's name should appear in literature about Warm Springs I really can't see—the literature is not about me." He marshaled his points as in a debate: "Furthermore Dr. M. has been constantly begged by me to come down here and look things over. Finally, as Dr. M. is not an orthopedist, none of the orthopedists here would care to have him associated." The last, if somewhat removed from the issue, clinched his argument; his mother had no more to say on the subject of Warm Springs brochures.

He went on trying to put his property on a paying basis. Other spheres of development came into the orbit of his mind's eye. He would have Ed Doyle try raising other crops besides cotton. Cattle: why not cattle in Georgia as well as Texas? Pine Mountain Valley could be developed as farmland; not nearly enough of the soil there was being worked; some of the farmers trying to eke out a living from the less fertile areas in Georgia might be brought here by a homestead movement . . .

When he went to New York in the spring (his half brother Rosy died early in May and there were affairs to be settled), the resort was barely making ends meet, but he had high hopes for its future and the greatest enthusiasm for its achievements so far. He contacted friends and relatives to aid in spreading the word. To Eleanor's "Auntie Bye" (Mrs. W. Sheffield Cowles, whose home they had rented during the Navy years in Washington) he wrote:

I am sending you some of our folders about Warm Springs. The work of starting a combined resort and therapeutic center has been most fascinating for it is something which, so far as I know, has never been done in this country before.

We have already 30 patients there this summer and our total capacity for this coming year will be only 50, a figure I think we shall reach in a few weeks. Most of the patients are suffering from infantile paralysis though we have two arthritis cases at the present time and expect several others, and also hope to have a good many people come there next winter for a few weeks of after-cure succeeding operations or serious illness. It ought to be a success as the doctors are most enthusiastic . . .

Aside from the therapeutic value, we have so many natural resources for the families of patients that the swimming, golf, riding, and quail shooting ought to appeal to those in perfect health. The whole property I have put under the Georgia Warm Springs Foundation and am now busily engaged in trying to raise two or three hundred thousand dollars to carry out the improvements and pay the mortgage on the property.

Oh, I do wish that you could be wafted down there and placed gently in a chair and slid gracefully down a ramp into the water. You would love the informality and truly languid southern atmosphere of the place! My one fear is that this gentle charm will appeal to some of our rich friends who are suffering from nervous prosperity and that they will come down there and ruin our atmosphere. . . .

Do send me some nice souls this coming winter, but not the kind who would insist on full dress for dinner every evening.

A look at the books with Basil O'Connor in the office at 120 Broadway showed a balance of $26.85 cash on hand in the First National Bank of Columbus and $24.22 in the Bank of Manchester. Less than $12,000 had been donated by philanthropists and friends. (The glass-enclosed pool was started, but Ford had not yet sent the check.) There was perhaps another $600 in the strongbox at the Meriwether Inn. Not very promising for a first venture, but Roosevelt was playing a hunch, and his businesslike law partner understood: the potentiality of Warm Springs lay in a factor that went far beyond any figures in a ledger, and that was its *spirit*. And the particular elixir that kept it going was not only the cheerful co-operation of a handful of hopeful patients and benefactors—the charitableness of Warm Springs— but a kind of force that yeasted and foamed beneath the surface and would one day become powerful enough to attack and destroy the disease that had brought so much destruction to people's lives.

"The place will burst its seams some day," O'Connor said.

"All we need is a professional fund-raiser, a good promotion scheme, and a first-rate administrator at Warm Springs—one who'll be on the job all the time—not a politician about to throw his hat in the ring!"

Roosevelt laughed and told his partner not to worry. He knew O'Connor was referring to the rumors that he would be running for governor of New York, since he was promoting Al Smith for the presidential nomination again. However, he had no intention of running for any office until his legs were much stronger, until he had mastered the trick of standing alone (for more than a few minutes at a time, as he did now), and, if possible, of walking alone.

"And don't worry about Warm Springs either, we'll find a couple of men," he added confidently.

During the summer he and Louis widened their political contacts in the interest of Smith's candidacy; Franklin was convinced of the merit in Smith's domestic policy—the worth of his "kitchen" cabinet in New York State was undeniable—but his foreign policy, or lack of it, was a source of concern. Nevertheless, Franklin considered Smith's progressiveness of enough value to discount his weakness and place him far ahead of McAdoo, the only other choice.

He was in Warm Springs again by September and spent the whole year concentrating on the development of his legs and the Warm Springs Foundation, always, of course, doing his best to build up the Democratic Party and his own position as one of its national leaders.

A young man by the name of Arthur Carpenter came to Warm Springs with his family; he had been advertising manager of *Parents'* magazine when infantile paralysis struck him down six months before. Like Franklin, he was a man of too much energy and drive to settle down in a wheel chair, and he had not been at the colony long before he was full of ideas for improving Warm Springs. Franklin, who recognized his ability, was glad to listen; he had rented his mother's cottage to the Carpenters and was often a visitor there. When "Carp" invited his friend Keith Morgan, a successful insurance man, to come down for a look at the wonder of Warm Springs, Franklin, with his in-stinctive judgment of ability in people, knew that he had found the two men he and O'Connor had talked about. Carpenter became business manager and Morgan took on the job of raising money for Warm Springs. They were to prove a highly successful combination.

More patients came. There were eight treatment tables lined up in one end of the pool, and eight physiotherapists. If a patient needed financial help to stay the necessary five weeks—a mini-mum in order to show real improvement—there was now some-thing called the Patients' Aid Fund, to which they could turn. The number of patients grew, and the regular guests decreased. Franklin's optimism was not in the least dampened by the fact that his idea of combining a resort with a therapeutic center was not working out; they would concentrate on the center, that was all. If one tack did not work, another would.

The glass-enclosed pool was nearly finished (Ford had sent his check for $25,000) and would be ready for use in December. A cement sidewalk equipped with iron bars had been laid, and walking practice was a regular feature of the daily routine. Patients cheered each other on, criticized each other's gait. Frank-lin could not walk as well as some, but he was the first to get up and make the effort to move as much like a normally healthy person as possible. His height was always a hindrance. His weak left foot still described an arc as he dragged forward in taking a step, but the right foot was flexible enough now so that he could put weight on it, balance, and lift his leg more naturally. Sometimes, as he had done in Marion, he took the right brace off and the leg held, functioning without support, but Mahoney and the doctor (as well as his own common sense) told him that he would have to wear both braces in public for safety.

Often, in the evening, he had extra practice sessions with Ma-honey, who would come over to the cottage after dinner for an hour or so. He showed her how he had taught himself to stand and they worked out a way for him to hold his balance longer, gripping the back of a chair or the edge of the desk for support; if he could hang onto the rostrum when he spoke in public, he could look like any one of the speakers who faced an audience, and his listeners' attention would not be distracted by crutches or canes.

The Democratic convention was to be held in Houston at the end of June, and Smith, as a matter of course, asked "Frank" to deliver the nominating address as he had done in 1924 and at the state convention in 1926. This time he was determined to appear unencumbered. In the living room at Warm Springs he and Mahoney tried using the arm-support method of walking, with a cane instead of one crutch; he could do without crutches entirely and walk with only one cane if he had a good, strong arm to clench. He sent for Elliott, who was now eighteen, tall, and huskier than Jimmy, to come to Warm Springs as soon as school was out. It would be well for all of his sons to learn the technique of walking with him—certainly the two older ones should know. (Elliott's resentment against Groton had not softened, and now he was balking the idea of going to college; perhaps being at Warm Springs and going to the convention would have the same effect as the cruise aboard the *Larooco,* when he seemed to be more reasonable. He wanted to work on a ranch during the summer, and Franklin made arrangements for him to go on from Houston to one of the big cattle ranches farther west.) Like all the Roosevelt children, he was lively company and joined the practicing with vigorous interest. Mahoney showed him how to hold his right arm with a clenched fist against his middle so that his biceps stood out with iron strength for his father's grasp.

Franklin had learned to handle a cane in such a way that it gave him extraordinary support; he kept the forefinger of his right hand (which held the cane) glued straight down along the side of the rod, where it not only prevented the cane from slipping but sent the weight from his powerful shoulder and arm directly through to the tip. He would balance himself against the wall with the cane in his right hand, and Elliott would get on his left side. Then, slowly, under Mahoney's watchful eye, they would start across the living room to the opposite wall.

Like James, Elliott had to get used to his father's tense grip on his arm, to the uneven gait, which produced a kind of awkward rhythm as the cane tip touched the floor, the right leg lifted, the pressure on his arm increased, and the left swung stiffly forward in an arc. He learned, too, how to pace his own steps to fit in with the strange rhythmic groping of his father. Their initial attempt to cross the room seemed endless and, when Franklin leaned his hips against the wall, telling his son to relax his arm, Elliott noticed the beads of perspiration on his face. The cross back was a little easier and, by the third time, Elliott was catching on. Then Franklin taught him to smile, to joke with Mahoney just as *he* did while they were wending their way back and forth, back and forth, across the long living room. At the convention they would have to smile at people, greet delegates . . .

It was sweltering in Houston, and the convention hall was packed with Democrats seeking the nomination for their choice of candidates. Franklin was able to enjoy the excitement with an attitude that was interested yet detached. (He afterwards wrote to a friend: "The only remark of the convention which will live was that of Will Rogers, who said that in trying to mop his brow in the Rice Hotel mob, he mopped three others before he reached his own.") Because of his life at Warm Springs, he possessed a certain serenity which he had never exhibited before and which enabled him to move calmly, surely, along the platform to the podium. Elliott's arm was firm; the cane was steady as he rammed the tip to the floor each time; his legs were steady, more so than they had been at any time since his illness. . . . The cheering increased as they moved toward the rostrum.

He whispered to Elliott to "shake the pulpit," and when he

found it strong enough, he clamped one hand on the edge, leaning heavily on it, yet balanced with his braced feet wide apart so that from the audience he looked, as he had hoped, like any of the speakers on the platform. With his free hand he could even wave to the cheering crowd, a smile of joyous triumph lighting his face. He spoke, once the cheering died down, in a quiet, intimate way, as if he were talking to friends, not delivering convention oratory. The silver tones of his voice, which here, too, went out over the radio to thousands of homes, were "wellbred and gentlemanly" but not aloof. Al Smith had refused the microphone because it only intensified the rasp in his voice and it made him nervous to talk into "that pie-plate." Not so Roosevelt: with his sense of showmanship, he made the most of his resonance and good diction to reach, through radio, more voters than he had in 1926. As he wrote to Walter Lippman, "I tried the definite experiment this year of writing and delivering my speech wholly for the benefit of the radio audience and press rather than for any forensic effect it might have on the delegates and audience in the convention hall. Smith had the votes anyway, and it seemed to me more important to reach out for the Republicans and independents throughout the country." And he was highly successful in his aim.

Even the Republican *Chicago Tribune* carried an editorial entitled "The Twilight of the Silver Tongues" and paid Roosevelt the dubious compliment of being "the only Republican in the Democratic party." The *New York Times* called it "A High-Bred Speech" of "a gentleman speaking to gentlemen," and elaborated: "There was nothing strained or fantastic or extravagant in what he said. It was the address of a fair-minded and cultivated man, avoiding the usual perils of national convention oratory, and discussing in an intelligent way the qualifications which should be sought for in the President of the United States and the ability of ALFRED SMITH to meet every fair test of capacity . . . It is seldom that a political speech attains this kind of eloquence. Indeed, the entire address of Mr. FRANK-

LIN ROOSEVELT is a model of its kind—limpid and unaffected in style and without a single trace of fustian." (Al Smith sent a blue-penciled copy of the article to Franklin, along with a note in the margin: "Dear Frank: This must be right because it brought tears in the Mansion when you spoke it. Al.")

The *New York World-Telegram* ran a glowing eyewitness account of the speech by Will Durant, who was covering the convention:

Here on the stage is Franklin Roosevelt, beyond comparison the finest man that has appeared at either convention; beside him the master minds who held the platform at Kansas City were crude bourgeois porters suddenly made rich.

A figure tall and proud even in suffering; a face of classic profile; pale with years of struggle against paralysis; a frame nervous and yet self-controlled with that tense, taut unity of spirit which lifts the complex soul above those whose calmness is only a stolidity; most obviously a gentleman and a scholar. A man softened and cleansed and illumined with pain. What in the name of Croker and Tweed is he doing here? . . .

Hear the nominating speech; it is not a battery of rockets, bombs and tear-drawing gas—it is not shouted, it is quietly read; there is hardly a gesture, hardly a raising of the voice. This is a civilized man; he could look Balfour and Poincaré in the face. For the moment we are lifted up.

That Al Smith was nominated on the first ballot was undoubtedly the greatest tribute to Franklin's address; up until then the convention had displayed a marked disunity of choice. Smith considered his overwhelming victory a personal triumph. For Franklin it was also a triumph—a double-edged victory. Not only had he increased his stature in the party and his national following among the voters, but he had proved to himself that he could manipulate his legs in public so that people would not realize how crippled they were, even now. He had vowed a few weeks before the convention, "I'll walk." And he did, in a sense. But he knew he had a long way to go until the phrase became a truthful one.

CHAPTER XII

Crucial Choice

BEFORE HE LEFT HOUSTON, Franklin was approached by the Smith forces on the possibility of his taking the nomination for governor, but he met them with a firm refusal: he would need at least another two years' work on his legs before he could think of holding public office. The coaxing of victory-flushed Al Smith that "Frank" as the gubernatorial candidate would insure a Democratic landslide in November did not sway his decision. He returned to Warm Springs right after the convention—as if he could hardly wait to push ahead with the rehabilitation, now that he had come so close.

His next goal was to get rid of the braces; he was convinced that with another two years of treatment, of stimulation by the warm mineral waters of the pool and regular exercise followed by rest, he would be strong enough to hold himself upright without the confining ridges of steel that brought him so much discomfort. He was elated at the very thought of being able to cast aside his braces, not merely for the sake of greater comfort and freedom, but because he felt that the stronger he was, the better job he could do politically, and he was eager to get on with the therapy.

At the pool, he asked Mahoney to bring him the chart of the

179

muscle test she had given him before he left for Houston. They went over it carefully: every muscle in his legs had increased in strength since the previous test; it was amazing.

"If we keep on at this rate, I won't have any excuse to turn down the nomination in two years," he grinned happily.

He spent a couple of weeks adhering strictly to routine—underwater exercises on the treatment table, swimming, sun-bathing, walking practice. Then a telegram from the National Democratic Committee summoned him to New York, where he was offered the chairmanship, but this, too, he turned down. He was determined not to let politics keep him too long away from achieving final recovery. Moreover, he and Louis Howe had decided that 1928 was a bad year politically; it was Louis' plan to have the governorship come in 1932, and, in 1936, Franklin would be ready for the presidency.

By the end of July he was in Warm Springs again, working away at the business of getting the Foundation, as well as his legs, in condition. He answered one of the many pleas he received from politicians and newspaper editors to run for governor with the valid excuse that "I have got so much tied up in the Georgia Warm Springs Foundation that I have to devote a lot of time to that . . ."

The languor of summer lay over Pine Mountain slope, allowing the patients to be out-of-doors till it was time to go to sleep. There were frequent picnics on the "Knob" and rides down the mountain in the moonlight. Like any group of close community interests, the Warm Springs colony of patients and staff found its share of romances—usually between girl patient and pushboy or physiotherapist and male patient—blossoming in these months. Occasionally two patients fell in love, and a friend of Missy's, who came to visit her the summer before, had married young Curtis, the manager of the hotel before Carpenter's appearance. Franklin was not one to discourage a healthy response among his companions, and suggested building a chapel on the grounds for the convenience of those who had discovered the best therapy of all. Miss Georgia Wilkins, who lived up on the hill and was one of the original owners of the resort, offered to sponsor the construction of a small sanctuary for worship and weddings.

Franklin had expected the Smith forces to call on him constantly for advice on national issues in the campaign, if not to act as one of the key organizers in bringing out a nationwide vote for Smith. But the Governor, who had asked businessman John J. Raskob to be the national chairman when Roosevelt refused the post, had his own limited ideas and stuck to them. To Franklin's dismay, he concentrated on Prohibition, religion, and power politics in New York State, which held little interest for the farmers across the country and scarcely endeared him to the dry South, already hostile on the subject of Smith's Catholicism. Nevertheless, Franklin arranged to make campaign speeches for Smith in Georgia, and carried on a correspondence campaign for a progressive economic policy in contrast to the Coolidge-Hoover conservatism. As Smith's original sponsor for the presidency, he felt obligated to do all he could to get his man elected. Anti-Smith handbills were being distributed all over the South, and Franklin strove to combat them in any time that he could spare from the treatment.

One night, just after he had comfortably settled himself in bed and was starting to sort a few stamps for relaxation, he heard footsteps outside and a rustling near the window. Turning the lamp directly on the screen, he recognized one of the villagers and called out to ask what he wanted. The man hesitantly whispered hoarsely that he wanted to "ask Mr. Roosevelt a question."

Rather than call for his valet and disturb the whole household, Franklin slid out of bed to the floor and crawled on his hands and knees to the window. The burning question on the man's mind concerned Smith's Catholicism. At the town meeting, attended by "Methodys" and Baptists, there was a good deal of discussion on the Roman Catholic policy of not recognizing marriages made outside the church. If Smith were elected, would

there not be a danger that all non-Catholic children would
be considered illegitimate?

Franklin's reply, made with a perfectly straight face (which he
had some difficulty in maintaining), was to tell his nocturnal
guest that the Roosevelts were both Protestant, had five children,
and were not in the least worried about their legal status. Relieved, the caller thanked him and disappeared into the shadows.
Franklin crawled back across the floor and pulled himself up
into the bed, where he smothered his roar of laughter under the
pillow.

The incident made him realize, however, what the Democratic
Party was up against in the South with a candidate like Smith;
he had been fully aware of the opposition, but not to what
lengths it would go. He would have to schedule more speeches
in Smith's favor.

Whatever the differences of opinion might be on national
policy, Al Smith and his contingent still kept after Franklin to
run for governor. They needed him desperately to insure not
only a wider national vote but the upstate New York vote,
usually Republican, without which Smith could not even carry
his own state. During August and September Franklin was
besieged with phone calls and wires from Smith, begging him
to run; almost as many came from Louis in New York, exhorting
him to decline on the basis of his health. One of his telegrams
warned: "There is no answer to the health plea, but any other
reason will be overruled by the governor himself."

Boss Ed Flynn of the Bronx called several times. Al called
from Milwaukee, where he was making a speech, to plead and
coax, but Franklin was immovable. Al finally conceded, "You're
the doctor, Frank," and disconsolately hung up. Franklin, disturbed by the pressure he had had to resist, sent Smith a wire
at the state convention in Rochester, where the Governor went
directly from Milwaukee. Missy typed the telegram: "Confirm-
ing my telephone message, I wish that I might even consider the
possibility of running for governor this year, especially if by so

doing I could further help you, but there are two considerations which are compelling." The first was that Smith's own record as Governor would assure the state vote anyway; the second was his health: he was only forty-six and owed it to his family to "give the present constant improvement a chance to continue. It probably means getting rid of leg braces during the next two winters, and that would be impossible if I had to remain in Albany . . ."

Missy sent the wire off to Rochester, but Franklin had a premonition that he had not heard the end of the matter. He was scheduled to speak the following night in Manchester, but he told Missy to see that he had plans that would keep him "out of reach of a telephone all day." He did not want to be tempted . . . It might be a good idea to have a picnic . . . Missy spoke to Fred Botts, who, with Carpenter and some of the others, started making arrangements for an outing on the "Knob" the next day.

Franklin's hunch was more than justified; while he was still in the pool the following morning (October 2), the first phone call came from Rochester. He sent a message that he "was out somewhere on a picnic and would be away all day." Then, to make it honest, he called to the others, "Let's get going!"

While the New York telephone operators had instructions to reach Franklin D. Roosevelt *anywhere in Georgia,* he was up on the "Knob," enjoying a picnic lunch with his companions, sitting on a big rock, his braced legs stretched stiffly out in front of him for support. The telephone in his cottage kept ringing, telegrams were delivered. . . . When he returned from the "Knob" late in the afternoon—he would not have come back then, except that he had to change clothes for the trip to Manchester—he found a wire from Anna, who urged him, "Go ahead and take." He chuckled at his daughter's brash advice, and took the time before he went to Manchester to send her an answer: "You ought to be spanked." But he could not have told whether he felt more like kissing her or not . . .

At the convention, Smith had by no means given up. He conferred with Herbert Lehman, the candidate for lieutenant governor if Roosevelt ran, and persuaded him to call Roosevelt with the offer to take over in Albany during the times Franklin had to be in Warm Springs. Next Smith asked Tom Lynch, the man who was responsible for Roosevelt's first appearance in politics, to make a long distance plea with his friend; and he sounded out John J. Raskob on the possibility of that tycoon's making a sizable contribution to Warm Springs, which would relieve Roosevelt's financial burden. All three put in phone calls to Warm Springs, but could not reach their man; the first two Franklin refused; by the time the third came, he was on his way to deliver the campaign speech for the presidential candidate.

As a last resort, Smith cornered Eleanor, who had come to the convention with great reluctance, and began trying to induce her to phone her husband. She found her position extremely embarrassing; she had agreed with Louis that Franklin should wait another two years before running for governor, but the pressure was beginning to wear her down. A few days earlier she had written to Franklin, "They feel so strongly about your running and even good explanations can be made to sound foolish." Now she parried with the leaders who had approached her. "I feel that this is Mr. Roosevelt's own problem," she said calmly. "I am not trying to influence him either way." Al Smith had his answer ready. "All we want you to do is to get him on the phone; we'll do the influencing!" In the end she agreed to do only that and no more.

By this time, Franklin had arrived at the schoolhouse in Manchester where he was to speak in the auditorium, three flights up. He had to haul himself up, step by step, hanging onto the railing—there was no other way—and in the auditorium he had to be lifted up to the platform. It was only a few steps to his chair, but he found them difficult to make by himself; the cane was not enough support and none of the local politicians he came with knew the "arm method." As he dropped heavily into his chair, he made a mental note always to be accompanied in public by someone trained to assist him in walking. While he was waiting to be introduced, a messenger brought him word that Mrs. Roosevelt was on the phone at the corner drugstore. He could not go then, and when he saw the messenger approaching the platform again during his speech, he talked for half an hour longer than he had intended. After all, he was praising Smith . . .

As he was acknowledging the applause, a third message came—the Rochester call was still waiting. . . . He finally got to the drugstore, where he discovered he had to talk from a phone booth—if he could manage to get inside. The men with him lowered him to the little seat, and he leaned against the rear wall, his braced legs sticking out of the booth. He picked up the receiver. To avoid the subject of his nomination, he began telling Eleanor with great relish how he had purposely kept away from the phone all day, but she cut him short by saying that she had to catch the train to Providence (for her teaching job in the Todhunter School) and that several people wanted to speak with him. She handed the phone to Al Smith, whose rasping "Frank?" he could barely hear. The connection was dreadful. Raskob tried, but a constant humming drowned out his words. Then the operator broke in to suggest that as soon as Mr. Roosevelt got back to Warm Springs he should go to the telephone in the Meriwether Inn.

He drove fast, but silently, back to Warm Springs, trying to prepare his answer to the arguments he knew he would have to face if the call came through. Missy wondered aloud what he was going to tell them, but he was not sure. For the first time, he did not know what he was going to do. He was thinking as fast as he drove, striving to come to a decision. Half an hour later, when the call came through, he was no closer to making up his mind. However, he could feel a hunch coming upon him, his intuition and a sense of timing that acted outside of reason . . .

Al's voice was painfully clear now; "Frank" had handled himself so expertly in Houston—what more did he want?

Franklin mentioned his obligation to Warm Springs; he was determined to see the Foundation through to success.

This was Smith's cue to put Raskob on the wire; he solved that problem with a single sentence: "Damn the Foundation! We'll take care of it!" He pledged a personal contribution of $25,000 as a start, and offered to loan Franklin $250,000 to pay off the mortgage.

Al took over again and argued that all Franklin had to do was to make a couple of radio speeches, be elected, and go back to Warm Springs.

He could go to Albany for the inaugural address, send a message to the State Legislature, and return to the resort for another two months. After that, he would just have to be in Albany to get the thirty days' bills out, and he could spend the whole summer at Warm Springs.

Franklin's laughing reply was a leaf from Al's own book: "Don't hand me that baloney!"

Momentarily stopped, Smith put Lehman on. The prospective Lieutenant Governor promised to "spell" him whenever he needed a rest. Franklin could see the room in the Seneca Hotel in Rochester, the tense faces of the cluster of men around the phone . . . Before he could say anything more, one way or the other, Smith came back with "just one more question": if Franklin was nominated the following day by the delegates at the convention, would he refuse the nomination?

He hesitated, and in that moment of hesitation changed the whole course of his life. He then told Al Smith that although he could not sanction the presentation of his name, he did not know what he would do if he were actually nominated.

His words were enough for Smith, who shouted, "I won't ask you any more questions," and jubilantly banged up the receiver.

At the Meriwether Inn, Franklin replaced the receiver with a far different gesture—one of thoughtfulness and finality, as if it designated the end of an era for him. Picking up his crutches, he made his way slowly across the big shabby old parlor—if the money came through, one of the first things he would do now would be to raze this rotting fire trap of an inn. He felt somewhat stunned by the sudden turn of events, but he could still focus on detail with an attentive eye and respond to the expectant smiles of the patients sitting around the parlor. Usually he was part of the evening activity—a bridge game, a song around the piano—but tonight he stopped only for a word or two with the companions closest to him: Fred, and Toi Batchelder, a pretty teen-age girl who had made remarkable progress since her arrival at Warm Springs two years ago as one of the early patients. (Toi had been "teaching" him to play bridge.)

Two of the pushboys hoisted him into the Ford, and he drove to his cottage. McDuffie helped him undress and take off the braces, but he told the valet he did not want to get into bed just yet; he would sit in front of the fire and relax, enjoying the freedom of his legs. The October days were warm, but the nights grew cool on the mountain slope, enough to make a small fire a comfort. As he sat gazing into the flames, Franklin considered what lay ahead of him; he had told Al Smith he did not know what he would do if he were nominated, but he did not have to ponder the matter. He was well aware that his ambiguous answer to Al constituted an agreement to run for governor, and he conjured up in the firelight the future as it would probably be in contrast to his present way of life. (It was true that he and Louis had planned his ultimate nomination for governor and then president, but he was unprepared for the precipitation of events by four years.) He recognized the fact that if he won the governorship it would mean the virtual end of all concentrated treatment on his legs, but he sometimes wondered, though he scarcely admitted it, even to himself, whether he had not already reached the maximum improvement he could attain. Then there was Raskob's offer to underwrite the Foundation; while he did not think it would be necessary to accept the loan, he was glad to learn that the financier was willing to take the risk. More important than his own recovery, now that he could manage to get around, was the rehabilitation of thousands of human beings, from the little children to adults like himself, who might be brought back to a normal life, not to mention the millions who might be saved by prevention from attack, if science could find the formula. For some time he had seen the Foundation in his mind's eye as a source for the furtherance of research which would lead to the discovery of some serum or vaccine. Dr. Draper's findings proved to be only a stab in the dark; on a large scale the fight against infantile paralysis would have to be organized, supported by publicly-donated funds. He would not have called himself a visionary—he was far too practical—but he saw things as they had the power of being, with every ounce of that potential realized. Now he was fully aware of the task he was undertaking.

Finally, of course, there was the lure that politics had for him, the sense of excitement he had in Houston; and he could not deny that he had a sense of obligation to the party, to the people who were begging him to run for office. Psychologically he felt the time was ripe—call it a hunch, a premonition . . . Louis would have a fit, but this time Franklin was going to make a political move entirely on his own . . .

Once he had clarified his decision, he called McDuffie to help him to bed, and slept soundly until morning.

He was nominated by acclamation the following afternoon at the final session in the Seneca Hotel in Rochester. The reporters, flabbergasted, showed Al Smith the Atlanta dispatches saying that Roosevelt would not run. Smith told them plainly, "The convention has the consent of Mr. Roosevelt to do what it did. It nominated him and he will run."

Almost immediately the telegrams came flooding to Warm Springs. Eleanor wired: "Regret that you had to accept, but know that you felt it obligatory." (Her statement to the puzzled newspapermen was somewhat longer: "In the end, you have to do what your friends want you to. There comes to every man, if he is wanted, the feeling that there is almost an obligation to return the confidence shown him.") Louis' terse telegram read glumly: "Mess is no name for it. For once, I have no advice to give."

Franklin laughed to himself like a schoolboy who has outwitted his teacher; this time he had not asked Louis' advice.

In the pool the day the news broke, his laughter rang clear, more buoyant than ever. His companions regarded him with pride, not unmixed with awe. His earnestness during walking practice showed them what it must mean to get up before masses of people whose prying eyes would be quick to detect physical weakness. Yet he appeared confident, undisturbed, almost eager to start on his first real political adventure in seven years. His attitude gave them the strength to follow his example; his whole being seemed to say, "If I can do it, you can do it."

Whether they could or not, he gave them hope, and when he left to accept the nomination in New York, their love went with him.

CHAPTER XIII

Back to the Political Battlefield

PUTTING THE NATIONAL CAMPAIGN ahead of his own, Franklin went out to the Middle West, where he made two speeches for Al Smith's candidacy before going to Hyde Park to receive official word of his nomination. In his speech, he said, "I accept the nomination for governor because I am a disciple in a great cause. I have been enlisted as a private in the ranks for many years and I cannot fail to heed a call to more active service in a time when so much is at stake." He did not mention the state of his health; he thought it would be obvious to those who saw him that he was exceptionally well, and he certainly was not going to advertise his handicap.

"No sob stuff!" he warned the reporters who came to interview him before his address. He made it clear that he wanted no quarter because of paralysis still in his legs, and both reporters as well as photographers respected his request. Directly after his nomination, however, Republican newspapers tried to discount his chances for winning the election by editorial portraits of Roosevelt as a man who was seriously ill, risking his life to gratify Smith's ambitions for the presidency.

"There is something both pathetic and pitiless in the 'drafting' of Franklin D. Roosevelt by Alfred E. Smith," the *New York*

Post, then in Republican hands, declared in a patronizing tone. "Stung by the Presidential bee, driven by the necessity of getting New York's electoral vote, the Governor made this most loyal of friends agree to serve his ambition at a price that is beyond all reason." It went on to speak of Roosevelt's struggle to walk, his refusals of the nomination and acceptance only under duress, and concluded, "But even his own friends, out of love for him, will hesitate to vote for him now." Other papers spread the rumor that Lehman, as Lieutenant Governor, would take over as soon as Roosevelt got into office.

Franklin was angry at such tactics and squashed the rumors at the outset with a heated statement to the press: "I am amazed to hear that efforts are being made to make it appear that I have been 'sacrificed' by Governor Smith to further his own election and that my friends should vote against me to prevent such 'sacrifice.'

"I do not believe that appeals to personal friendship should form any part of a plea to the electorate. But if I did, my own appeal would be: 'Not only do I want my friends to vote for me, but if they are my real friends I ask them to get as many other people to vote for me as possible.'" He ended sternly, on a businesslike note:

"I trust this statement will eliminate this particular bit of nonsense from the campaign from the very beginning."

Al Smith added his retort to the rumors of his candidate's physical inability to hold office with a quip that was widely printed: "A Governor does not have to be an acrobat. We do not elect him for his ability to do a double back-flip or a handspring."

When Franklin came to the Biltmore Hotel in New York City to open his headquarters before starting on the strenuous campaign Louis and he had set up, he assumed the same sort of joking attitude with the reporters who were waiting curiously to see how he handled himself. The *Herald Tribune* wrote that he came in . . . "supporting himself on the left side with a crutch and on the right side with a cane, and leaning forward on these supports so that he could draw his feet after him in a sliding gait."

"How's the state of your optimism?" he was asked.

"Fine," he said. "I told them in Poughkeepsie this afternoon that most people who are nominated for the Governorship have to run, but obviously I am not in condition to run, and therefore I am counting on my friends all over the State to make it possible for me to walk in."

To another newsman, who inquired if it was true that he would go to Warm Springs between sessions of the State Legislature, he answered with a grin, referring to Lehman, who was a banker, "I can leave the combination of my safe to Colonel Lehman, knowing that it will be in safe hands." His joking, happy frame of mind won the admiration of the reporters and made the opposition press so apprehensive that the subject of his poor physical condition was dropped like a hot chestnut. Any attack would have to be strictly on political grounds.

Franklin was determined to prove that his health was not a factor in his endurance or efficiency. "I'll go more places and make more speeches than any man who ever ran for office in New York State," he announced to the organization Louis had set up in lightning order. Now that the die was cast, the little man worked with powerhouse energy around the clock to form a campaign committee that was not only skillful but hard-working and vote-winning. Men like Jim Farley and a young lawyer by the name of Samuel Rosenman, who had aided in the research for Smith's speeches, were part of the group that strove to swing the vote for Roosevelt.

The strategy was simple enough. Tammany Hall would take care of the Metropolitan Area; Franklin would campaign almost entirely in upstate New York, the Republican stronghold he had assailed in 1910, when he flashed about the State in the red Maxwell, a singular sight among the farmers. The car he was to use now was unique, also, for a vastly different reason. A reinforced steel rail was put into the back of the front seat, so that he could pull himself up by it with the strength of his powerful arms and, with his braces locked tight, stand in the car to greet the crowds, have his photo snapped, and make a short speech.

At home, he and Eleanor conferred as to whether she should do any campaigning for him; she was already heading up the office work of the women's division under Belle Moskowitz, Smith's aggressive adviser, and Franklin thought it was more important for her to remain at that post than to stump for him. He asked Anna, however, since she had urged him to run, to come along as one of his secretarial aides, and she was more than ready to accompany him on the campaign tour.

From the first, he enjoyed himself immensely, in spite of the difficulties he had to face merely to pull himself up or get out of the car. He accepted and acknowledged his handicap—made jokes about his legs—but at the same time he overlooked or rose above the inconvenience and discomfort. He had reached a point of objectivity that was astounding to his colleagues and his listeners. (At Rochester, where he emphasized the humanitarian program of the Democratic Party, which included aid to crippled children, he was able to say, without self-consciousness: "I suppose that people will recognize that I myself furnish a perfectly good example of what can be done by the right kind of care. I dislike to use this personal example, but it happens to fit. . . . By personal good fortune I was able to get the very best kind of care, and the result of having the right kind of care is that today I am on my feet." What private means had done for him, he pointed out, state aid could do for unnumbered victims; and the cost of restoring these cripples to an active, useful life would be comparatively small—much smaller than keeping them dependent for the rest of their lives, a financial burden to their familites and, therefore, to society.) Most of the time he brushed aside, if he mentioned it at all, his disability, as if it were of minor importance, and turned to the issues of the time—labor problems, labor laws, public power plans, religious prejudice (when he campaigned for Smith); but when, as in Rochester, he touched on the subject of the handicapped, it was almost as if an outsider was speaking, even though he included himself. His approach was scientific, completely devoid of self-pity: when he was humorous on the subject, it was without egotism; he was not seeking to draw attention, but to laugh it away. If he had been in treatment with Freud himself, he could not have made a better adjustment.

The tour began on October 17 at Binghamton. Here he met Rosenman, who was loaded down with big manila envelopes of "material" for campaign speeches, but for several days Franklin did not even ask him to open them. He had his own ideas for subject matter, and they were concerned principally with the national election. Rosenman had never met a politician like Roosevelt, whose manner was "cordial, but not gruffly so." Franklin's impeccable English, cultured accent, and country-squire appearance—he usually wore a soft collar and loose tweed suit for comfort's sake, and because soft, loose-fitting clothes were easier for him to get into—was something of a surprise to Rosenman, who was used to self-made-man Al Smith, with his snappy suits and brown derby. (Franklin insisted on campaigning in his battered old brown felt, which he had worn in the 1920 campaign, in spite of Anna's pleas that he buy a new one before they left New York City. This ancient, well-creased fedora was like an old friend; it would bring him luck, he maintained.) Furthermore, Rosenman had heard that F.D.R. was "something of a playboy and idler," but the man he met, who stood so straight and tall on his rigid legs once he got himself up to speak, did not fit that description at all—"the broad jaw and upthrust chin, the piercing, flashing eyes, the firm hands" delineated no lightweight amateur politician, but a professional of championship caliber who would put up a stiff fight and who, indeed, seemed confident of winning.

Yet Rosenman was puzzled because Franklin, although amiable

enough, ignored him and his envelopes for at least three days, and the tour was to last only two weeks. At Binghamton, where he made one of his major addresses, Franklin launched an attack on the anti-Catholic propaganda against Smith and the evils of religious prejudice in general; he spoke in an auditorium and made sure there was someone with him—on several occasions it was Jimmy—who had practiced the arm-and-cane method of walking, and, except for the two or three minutes until his stance was fixed behind the rostrum, the audience hardly seemed to notice his handicap. His glowing smile, his attractive way of speaking, and his arresting phrases (for which he had a special knack) absorbed their attention almost immediately.

At the crossroads stops during the next few days, he developed a different technique. He rode in the touring car of the little automobile cavalcade that carried the campaign retinue through Republican towns, and he did not seem at all bothered by Hoover buttons or by the small groups of doubtful Democrats that turned up. At every stop, he reached forward for a firm grasp on the iron bar and pulled himself to his feet, his biceps bulging under the sleeves of his tweed jacket, his straining shoulders as broad and hard as an athlete's. Snapping his braces to be sure they would hold him up and clamping one hand on the rod, he waved to the people with the other and smiled happily, as if this were a sociable gathering. All they saw was the strong upper half of his body, his handsome, friendly face. He pitched into a brief sketch of his reasons for becoming the Democratic candidate. The *Herald Tribune* recorded his usual pattern as including "a few words of fulsome praise for Alfred E. Smith, a reference to his last call in the town . . . an allusion to himself as an 'upstate farmer, too,' a description of the campaign as one of reactionaryism versus progressivism, and an invitation for the crowd to take a look and judge for itself the state of his health." What they saw was a robust-looking man, but a fine-grained one, well spoken, highly intelligent, and one of them, a farmer. They could not see his weakened legs, or realize the tremendous effort it took for him to stand there talking to them.

Sometimes he would ask, with an edge of satire: "Do I look like a sick man?" and everyone would laugh, everyone would feel at home with him. At that point he would sit down again on the back seat and the Democrats in the crowd would come up to shake hands with him, to talk over their problems and report any progress that had been made in the area. Here the habit of listening that he formed during the past six years stood him in good stead. People whom he once would have considered bores, back in the days when he was a State senator, when he could (and often did) turn and walk away from them, he now found himself listening to, not only because he could not help himself, but because he was interested in their project, in finding out what Mr. Average Man thought, felt, and did. (It also became a kind of game for him to draw his constituents out with pertinent questions—as he did with a band of dour and somewhat dejected Democrats in Utica—and watch them expand and glow with a sense of importance at receiving attention.)

From one small town to another he traveled, exuberant and energetic. After four days of constant touring and speaking, he was in better shape than the rest of his group, one of the papers reported; he would probably wear them out before the end of the campaign. Rosenman began to wonder, with his unopened envelopes, why he had been asked to come along. Then a couple of telegrams arrived from State leaders: "Remind Roosevelt that he is running too"; and, even more imperative, "Tell the candidate that he is not running for president but for governor and tell him to stick to state issues."

When Rosenman showed the wires to "the candidate," he grinned good-naturedly. "All right, let's draft a speech about labor," he agreed. And in a "one-horse town" hotel they sat up half the night hammering out one of his most successful addresses, given in Buffalo. It was the beginning of an association that lasted seventeen years. Rosenman, used to Al Smith's custom of speaking extemporaneously from general topics jotted on the backs of envelopes, was surprised when Franklin asked him to write the first draft for several speeches on separate state issues, including labor, public welfare, power (public utilities), farm problems, and other subjects of State concern. Then he would go over the drafts with the utmost care, smoking a good deal but saying very little; he had enormous powers of concentration, Rosenman discovered. After he had gone through the material several times, he would add touches to the final draft which gave a speech color and drama. He had a particular genius for livening up a routine topic with an unusual, often original, phrase or an unexpected slant.

Newspapers sat up and took notice. Reporters were able to send in clear-cut stories every day. What he said, and the way he said it, became of primary importance; the physical difficulties in making appearances faded into the background. In this, the reporters and photographers, who saw what he had to go through merely to stand up before an audience, were in large measure responsible. Reporters kept mention of his health at a minimum. Except to state that it was excellent, or to quote his own quips on the subject, they did not discuss it. Men from opposition papers—and most of them were—treated him as if he were perfectly normal: they attacked his politics and wisely dropped the question of his physical ability. Photographers, who often had opportunity to catch him in an awkward moment, trying to get his balance, haul himself up in or out of the automobile, cooperated to the fullest. (When the campaign was over and Franklin prepared to vote in the Hyde Park Town Hall, a group of newsreel men and photographers had their cameras ready as he pulled forward and extended his stiffly held legs out of the door, his face a study in concentration. He looked up and smiled briefly. "No movies of me getting out of the machine, boys," he suggested pleasantly; and they stood aside, busily adjusting photographic equipment until he had maneuvered his long body through the little doorway, grasped the arm of his driver, locked

his braces, and leaned on his cane in a nonchalant pose. Then
the cameras started clicking.) The sportsmanlike policy of taking
pictures of F.D.R. from the waist up or in a pre-posed standing
shot was to continue through all the years of his public career.

His popularity picked up as the campaign gathered momen-
tum: Buffalo, Rochester, and Syracuse; Watertown, Oswego, and
Utica; and Republican-controlled rural areas, where the results
began to show up dramatically. Franklin described it at the end
of the upstate hitch: "We got to Herkimer, where we all made
speeches; then we expected to come through to Schenectady, but
when we got to Fonda, there were forty or fifty automobiles in
line blocking the road, and we were literally kidnapped. We
were told that in that neck of the woods, Gloversville, where in
the past there had been occasionally two Democrats and sometimes three, that had gone to the polls, there were two thousand
people waiting for us on the street, so we changed our plans a
little and went up to Gloversville. We got to Amsterdam. We
expected to go through Amsterdam just as fast as the traffic cops
would let us, but there were sixteen hundred people in the
theatre in Amsterdam, waiting. They had been waiting there
two hours. And then, for good measure, we just dropped into
Schenectady"—barely in time, he might have added, for one of
his major campaign speeches—"and spoke there earlier in the
evening, and now here we are in Troy." He could not resist a
final shot: "Too bad about this unfortunate sick man, isn't it?"

Things were going well at headquarters in New York, too.
Louis wrote on October 22 that they had already piled up
$100,000 in campaign funds and expected more. Feeling much
less gloomy about the outcome that he had at first, he predicted,
"I am horribly afraid you are going to be elected."

By the end of October, the betting odds, which had been two
to one on Ottinger, the Republican candidate, became two to
one in favor of Roosevelt, and his chances of carrying the State
were now eclipsing those of Al Smith. Certainly he had proved
his physical fitness for the job in Albany, and, in so doing, he

had increased as well as regained his popular following as a
fighting campaigner and an exciting political figure. When he
arrived in New York City on November 1 to wind up the campaign with Smith in a tour of the Metropolitan Area, he was
hailed with wild enthusiasm by the crowds which packed the
halls.

He spoke wherever he was scheduled, in spite of the hazards
which arose when the enormous crowds made it impossible for
him to enter the front of a building and make his way up the
aisle to the stage. The rear entrances were risky. In Brooklyn
a steep fire escape led up to the stage door; it was too narrow to
allow men to carry him, he decided. He handed his cane to one
of the men and shook the railing; it seemed firm enough. "I
think it'll hold me," he announced hopefully. He got a tight
grasp on the rail with his right hand and leaned his left palm
against the rough brick wall. He lifted his stronger leg and
pulled his weaker one up to the first step, as his body swung
forward by means of his powerful shoulders and arms, his strong
wrists and large firm hands.

"It's all in knowing how," he grinned. Step by step, he began
laboriously pulling up to the top of the steep flight. Anna,
watching him fearfully with the others, followed directly behind
him and noticed that the back of his neck was wet with perspiration, the cords distended with strain. Once his hand nearly
slipped away from the wall and he swayed, balancing. When
he finally managed to reach the top, he was completely out of
breath and leaned heavily against the doorframe while Anna
mopped his steaming face with his handkerchief. Two of the
men who followed her rushed to support him.

It took a moment or two till his pulses stopped pounding and
he could breathe naturally again, and he said the chairman
should begin the introduction. They could hear the words and
then the applause coming up with a roar . . . He flexed the
fingers of his left hand, sore from scraping against the brick, and
gripped his helper's arm; taking his cane from Anna with the

other hand, he put it into position with his forefinger out along the rod and started for the stage in his slow, uneven, but steady, gait. When the spotlight caught him his head came up automatically and his beaming smile, warm and appreciative of the ovation, did not betray his sense of secret triumph at having physically overcome a tremendous obstacle. The cheering audience, seeing only the strong upper part of him behind the podium, one hand on the edge of it, knew nothing of his recent ordeal. And as soon as he began to speak, he himself forgot about it. Such trials were a part of the game—if he was going to campaign, he had to expect them.

At another hall an emergency ramp had been laid down leading to the stage, and he thought he would have little difficulty getting there; but the crowds were so great that, although there were policemen present to control them, they kept pushing forward to get a good view of him. His pathway had to be cleared every few steps and, with his slow tread, it took him a full five minutes to reach his seat on the platform. But by now his popularity kept the crowd cheering and waving flags the whole time.

In Yorkville the auditorium was small and packed to the doors. It was impossible to consider trying to get in the front entrance. Here, too, there was a fire escape in the rear, wider than the one in Brooklyn, and, although he hated the humiliation of being carried, he thought it wiser than to use up undue energy in struggling to the top by himself; moreover, it ended in a window back of the stage. He had to be shoved through by the strong arms that held him. . . .

Frances Perkins, who had known him slightly in his early years as State Senator, was one of the fifty-odd people to be on the platform that night, and she stood in the wings, watching with "a mixture of consternation and admiration," her hand on her throat, as he was brought in over the fire escape and through the window. She recorded that he "came up over that perilous, uncomfortable, and humiliating 'entrance,' and his manner was pleasant, courteous, enthusiastic. He got up on his braces, adjusted them, straightened himself, smoothed his hair, *linked* his arm in his son Jim's, and walked out on the platform as if this were nothing unusual." That she was able to use the expression "linked his arm" is testimony to the impression of casualness he was able to give when his fingers were locked in a tight grip on Jimmy's arm and his knees were shaking a little from having his weight put on them suddenly when he was set down. He immediately launched into his speech, and the audience went wild; but Frances Perkins scarcely heard what he said. To her, and to the other colleagues who saw him from the wings, the important thing was his courage. No matter how much his contemporaries might disagree with him at various times, they could not deny his valor, the creative quality in his brave acceptance of the hard blow fate had dealt him.

Franklin himself was exhilarated and, indeed, seemed to thrive on the campaign, no matter how rigorous it might be. Louis said all he had needed was "a sound exciting dose of politics" and he agreed. In one of the last campaign speeches at Yonkers, he declared happily, "If I could keep on campaigning twelve months longer, I'd throw away my canes."

However, he had to stop, because election day was at hand. He cast his ballot in Hyde Park shortly before eleven on the morning of November 6, and went in to New York with his mother to be at the Biltmore headquarters when the returns came in that evening. Early figures were not encouraging as far as the national picture was concerned, and long before midnight it was apparent that Hoover would win the presidency. Smith was losing even in New York, and by twelve o'clock the Democrats had conceded his defeat by an overwhelmingly victorious Hoover. The contest for governor was much closer— Franklin sat quietly, listening for the returns from upstate districts—but it looked as though Ottinger would be carried into office by the Republican landslide. A cloud of disappointment hung over the group of committeemen at Democratic headquarters; they had come so close! Louis was heartsick, but Franklin told him to cheer up, the end had not come yet.

At around one o'clock a few scattered returns trickled in from districts they had covered in the tour, and the balance began to tip in Roosevelt's favor. Ed Flynn, drawing up a tally, figured a narrow victory for their candidate if the good returns kept coming. They were slow. . . . Then some poor returns showed up; it was discouraging, but Franklin's spirits did not sag like the others'.

"I think the politicians there are up to their old tricks," he remarked to Sam Rosenman. He meant they were delaying returns until they saw how many votes they would have to stuff into the ballot boxes to beat Roosevelt's slight lead in New York City. "We've got to speed up those returns!" he insisted. He got on the phone and began putting in call after call to the sheriff's office in every hamlet and town he had visited and many that he had not, demanding that the officers of the law supervise the count. Ed Flynn sent a statement to the press at two in the morning, charging the Republicans with fraud by delaying returns. Franklin stayed on the phone until six in the morning. The results began to tell: the returns, which came in steadily, gave a slim margin to Roosevelt, which finally added up to a hairline victory for him. In the final count, which was not settled for several days, he received 2,130,193 votes to Ottinger's 2,104,629; he had won by 25,000 votes!

He joked about being a "one-half of one per cent governor," but he was jubilant over his victory, and, now that the whirlwind of electioneering had died down, exhausted. (He was also extremely disappointed at Smith's defeat; more, perhaps, for what it meant in terms of the Democratic Party as a national force than for concern about Al.) Ten days after Ottinger had finally conceded, Franklin was on his way to Warm Springs for a well-earned rest, accompanied by Eleanor, Missy, and a new secretary who was to be her assistant from that time on: Grace Tully, who had joined the staff on the tour. A group of state Democratic leaders followed within a few days to help him make plans for the governorship while he was "resting."

His companions at Warm Springs were fairly bursting with pride over his election and met the train with a parade led by

Fred Botts, in a tall silk hat and cutaway, driving the ancient coach from Meriwether Inn, followed by a string of automobiles loaded with patients and a number of villagers who wanted to wish him well. Franklin was touched and, although he was tired, took the time to say a few words and visit with his friends before driving to his cottage. The politicians who came down to consult with him were impressed with the way things hummed at the little resort; the new glass-enclosed pool was ready for use and ground had been broken for an infirmary; the townspeople went out of their way to do favors for Franklin and did all they could to make the politicians comfortable. (One of them said to another, "Our boy Franklin's really got 'em on the run down here.")

There were conferences by the dozen in the little cottage. Missy and Grace Tully had a hard time handling the traffic. Men came to meet with the governor-elect in his bedroom before breakfast and gathered in little groups in front of the fireplace before he went to bed. Basil O'Connor came down and moved briskly around the resort, making notes, not colliding with the politicians if he could help it. He was interested in expanding Warm Springs. Franklin bathed in the new pool and, if the sun was warm enough, lay in its rays for a while; but on this trip he could not devote much time to the recreation or to the exercises and the walking court. He had had plenty of exercise and, when he was not conferring, needed to rest.

In New York, Louis was busy at his wizardry, making up a political brew that would be ready in 1932. All over the country, Democrats were talking about the man of the hour, the governor-elect, the logical candidate, the one man who could hold the Democratic Party together. Will Rogers sent a check for Warm Springs, with the note: "I don't know how the Party can ever get through paying you. You pulled them out of a tough hole."

On Thanksgiving Day, Franklin had dinner in the dining room at the Inn, surrounded by his "gang." He carved four turkeys and said this would be the Founder's Day at Warm Springs, because it was the first Thanksgiving they had spent together. And in his heart there was probably a private prayer of gratitude.

CHAPTER XIV

Victory in Albany

HE WAS GOVERNOR. He was sworn in on the first of January 1929, taking the oath of office with his left hand on the old Dutch family Bible, published in Holland in 1686 and used for the ceremony at his request; he held his right hand in mid-air, repeating the oath, and stood straight and strong; only the tips of his steel braces, showing beneath the striped trousers, betrayed the fact that there was a weakness in his physical make-up. He used neither crutch nor cane for support. At Warm Springs he had taught himself to stand alone with the distant purpose of such public occasions in mind, and he was making use of the accomplishment sooner than he had expected. He was able to maintain his balance without strain or fatigue during the ritual —he wanted to assume the office of the governorship on his own.

It was symbolic of the way he had already assumed the executive responsibility by making his own appointments, even though his action had caused a schism between him and Al Smith, who had expected that "Frank" would take over not only the state program of social legislation and reform that he had begun, but his group of advisers as well. His particular recommendation was Belle Moskowitz, who was responsible, most people admitted, for much of the progressive policy the State had adopted during

his governorship. She was "able, high-minded, intelligent"—
and "shrewd" and "domineering." She had served Smith loyally,
to the point where there were those who claimed that she ran
the office of governor for him. She would be ideal for "Frank,"
Al thought. With Belle as the official Governor's Secretary, Frank
could go to Warm Springs whenever it was necessary, and rest
assured that there was someone in Albany who could look after
things.

Franklin had listened to him, had agreed that Mrs. Moskowitz
was able, reliable, and had done a great deal for Al and for
good government in the State; but he would not commit himself
on her appointment as Governor's Secretary. He wanted to appoint his own aides. He felt this was doubly important in his
case, in order to prove his mettle as an executive and as a physically healthy man. But to Al he said nothing one way or the
other. When the ex-Governor, getting nervous as Inauguration
Day drew near, sent various people to give him a nudge, he still
would not agree to Belle, although he offered no clue as to
whether or not he had anyone else in mind.

To Frances Perkins, one of Smith's emissaries, he admitted,
with a striking degree of self-analysis, "I didn't feel able to make
this campaign for governor, but I made it. I didn't feel that I
was sufficiently recovered to undertake the duties of Governor
of New York, but here I am. After Al said that to me I thought
about myself and I realized that I've *got* to be Governor of the
State of New York and I have got to be it MYSELF. . . . I feel
sure that if I had Belle Moskowitz there, she is so accustomed
to running and planning everything, she would inevitably plan
and develop the work of the Governor of New York in such
a way that I would not really put *myself* into it. I have to do
it this way by myself without Mrs. Moskowitz. I am awfully sorry
if it hurts anybody, particularly Al."

Yet he was not sufficiently concerned to give Al an inkling as
to the person he might appoint, if he knew who it was going to
be. Although he was giving the matter a good deal of thought,

he probably had not made up his mind. One of the reasons he objected to Belle Moskowitz may very well have been the fact that he had had to cope with a domineering woman in his mother, and he did not want the same problem in Albany that he had in Hyde Park. It was true that his mother had come around beautifully on the matter of his political career; she had been extremely gracious during the campaign, had not uttered a murmur when the house and grounds at *Hyde Park* had been overrun with politicians, and no one was more proud of Franklin's victory than she. However, she still held the reins at *Hyde Park* and Franklin had long ago accepted this as her province; he usually had things the way he wanted them in the end, but it took some maneuvering. He did not want to have to "handle" Belle Moskowitz, who was, if anything, more touchy than his mother when her judgment was questioned. She was naturally resentful of his failure to snap up her services now, and in her bitter complaints to Smith probably broadened the break between the two men.

Not until the night before Inauguration Day did he let Al know that he had appointed Guernsey Cross, a competent worker in the Party, as Secretary to the Governor. Then he explained, "You know I need a great, big, strong man as secretary. I need someone whom I can lean on physically, if necessary, and I think it will be better, Al." He had presented Smith with a fait accompli, and nothing could be done about it at that late hour, but the ex-Governor was offended beyond reconciliation.

Soon after he was inaugurated, Franklin called the first of the informal conferences of state officials, which he initiated to discuss casually with his co-workers matters slated for legislation. He wanted to get acquainted with the people in State government, and he wanted them to feel that he and they were all working together. The meeting was held in the Executive Chamber in the Capitol; an ornate room originally designed as an audience chamber, it was decorated in red velvet and gold, and the impressive drapes were embroidered with the coat of arms of New York. At one end of the long room stood a huge desk behind which the Governor was supposed to sit during hearings. At the opposite end was the door by which he entered, leading from his private office. Between the two stretched the entire length of the Chamber, but no one realized, until it was too late, that this would present a difficult problem for the new Governor. At least a hundred people had gathered for the conference, many of whom Roosevelt did not know.

He came in, holding onto Guernsey Cross's arm for support, his cane in his right hand. As a matter of custom, everyone stood up when he entered, waiting courteously until the Governor was seated before they sat down. The Secretary had practiced walking with Franklin, but it seemed to take them an endless time to reach the desk. The floor was polished and Franklin had to put the tip of his cane down with extra care, so it would not slide. . . . The audience watched him uneasily, growing tense as they stood and waited, while he moved slowly in his awkward, dragging gait toward the desk; they began to wonder, with dread, whether he would be able to reach it.

He was not quite halfway across the room when he sensed the anxiety and tension of those who were watching. He looked up and smiled, nodded at Frances Perkins and one or two others he knew, and in a carefree gesture threw back his head, his strong chin jutting out. With a quick wave of his cane, he assured them lightly, "That's all right, I'll make it!" He set everyone at ease; a ripple of relieved laughter crossed the waiting crowd, and it seemed only a moment later that he was behind the desk and they all sat down and went to work.

Franklin wasted no time in getting down to cases, and those who conferred with him that day discovered that he was easy to work with because he was quick to grasp a situation and to act on it. He asked pertinent and stimulating questions and, in the main, accepted judgments from those he felt were qualified. He continued to make his own appointments when a post had to be filled, and one of these was to promote Frances Perkins from Chairman of the Industrial Board to Industrial Commissioner, again disregarding Al Smith's advice. Al had appointed Frances when "women had never been appointed to anything" and he thought she was "first class," but he thought the Commissioner should be a man. Franklin argued that her record showed she could handle the job as well as any man and a good deal better than the one she was replacing. He had known her since his first Albany days and was convinced of her ability. She proved that his estimate of her was entirely accurate; Frances was neither aggressive nor domineering, like Belle Moskowitz, but she was firm; and she had a keen grasp of labor affairs. She became, like so many of the people he dealt with, a friend of the Roosevelt family, a close associate for the rest of his life.

He selected his friend and neighbor, Henry ("the Morgue") Morgenthau, Jr., as head of the Agricultural Advisory Commission because he had worked hard during the campaign and was a good farmer.

The official family at the Executive Mansion included Missy and Grace Tully, who served as secretaries to both Roosevelts. Eleanor divided her time between Albany and the Todhunter School, her busy schedule requiring her to be away teaching from Monday to Thursday night. Often, when she was not there, Missy acted as official hostess. Louis, of course, was in and out, his head buzzing with plans for the future. He usually saw Franklin early in the morning, while the latter was having breakfast in bed, and before the state duties began. (Louis' eye was on the White House. Happy as he had been over Franklin's victory, he regarded Albany merely as a junction on the way to Washington.) Samuel Rosenman, who became Franklin's counsel, was there off and on. Jim Farley, one of the most ardent campaign workers, frequently came there with Louis to plot the course of the Democratic Party on the national scene; and, in the second term, a young reformer by the name of Harry Hopkins was very much in evidence at the Executive Mansion.

On weekends and holiday vacations the house was overflowing

with boys of varying ages; from Jimmy, who was now at Harvard, to fourteen-year-old John at Groton, they came, sometimes all at once, each one bringing a friend. In winter there were skis parked in the hallway, and in spring baseball bats and tennis rackets stood around. The chairs were strewn with jackets and sweaters (no matter how much Eleanor kept after the boys to put away their wraps), which gave the stuffy Victorian "Mansion" a homey, lived-in atmosphere it had probably never experienced in the history of the State. And when Anna visited her parents with her year-old daughter, there were evidences of an infant around the house. (A "four-generations" photograph was taken at this time, showing Franklin with his mother, daughter, and granddaughter.) Nieces and nephews, aunts and uncles, cousins and family friends came for visits at various times; Eleanor's friends, Marion Dickerman and Nancy Cook, who were living in the cottage at Val-Kill, where they were setting up the furniture factory, were accepted in the household as part of the family.

In this kaleidoscopic picture of domesticity mixed with his professional interests, Franklin was happy to pose as the head of a large and growing family. After he reached the White House he often referred to himself as "Papa." The constant commotion did not upset him in the least; on the contrary, he relished the confusion, for the fact that he could move through it without being disturbed was a sign of radiant health, of his complete return to a normal active life in the fullest sense. His renewed vigor was a source of joy, and even wonder, to him when he stopped to think about it, which was not often, because he was too much occupied with the affairs—and problems—of state.

During the first two months of his administration he spent time setting up his own organization, by which he could carry on the program started by Smith. He was in full accord with the reforms, but he wanted to continue them by means which gave him the most facility. Besides lining up personnel of his own choosing, he made certain physical alterations to help him get things done. He had ramps put over the steps leading to the

Executive Mansion and at the underpass leading to his office in front of the Capitol; he saw to it that the furniture was moved around so that it would be accessible, with the fewest possible steps taken to reach the desks or chairs he used; he had filing cabinets within easy reach in his private office.

Toward the end of February, after he had delivered his address to the Legislature, in which he asked for a record budget, immediately causing a furor, he went to Warm Springs for a brief rest. When he traveled from this time on he had to be accompanied by bodyguards. He picked out two former state troopers—Gus Gennerich and Earl Miller—strong, muscular men, who could be relied on for support as well as protection. Between Gus and the Governor a camaraderie sprang up immediately. The police guard, taking his cue from Franklin's first-name habit of addressing people, treated the new Governor with very little ceremony, and Franklin was delighted. They would indulge in a kind of horseplay that astonished onlookers who happened to see them during an informal moment. One trick Gus liked to pull was to bark out "Alley-oop!" when he was helping Franklin into the Ford, giving him such a terrific shove as he lifted him in that the whole automobile shook (even the new blue Model-A he bought, which was considerably stronger than the old Model-T). Franklin would make a pretense of absolute stillness, and then, with a sudden shout back, would grab Gus around the shoulders and wrestle him down to the car door or throw him back away from the running board. Gus, panting and twisting, would wrest himself out of the hold as fast as he could, because the "Boss," when he was sitting down, had terrific strength.

There was no one who could assist Franklin in walking as well as Gus; he had an arm of steel, and yet his nervous system was so highly geared that he knew just how to gauge his steps to coincide with Franklin's gait, how to help him at curbs or up a flight of stairs, if that became necessary, and occasionally it did.

Earl Miller taught Eleanor, who was on the trip, how to ride

horseback really well—she had always been a timid rider—and
he encouraged Franklin to try getting on a horse more often,
showing him a way to straddle so he would not be too uncomfortable. Franklin could not endure the jolting for very long;
the tops of the braces cut into his hips and his legs could hardly
grip the sides of the horse. But he did try riding a gentle mare,
and on one of the trails his horse ambled along he discovered
the ideal spot for a house he would build—high up on the slope,
on a little hill overlooking Pine Mountain valley. His home
would have a porch in the back, a place to watch the sunset
over the panoramic view; in the front it would be level with
the ground, so he and his gang would have no trouble getting
inside. . . .

The new infirmary, which was taking shape, also was designed
with an entrance devoid of steps—a one-story building of southern
colonial architecture, with columns across the front, and wide
windows looking out on what would be the green lawn of the
campus. Things were shaping up. Edsel Ford had donated
$30,000; Raskob about $50,000 (and over the next three years
he would send checks amounting to $113,000). Keith Morgan,
the official fund-raiser, had lined up a good many more contrib-
utors, and Arthur Carpenter was managing so well that the resort
was showing a slight profit. Franklin could relax on the administrative end of his "investment" and enjoy a good rest. Characteristically, however, he soon discovered a new project—slum
clearance in Atlanta—linking up the work that was being done
in New York with the problem in Georgia.

He returned feeling refreshed and ready to fight for his budget,
which he finally won. His first big hurdle as Governor was taken
in stride, and during the next nine months he set about continuing the reforms: workmen's compensation was speeded up;
safety codes for factories were improved; industrial hygiene and
preventive activities in the Labor Department were developed.
He pushed for a wider utilities program, as well as a reforestation project.

In all of these Franklin used the "human" approach; he had to see things in terms of human experience before he could deal with the statistics. He had Frances Perkins give him a graphic picture of the conditions discovered by the Labor Department: how men contracted silicosis from polishing the insides of glass milk tanks; how girls painting illuminated dials on clocks and watches picked up radium poisoning from shaping the fine hair brushes in a point with their lips; how an old carpenter who lost his arm was cheated out of his workmen's compensation. When he heard stories like these, he could get ideas for improving the situation and set the wheels in motion for proper legislation.

When summer came and the Legislature disbanded, a good many measures had been passed to further the reforms of Franklin's predecessor. He spent most of the summer at *Hyde Park,* where he could be close to Albany and New York City in case he was needed for consultation on state or national politics. He could bathe in the little pool at Val-Kill, do his morning exercises on the south lawn, and be ready by noon to entertain visitors, most of them political associates. A great many people who wanted to have private talks with the Governor came to see him in Hyde Park, and more often than not were invited for lunch, afternoon tea, or dinner; sometimes they stayed overnight—a custom Sara Roosevelt preserved from long years of country living, when people who came by horse and carriage rarely returned the same night and one had to be prepared for guests who might stay several weeks. (Now that Franklin was Governor, she put herself out to be charming to those who worked with him. "I think a mother should always be friends with her children's friends," she would say benignly, making it obvious that she would never be friendly with these people if it were not for Franklin.)

It was not unusual for a sizable gathering to be assembled by lunchtime, and they would all sit down at a long table on the porch, enjoying the breeze that blew off the Hudson; if nothing else was on hand, Eleanor could always serve scrambled eggs and Franklin would be well satisfied with the menu. He sat at the head of the table, a genial host; he talked to everyone and kept up a running banter with the boys, who were home for summer vacation and making the most of their freedom from school discipline. They loved to tease their father and argue with him as they could never argue with teachers, and he encouraged them. One prank they all liked to play was to give out with some tall tale when a distinguished guest was present; the more preposterous the story the better, and it did not matter whether they were able to pull it off or not—they would burst out laughing, Franklin along with them.

For private conferences, Franklin still used his little study off the back hall, the same one he had used as a boy and for the first political conclave he had had in 1910 with Judge Mack and Tom Lynch. His mother often remarked, "I do wish he'd let me fix him up a nice study, now that he is grown up and is the Governor." But Franklin's answer, when she broached the subject to him, was always, "This is plenty good enough for me." He liked it just the way it was—a small room nearly filled by a big desk, an old easy chair and a couple of straight-backs, a bookcase close by, a row of pipes, a few ash trays, knickknacks—"everything right within reach," he often said; and he wanted it to stay that way. Here he conferred with state dignitaries, went over the budgets for different departments, and did all sorts of writing, from messages to the Legislature to Thanksgiving proclamations.

Later he went to Warm Springs, and his companions were so glad to see him they immediately planned a picnic on the "Knob." Someone had dragged a car cushion onto one of the big rocks for him, but after a while he decided to move over to the barbecue pit. As he heaved himself up, one of his braces broke and he went clumping to the ground. The electrician of the Foundation, John Riehle, helped him back to the cushion and asked to see the brace. Franklin opened his belt, reached into his trousers, and unbuckled the straps, and John pulled the brace out through the bottom of his trouser leg. If the electrician could fix it, Franklin thought, a lot of time could be saved; otherwise, he would have to send the brace all the way to Boston to be repaired.

"Can you fix it?" he asked.

"Maybe." John was hefting the brace. "How much does this thing weigh?"

"About seven and a half pounds." Franklin made a face. "Feels like a ton."

The electrician nodded. "There's no need for braces to be so heavy. With the right metal I'll bet I could make one around three pounds—for children, about a pound and a half."

Then and there the idea for a brace shop at Warm Springs came to Franklin's mind, and he acted on it at once by consulting with Arthur Carpenter and others as to the cost of a machine shop equipped to fashion and forge braces of the lightest metals which would be strong enough. Patients could be fitted right there, and adjustments could be made immediately; no long gaps while the contraption was sent back once, twice, and even three times before it was tolerable—or if it was damaged, as Franklin's was on that memorable picnic. John mended the broken hinge in the machine shop back of his cottage, but the repair job was only temporary. At Franklin's suggestion, John was sent to the Children's Hospital in Boston, where he took a training course in the art of brace-making. When he came back, he did some experimenting with aluminum and other metals.

Eventually, Franklin had a pair of braces which were much lighter, weighing less than four pounds apiece instead of nearly ten. In Boston, John learned to make the type of brace Roosevelt had had before, designed especially for heavy patients, who need a lock on each upright or side—a double, automatic lock called a "bail," which was a thin, semicircular metal ring back of the knee joint. When Roosevelt stood up, it automatically snapped tight against his leg; when he was sitting down and wanted to release it, all he had to do was to press his legs against the edge of the chair. The uprights were painted black all the way down, so that the tips, which used to show beneath his trouser legs, were unnoticeable, even at close range.

These were more comfortable than his old braces (if any could be described as "comfortable"); he was able to walk more naturally in them; his left foot did not drag nearly as much, relieved of the constant heavy load on it all the time. The last pair was made for him in April 1940, and he wore them until near the end, when he felt too tired to wear braces at all. (He often thought that this was a most fortunate accident on the "Knob"!)

In October the stock market collapsed and, although some people claimed—after the frenzy had subsided—that this was merely a Wall Street crisis, it soon became apparent to those who were in governmental posts that unemployment was spreading and that the country was heading into a depression. With the same spirit of pioneering that led him into so many projects, Franklin set out to find a way to solve the problems of unemployment. It became one of his main contributions as Governor of New York and foretold much of the monumental work he would accomplish a few years later.

If he did not know, any more than other leaders (including Hoover, who stood by helplessly while the country floundered), what was to be done, he could at least study and learn, and this he did with intensive application. Just as he approached his recovery with a scientific outlook, a willingness to try any new method he thought might help him regain the use of his legs, so he now prepared to try various remedies for the unemployment situation in New York.

First of all, at the suggestion of Frances Perkins, he modernized the State Public Employment Service offices and developed the personnel department. (Here again it was the story of a particular office—dingy, unventilated, devoid of electricity or daylight, and without benches ["the men would only steal the light bulbs, and go to sleep on the benches," the manager said]—which helped Franklin to see the needs and go into action.) Other moves to stem the tide of rising unemployment were the strict enforcement of the child labor laws, adoption of a five-day week as a means of sharing the work, part-time work or work for a few days a week instead of flat layoffs, and "made work" drives in every city, so people would have some kind of employment, even odd jobs, that would bring in some kind of a living. These measures could not actually be taken, but were recommended to employers. Many businessmen, however, becoming desperate enough to be open to suggestion, acted on the ideas. And they came to look on Roosevelt with greater respect. Those who had been doubtful about either his ability or his liberalism began to feel reassured on both counts.

Most of 1930 Franklin devoted to a study and investigation of the cause and cure of the great economic illness. New skills were developed in determining the number of unemployed. He felt that people in general should be educated not only in ways to relieve the prevailing malady but to prevent it, if possible. He was observing, absorbing, learning, and, as usual, his reaction was creative. He set up a Commission on the Stabilization of Employment, significantly choosing a positive title instead of the negative "Unemployment Commission" which had been suggested. In his eyes, it was better to focus on the bright side of a picture rather than the dark. He was a builder, one who would always emphasize the constructive instead of the destructive. He kept close track of the study to stabilize employment, of the hearings that were held in rural as well as industrial areas; and he early made it known that he expected the results of the studies to be distributed for the education of the general public as well as government officials. His idea was that men and women out of jobs, and small businessmen whose industries were failing, should learn ways and means of preventing such crises in the future. On a miniature scale, he had seen the value of education and participation among the patients at Warm Springs, and he sought to apply the same principle to the people of New York.

And the people responded. When the time rolled around for the 1930 campaign and Franklin toured the State for re-election, the voters of New York turned out in droves to listen to their Governor. He was doing something about the business crisis which was rapidly deepening into a depression; he was a man of action. He used much the same technique as in 1928—a caravan of cars rolled into nearly every district in up- and down-state New York, and he spoke from the back seat, as he had before, but he made these appearances more like discussion groups: he did speak, of course, but he encouraged people to ask more questions. He gave the impression that he needed everyone's help to solve the problems of the hour—and he was sincere: he had to have the support of his constituents to carry out the program he had started in the previous year. And his listeners were with him. If they had disregarded his physical condition in 1928 after the first few moments, when they got used to his braced legs and his slow walk, then they overlooked it completely this time. By now everybody's curiosity was satisfied; one could see that Franklin D. Roosevelt was far from disabled, that he had some good sound ideas, and the majority of the people had faith in the Governor's ability to see that the ideas were carried out.

Eleanor was of much assistance to him during this campaign. She still did not do any actual electioneering, but she went around meeting and talking with people in her easy, cordial way. At the state fair, which they attended together, while Franklin was driving over the grounds and shaking hands with everyone who came up, she went through the various buildings and tents where the livestock exhibits, the flower and vegetable displays, the jellies and preserves and other canned goods, and the patchwork quilts were lined up for all to see. Eleanor sampled the foods, admired the homemade quilts, bought flowers, and asked questions, like any fair-goer. The fact that the Governor's wife,

New York's "first lady," could discuss prize crops and blue-ribbon livestock, enjoy a taste of strawberry jam or pickle relish, and also show great interest in schools, health, and recreation made a lasting impression on those who met her; it added to the feeling that the state government was in good hands and should be kept there.

When election day rolled around, F.D.R. was voted into his second term as Governor by the enormous margin of 725,000, a mere 700,000 more votes than he had received in 1928. It was the most sweeping victory a Democrat had ever made in New York, with its traditional upstate Republicanism. At *Hyde Park* there was rejoicing which amounted to grand jubilation. Franklin had failed to carry Dutchess County two years before, but now these same doubters came to congratulate him. Sara Roosevelt's green lawn was trampled by well-wishers, politicians who had been traipsing in and out of the house since the campaign began. The place looked more like a recreation ground than a country estate; there was a hole in the living-room rug, burned by a cigar ash, and the furniture sagged under the strain put upon it by campaigners. Yet his mother was so proud of Franklin's victory that she could be cheerful about the damage. Louis Howe did a hornpipe for joy, his usually saturnine face beaming with satisfaction, although he warned that they had plenty of work ahead. Franklin himself was pleased and surprised, not that he had won—he had expected to win—but by the tremendous landslide. And the success was his—he had planned it, he had built it up. He had privately bet that he would win by 400,000 votes—by far the largest figure in the betting pool—and there were those who felt he was being overconfident. That he would win by almost twice as many votes—a good percentage of them Republican—astonished him no less than it pleased him. Since the Legislature was still largely Republican, the victory was his alone.

At Warm Springs, where he went for a rest as soon as the election was over, the patients were, of course, delighted; and the townspeople made a big fuss over him, especially a small upper-middle-class group who had settled in the permanent homes on the slope. One hostess suggested that they wear "black ties" for dinner when the Governor was present. Franklin was amused, but annoyed. "Let's not be silly!" he snapped. He had no more liking for dinner clothes now than when he had written Auntie Bye not to send hotel guests who insisted on dressing for dinner. He came to Warm Springs to relax and usually wore no tie at all, but a soft shirt open at the neck; when a cuff button was missing, he had been known to hitch his shirt sleeve together with a safety pin; and he was not going to start sprucing up at the resort just because he was Governor.

That fall Keith Morgan, the official fund-raiser for Warm Springs, took advantage of his insurance connections to provide for policies, in the name of the Foundation, with twenty-two different companies, amounting to $560,000, on Roosevelt's life; two eminent physicians, who examined him thoroughly for the companies, reported that he was in excellent health, as sound a risk as any normal man of his age. The Foundation was to be the sole beneficiary and to pay the yearly premiums on the policies, which could serve as a basis for loans in times of emergency. More important was the fact that conservative insurance firms were able to grant him policies, a fact which would serve, Franklin hoped, as positive proof to the public that his victory over his illness was complete so far as his general state of health was concerned. There could be no doubt that he was equal to the task of holding any political office—including perhaps, the presidency.

CHAPTER XV

Fresh Challenge

HE KNEW. With the same sort of prescience that enabled him to purchase a down-at-the-heel resort called Warm Springs, confident of being able to transform it into a health-giving center of national renown, Franklin had known for a long time that he was going to be President. It was true that Louis Howe had been promoting the idea for years and that his ambition had been fed by the vice-presidential nomination. The eight hundred speeches he had made in the 1920 campaign had brought him a national reputation; by the end of it, he was better known than James Cox, the presidential candidate. Democratic leaders hailed him as a man with a future, and the rank and file felt there had been no one like him since Teddy Roosevelt in 1900. Ever since he began to recover from the blackness of paralysis, Franklin felt that he had been spared for the specific purpose of becoming a leader and that his leadership would carry him into the White House. It was only a question of timing.

He sensed with his uncanny accuracy that the hour was at hand. Late in November, when he returned to Albany after Thanksgiving in Warm Springs, he sent for Edward T. Flynn, who had been so energetic in the 1928 campaign. As usual, he wasted no time in getting down to cases. "Eddie, my reason for asking you to stay overnight is that I believe I can be nominated for the presidency in 1932," he said frankly. They settled down for a long talk about the possibilities, with Louis joining the huddle after a time. They decided to call Jim Farley in on the consultation, and this triumvirate of veteran politicians took over the task of organizing an F.D.R. "Pre-Convention Committee" to line up delegates, collect funds, and alert Democratic leaders all over the country. Franklin himself kept in regular touch with every Democrat who could be useful; he wrote at least five thousand letters during his second term, although he was, all this time, principally concerned with New York State affairs.

The "economic crisis" caused by the stock market crash had become a widespread depression. In state after state factories were forced to shut down, more and more people were out of jobs. The figures brought in by the Stabilization Commission showed that unemployment was increasing at an alarming rate; the data also showed clearly that there would have to be some kind of insurance against the hazard of unemployment, but no one, least of all the President, seemed capable of making the slightest move. It was as if the country was being paralyzed by an infectious disease which no one could stop from spreading.

Franklin had followed the work of the Commission closely. He had studied the reports, discussed the various phases with different members, and had seen for himself the ravages of depression in a little sweater mill outside of Poughkeepsie one day. He had driven over from *Hyde Park,* where he had been spending the weekend: he had watched the faces of the frightened, confused workers, who had accepted wages of five dollars a week for a limited time to fill a backbreaking order, because it was better than being idle, earning nothing at all, as they had been for weeks. He conferred with the despairing employer, who was at his wits' end to know what to do next. The wholesalers had ceased sending orders for the "quality" sweaters made in his mill because the retailers could not "move" them; nobody had money to buy. Finally, he had been given a rush order for a much cheaper sweater at an impossibly low rate; he would not make any profit, and his 150 workers would have only bare subsistence for a few weeks, and then nothing again. Franklin talked to the workers; he listened to their individual stories. In this way, he was able to understand and interpret phrases like "descending spiral" and "seasonal employment" in terms of human experience; and because he had an honest affection for people, a deep understanding of suffering through his own ordeal, he was convinced that something must be done, and done quickly, before the damage became much greater. He realized that unemployment insurance was considered "radical" and that New York could not maintain the expense if the other states nearby did not carry insurance, because the competition would be too great. He decided to call an interestate conference of governors of the eastern states sometime before the annual conference of governors, which was to be held at Salt Lake City. He could not have made a wiser move, and he did it diplomatically, telephoning each governor to sound him out informally on the matter before issuing a state invitation.

Nearly all of the men were progressive—or, if not, they were so worried by the situation they were ready to jump at any suggestion of action—and were glad to accept. Among them were several who became Roosevelt's supporters as a result of this conference—John G. Winant of New Hampshire, Gifford Pinchot of Pennsylvania, and George White of Ohio. A three-day conference was held, prepared in record time with the assistance of a dynamic young economist by the name of Paul H. Douglas of the University of Chicago, whom Franklin liked instantly. At the sessions Roosevelt showed the natural genius he possessed for dealing with people, winning them over to his way of thinking by consulting with them instead of handing out advice or dictates. He presented the mountain of material the Commission had piled up for him with a masterful touch, merely by simplifying it. He could make his points crystal clear by changing the complicated phrasing, cutting out an unnecessary load of detail. He asked questions of his colleagues, inviting their opinions. The end results of the conference were far-reaching for him politically; the immediate results were the good will of the governors and their support for the stand he was going to take at the annual conference.

He went to Salt Lake City, where he delivered his speech over a nationwide hookup, standing easily in front of the microphone, his new braces allowing him to assume a more natural position. He cut out half the material Frances Perkins had given him on the statistics of unemployment insurance, and emphasized the basic philosophy of it: that the state is responsible for the people who comprise it; if they are deprived of a living through no fault of their own, the state *owes* them a livelihood—not a dole, but a human right. (He and Rosenman had worked until the last minute to get the greatest degree of objectivity into the wording.) Speaking clearly and forcefully, he said:

"In broad terms I assert that modern society, acting through its government, owes the definite obligation to prevent the starvation or the dire want of any of its fellow men and women who try to maintain themselves but cannot.

"While it is true that we have principally considered those who, through accident or old age, were permanently incapacitated, the same responsibility of the state undoubtedly applies when widespread economic conditions render large numbers of men and women incapable of supporting either themselves or their families because of circumstances beyond their control . . ."

His judgment was wise and accurate. Although a few critics assailed his motives or branded his ideas as "revolutionary," the majority of newspaper articles hailed him as a man of action, and the headlines played up his name: it was "Governor Roosevelt Comes Out for Unemployment Insurance," not the conference; the implication was that his idea was accepted, as in fact it was by the greater portion of governors.

What impressed the leaders in the country even more was the fact that he followed through, and was the first to act upon his beliefs. He called a special session of the New York State Legislature, on his return from Salt Lake City, for the purpose of voting public funds for unemployment compensation. He fought for other measures, in the main unsuccessfully, but his battle intimated the victories that were to come later on: control of public utilities (for which he established the State Power Authority), social security, reforestation, and other reform measures.

The outcome of his activity, plus the work of the Pre-Convention Committee and his own political correspondence, was a "Roosevelt-for-President" boom. Roosevelt clubs sprang up in the Bronx and other boroughs; and among Democratic leaders his name was mentioned more and more as the most likely candidate, although there were a number of contenders, including Al Smith. The opposition, inside of the party and out of it, could not point to any inefficiency in Franklin's administration as Governor of New York, so it took to the old tack—circulating rumors of his poor health, citing it as a hazard in choosing the man for the highest office in the land. The fact that Roosevelt was the picture of radiant health, slept like a top, and could outwork any member of his cabinet had no effect on the rumor-mongers, if they even realized the inconsistency.

Hints were dropped that he was still suffering acutely from the effects of poliomyelitis, that he was in pain a good deal of the time, that his spinal cord was damaged; one insinuation was that he was impotent, and another, squashed by doctors immediately, was that F.D.R. was in danger of going insane, since infantile paralysis attacked the brain in its final stage. Franklin saw that his medical tests for the insurance policies were of little value. He was discouraged at the thought that his "positive proof" was regarded so lightly. But he was determined to show the public that he was physically fit for the job of president just as he had been for governor. As a matter of fact, he was stronger than when he went into office; he had become used to working long hours, holding consultations one after another, attending official functions like receptions (although many of these he spared himself in order to conserve his energy for more important tasks), and giving speeches. He was nettled by the ugly rumors—what more proof could he give? he wondered.

Then a national magazine came forward to suggest a feature article which would include a full report of his daily routine and of his state of health after examination by a panel of doctors; he agreed at once. Three prominent specialists—Dr. Samuel W. Lambert, a diagnostician; Dr. Russell A. Hibbs, an orthopedist; and Dr. Foster Kennedy, a neurologist—moved into the Executive Mansion, accompanied by a staff writer, who began his observations of the Governor's day at breakfast time. Franklin was always awake early, and took his breakfast in bed so that he would have a half an hour longer to rest his legs. After he was up and dressed, the reporter followed him as he went down the ramp with Gus at his left side and was helped into the car. At the underpass in front of the Capitol, the reporter noted that Franklin always clicked his braces before starting the halting walk up the second ramp and down the long way to his office. Once he was comfortably seated behind his desk, he was ready for all comers, alert, interested, exuding a radiant energy that was maintained through a steady flow of appointments till lunchtime. He usually had lunch at his desk and, while he relaxed, he did not let down in spirits or energy; he chatted and laughed, made no reference to his handicap, and was ready for work again in a short time.

The three doctors gave him minute and extensive examinations, which also went on through the day, in order to gauge his endurance. Franklin let them probe him from head to toe, asked a few interested questions, and gave them a history of his case when they requested certain background information; outside of this, he scarcely paid any attention to them—he was far too busy to be concerned. To a great extent he went ahead with his affairs as if they were not around. When the telephone rang, the doctors had to wait to take his chest measurements or his heartbeat. Politicians and press men came and went, secretaries were in and out—affairs of state came first. Franklin knew he was perfectly well; the doctors had only to verify the fact. Their statement was unequivocal:

"We have today examined Franklin D. Roosevelt. We find that his organs and functions are sound in all respects. There is no anemia. The chest is exceptionally well developed, and the spinal column is perfectly normal; all of its segments are in alignment, and free from disease. He has neither pain nor ache at any time.

"Ten years ago, Governor Roosevelt suffered an attack of acute infantile paralysis, the entire effect of which was expended on the muscles of his lower extremities. There has been progressive recovery of power in the legs since that date; this restoration continues and will continue . . . We believe that his powers of endurance are such as to allow him to meet all demands of private or public life."

The technical details of the report were practically repetitious in their "normal" findings: "Heart: regular; rate 80 . . . no murmurs . . . Blood pressure 140/100 . . .

"Pulse: regular; rate 80—after examination by three physicians rate is 84, returning to 80 after 3 minutes . . .

"Lungs: No dullness, no changes in respiratory murmurs, no extraneous sounds or rales; no abnormalities in voice sounds . . . Chest expansion good . . .

"Abdomen: Liver and spleen not enlarged, no pain, no masses. Abdominal muscles show slight bulging on left. No hernia . . . No evidence of columnar degeneration of spinal cord. Both optic nerves normal. A false Babinski reflex is present on both sides [old polio symptom]. Right knee jerk absent. Left shows responses in upper and outer portion of quadriceps extensor."

So it went. Reading the report would make the examinations seem completely unnecessary, which was the effect Franklin had anticipated. The next item was hardly scientific: "Some coldness of feet below knees; cocktail makes them right." Then: "The lower erector spinae are slightly affected. Gluteus medius partial R. and L.

"Wasserman—negative with both alcoholic and cholesterinized antigen." The last notation was brief but definite: "No symptoms of impotentia coeundi."

He went ahead with his plans to enter the presidential race. The Pre-Convention Committee, through the efforts of Flynn, Farley, and Howe, had expanded to some seventeen or eighteen members, with both Mrs. Roosevelts, who worked with loyal enthusiasm, making it about twenty. Among the others were Frank D. Walker, Laurence A. Steinhardt, Jesse Straus, James W. Gerard, Joseph P. Kennedy, both junior and senior Henry Morgenthaus, William H. Woodin (a former Republican, converted by Roosevelt's logical, intelligent liberalism), Colonel House, and Lieutenant-Governor Lehman. (True to his promise, Lehman had "spelled" Franklin when it was necessary, but he never had to take over the reins while the Governor went to Warm Springs to rest. Those periods were brief, and taken at times when he could be spared from Albany. Recently, it was Franklin who had given Herbert some health advice. Lehman had come to the Mansion for a consultation on the most recent banking crisis; he had presented his solution, and they had both decided on the course to be taken. Franklin was satisfied, and immediately relaxed, but Lehman kept pacing up and down the room nervously. Finally, Franklin told him to "sit down and stop worrying" now that their decision was made: he could put his energy to much better use the next day in carrying out their plan, than by exhausting himself in pacing up and down that night, fretting about the soundness of their solution!)

In January 1932 Franklin made the formal announcement of his candidacy. He was way ahead of Smith in the New Hampshire primary, and won hands down in North Dakota against "Alfalfa" Bill Murray. In Georgia, where he had built up a

wide following because of Warm Springs, the leading citizens
had come out for Roosevelt in 1930. However, he lost California,
Connecticut, and Massachusetts; Hearst and McAdoo opposed
him; Raskob, who was still head of the Democratic National
Committee, was backing Smith, as was Tammany Hall. Franklin
and his preconvention committeemen would have to double their
efforts. He was equal to the extra strain added to the hundred-
and-one activities in Albany. He made speeches in and around
New York, one of the most famous, his "Forgotten Man" speech,
winning him the support of every liberal in the country.

Speeches caused him little, if any, fatigue. He responded to
the people, and they to his warmth and sincerity. The one great
test of his endurance came when President Hoover summoned
him and a number of other prominent governors to the White
House and, at a reception, kept everybody waiting for over an
hour. Franklin had to stand in the receiving line with the others,
waiting. He could feel his feet beginning to grow numb with
their usual coldness, which always increased when he had to
stand in one spot. The braces pressed against his legs, and
the hinges at the hips cut into his flesh, bringing a throbbing
ache in the small of his back. Eleanor, who was one of the
governors' wives to be invited, knew what he must be going
through and watched him anxiously. But he overrode the pain
and discomfort with supreme control and stood smiling, greeting
his colleagues, and conversing as if nothing bothered him. Underneath his cutaway, his white shirt was sealed to his back with
cold sweat, but he gave no outward sign of distress and there
were very few who ever knew that this was one of the toughest
trials in his career.

When the Legislature had completed its "thirty days' bills,"
and before the convention took place in Chicago, Franklin went
to Warm Springs for a "breather," to get in condition for the
political carnival to come.

At the resort, whose fame was steadily growing, to the point
where they had more applications from crippled patients than

they could accommodate, a number of changes had taken place.
Mahoney had contracted a kind of arthritis which prohibited
her from working in the pool; she was forced to leave, at everyone's regret, particularly Franklin's. As a means of prolonging
her usefulness, he had arranged for her to take a trip to Europe,
to do "research" at famous spas there. But, as she herself said
when she came back, the pioneering days at Warm Springs were
over, and she was a pioneer. She went into the hills of West
Virginia, where a state project was under way to get the cripples
out of hiding and rehabilitate them. Alice Lou Plastridge took
over as head physiotherapist at Warm Springs, a post she would
retain for twenty-one years.

With Mahoney gone, Dr. Hubbard, who was old, decided the
time had come for him to retire, and a new physician, a dynamic
orthopedic surgeon who had become famous for his operations
on clubfoot and weak-ankle conditions, Michael Hoke of Atlanta,
became the medical head of the center. He was pressing for
new equipment, greater hospital facilities, but there still was
not enough money for extensive expansion. Keith Morgan was
working hard, and funds were being donated, but too slowly
for large-scale construction. The rates could have been raised,
but that would have been strictly against the original policy
and Franklin would not hear of it. The Patients' Aid Fund still
contributed twenty-one dollars a week to those who could not
afford to pay the fee; and the signing of those checks was one
of the few jobs Franklin had not delegated to anyone else.

His hilltop home and the narrow winding roadway that had to
be built up to it were completed while he was there this time.
He invited his gang for the first of many dinners they were to
enjoy, prepared by his new cook, Daisy Bonner (who was to stay
with the Warm Springs household until the end). Daisy was
proud of her cooking, and the unpretentious cottage that was
to become the Little White House rang with good cheer on the
night of its initiation.

The patients, along with their leader, had grown in their

ideas and enterprise. They had begun publishing a monthly magazine called *The Polio Chronicle,* and its pages voiced the recognition of Warm Springs as a force in arousing and co-ordinating a nationwide interest through its spirit and remarkable experience in helping the handicapped. Franklin had been asked to write an editorial on the first page of the first issue. He made it a call to action and headed it: "WANTED—EN-LISTMENTS FOR A CRUSADE." The paragraphs that followed contained an urgent appeal for a national army of sympathizers to fight the disease on all fronts: first and foremost, prevention, which would eventually obliterate the enemy; then proper diagnosis (he remembered the damage that had been done to his own legs by Dr. Keene's erroneous opinion); proper treatment during the acute stage; and aftertreatment, the Warm Springs' specialty. Finally, he dwelt on hometown rehabilitation, which was of no small importance in bringing a patient back to life.

At last he had declared open warfare on the disease!

CHAPTER XVI

Triumph and the White House

WHILE THE AIR in the convention hall in Chicago sizzled with
broiling temperatures and burning rivalry among the half a
dozen Democratic candidates, Franklin stayed in Albany and
carried out his nomination maneuvers by remote control. Al
Smith had gone to Chicago with the backing of Tammany Hall
for the purpose of defeating his recent protégé, if he could not
win the nomination himself. When asked which candidate he
was supporting, he had so far lost his dignity that he snarled
at reporters, "I'm for myself!" Two other leading contenders,
"Pecan" Jack Garner of Texas and McAdoo of California, were
hardly less heated. All were frantically trying to secure votes.
Franklin was also attempting to gather support, but he was not
frantic. Over a loudspeaker hooked up in Louis Howe's hotel
room, he spoke to various groups of delegates as he sat in Albany
headquarters, working with the circle of professors Louis had
labeled his "brain trust," seeking to line up material on every
facet of American life and the elements which had led to the
depression.

After days of backbiting and weary wrangling, which included
a famous deal Farley made with the infamous Hearst, Garner
and McAdoo released their votes for Roosevelt's candidacy and

231

the nomination was his. Then Roosevelt made an unprecedented political gesture: instead of waiting to be notified at his home, according to time-honored custom, he took a plane to Chicago to accept the nomination in person. It proved to be a master stroke, planned down to the last detail with insight and precision. Will Rogers was holding forth behind the rostrum with his razor-edged tomfoolery as Franklin entered the hall, and, with split-second timing, Rogers sent one of his good-natured barbs at Roosevelt, focusing attention on the candidate himself, who feigned the greatest surprise and then threw back his head, leading the roar of laughter.

On this high note of merriment and good cheer he made his entrance, his hand on Gus's arm, the lower half of his body hidden from view by the cluster of close associates who moved with them—Flynn, Farley, and Howe, Rosenman, Tom Lynch, and one or two others. During the preconvention campaign he had perfected the technique for making public appearances, which he had started in *Hyde Park* eight summers before when he first practised "walking" with a firm hold on Jimmy's arm. Now, with the merest nod from him, the intimate friends who usually accompanied him on trips would gather around in a protective circle, laughing, joking, playing up to his animation, at the same time clearing the way for him and Gus as they went toward the rostrum or to his seat on the platform. He had increased the tempo of his pace somewhat, his head and shoulders stood out powerfully above those of his companions, and he moved with greater ease, so that his advance, still fairly slow, seemed quite natural to audiences or casual onlookers, who never noticed the strange uneven rhythm of his gait and could not see his stiffened legs, rigid in the braces. Occasionally, the little group would break out skillfully as he gestured with his head or lifted the cane momentarily in greeting; they parted just enough to show his head and shoulders.

As soon as they had safely reached the rostrum, the little circle of men would disband casually, as if the action was unrehearsed, allowing the audience to see the full figure of Roosevelt, tall and at ease, his left hand to all appearances lightly holding Gus's arm, his right expertly ramming the cane down at a jaunty but firm angle. Today he waved it at the crowd once or twice before setting down the tip to lean forward and whisper a few intimate words to Will Rogers by way of a wisecrack salute. Then he was behind the podium, securing his stance with a firm grasp on the edge, acknowledging the applause, the cheers, and the blaring of the band. His speech was not too long, but direct and forceful. In his acceptance, he made the first mention of the phrase "New Deal," promising the people a better hand in the game of life if they would only have faith in him and in themselves, if they worked with him to bring about changes that would replace despair with hope. It was a call to action, and the delegates responded with renewed spirit after the long haggling days of nominations. The band struck up once more the convention theme song, "Happy Days Are Here Again!" But this time it seemed to fit the occasion. A week earlier one commentator had deemed the musical slogan "a damn lie" in the face of the starvation and poverty that stared out from Chicago breadlines and pathetically filled park benches night after night; now the words were believable, and most of the departing delegates went home smiling over the choice that had been made.

In his hotel suite, Franklin was besieged with reporters, cameramen, and politicians of every rank and stripe. The happy triumvirate of Flynn, Farley, and Howe was busy plotting the campaign to follow; the brain trust, or "Privy Council," as Franklin called it, had already prepared a number of speeches at his confident insistence some time before the nomination. On every hand there were consultations, congratulations, and general jubilation. Tom Lynch brought out two bottles of champagne he had put away "just for this occasion" in 1918, before Prohibition. In the midst of the hubbub, Franklin was given a message that some young woman wished to see him; she walked with a cane and had been at Warm Springs. He had her shown in at once. It was Toi Batchelder, his pretty young bridge "teacher," now considerably grown up and vastly improved; she walked quite steadily with a cane and only one brace. She had graduated from secretarial school and had written to F.D.R. asking if she might be of some use on his campaign staff. He had dictated a few hurried lines to Missy, telling Toi to see him in Chicago, and he hailed her with a delighted, "Toi Batchelder!" over the buzzing of the crowded room. "This is grand," he said. He complimented her on the progress she had made and scribbled on his inevitable scrap of paper the name of the man she was to see. He wished he could have settled down for a chat about Warm Springs, but it was impossible. As Toi left, making her careful way to the door, the bit of paper tucked in her purse, he called after her, "Toi, how's your bridge game?" and she could hear his ringing laughter as she stepped into the hotel corridor.

Some of his advisers, including Louis, thought Franklin should make a "front porch" campaign from his home in Hyde Park. He could continue the effective use of the radio he had begun in 1926 and could reach the people without exhausting his energy before he was elected. But he would have none of such counsel. He wanted to see the people and be seen. He wanted to prove once again that he was physically fit for the strenuous job he knew would be in store for him if he won. Besides, he enjoyed campaigning and was not going to miss out on the excitement of a presidential election tour when he was the candidate; it was as simple as that.

He set out on a cross-country campaign that was to carry him into all but seven states for a total of 27,000 miles of travel. A new piece of essential equipment was a detachable ramp, which could be fitted over the steps of the train, allowing him to climb down and up again without having to be carried or even helped by a lift from someone's arm. The train steps, of course, were steep, so the ramp was at a sharp angle and he had to take it slowly, but he could do it on his own. He made every whistle stop, appeared on platforms all over the country, and was usually standing on the rear platform of the observation car, his hand firmly on the railing, his braced feet wide apart in the stance he found safest, when the train pulled in. He would say a few words of good cheer to the waiting crowd, lean over to shake hands with people who came up, or kiss a baby held out to him by the arms of a hopeful parent. The stop completed, he would stand there smiling as the train pulled out again, waving with his free hand. Only when they were well out of sight would he turn to go inside on Gus's arm. When he was settled in his compartment—the person helping him had to learn to let him down into the seat very carefully—the first thing he did was to loosen his trousers and unlock the braces. His valet, McDuffie, whom he had brought from Warm Springs, would help him take off and put on the trousers again. Delighted to be free, Franklin would immediately get down to work with Rosenman or A. A. Berle on the campaign material. Some minutes before the next stop, Rosenman or someone would warn him, "We'll be in Fostoria in fifteen minutes," and he would call for McDuffie, who helped him remove his trousers and put the braces back on, and he locked and tested them before getting dressed again. Then he would grab Gus's arm and start toward the back, squeezing sideways along the aisle. Sometimes the ride between stops would only last a couple of hours, but he could work more easily if his legs were unfettered by the braces; they gave him a feeling of being imprisoned. So, unless the time was very short, he always went to the trouble of taking them off after a stop and putting them on before the next. And, during the process, he would talk incessantly, hardly interrupting the line of thought he and his helpers had been hammering at.

If he had to leave the train for a major address in cities like Cleveland or Chicago or St. Louis, he would not come out until the ramp was attached and secure, and then would slowly, carefully descend to the ground or station platform, As a rule, there was a crowd of watchers gathered to catch a glimpse of the candidate if they could not hear him speak, and sometimes a murmur ran through the ranks as they witnessed the slow process, but the sound was one of surprise rather than pity, because most people never realized how difficult it was for him to move his legs. The murmurs would last until he had reached a waiting automobile, was hoisted in, had pulled himself up by the rail, and turned to wave, saluting the crowd with his big smile. Then people broke into cheers, and his handicap was once more forgotten.

One of the amazing qualities about his manner was the power of making others forget there was anything wrong with him. As soon as the physical maneuver was past, his strong personality and radiant charm took over and put an end to any awareness of his disability. Many of those who did not see him at close range, or saw only his pictures in newsreels and papers, never knew, unless they were told, that he was crippled. (One of his ardent admirers in the Middle West, on being told that Roosevelt was paralyzed, even denied the fact hotly with a flat, "Why, he is *not!*" and refused to believe it.) Those who hated him later for his "radical" policies felt no compulsion to soften their venom with pity, because he asked no quarter in the name of physical hardship, nor expected any. His colleagues more than half the time forgot while they were working with him that he could not get up to leave the room without help, and were reminded of the fact only when he called for somebody to assist him.

His joking, objective attitude when he did refer to his affliction in the company of close associates carried over to them. Basil O'Connor's frequent remark in later years, when Franklin would try to figure out the best way of navigating himself—"You walk on your *chin*, anyway!"—never failed to make Roosevelt grin fondly at his friend.

In front of audiences, his eloquence and delivery, coupled with the startling content of his speeches, especially on this first campaign tour, dispelled any consideration of his physical condition by those who were listening. The Democratic platform in 1932 was designed to meet the needs of a nation that was sinking into the sad coma of a deep depression and had to be brought back to life; it was like a shot in the arm to many parts of the country waiting for the remedies of the New Deal. Some of them had already been successfully tried in New York: unemployment insurance, a widened public works program, old age pension laws, greater control of public utilities, agricultural aid, plus repeal of Prohibition to act as a stimulant.

By September 23, the campaign train had crossed the country, and Franklin, giving one of his most important addresses at the Commonwealth Club in San Francisco, set forth the principles he was to follow throughout his career in office. He and Berle, who was responsible for most of the writing, had concentrated on this speech, which was a plea for economic as well as political democracy, or, as Franklin phrased it during the final hours of work: "the development of an economic declaration of rights."

Standing behind the rostrum with greater ease than at any time so far, he delivered his credo in forceful tones: "Every man has a right to live," he began simply enough, "and this means that he has also a right to make a comfortable living. He may . . . decline to exercise that right; but it may not be denied him." Now he came to the crux of his statement, and his own intense interest lifted him so far above the physical problems of his paralysis that no audience had a moment to speculate on them. "Our industrial and agricultural mechanism can produce enough and to spare. Our government, formal and informal, political and economic, owes to everyone an avenue to possess himself of a portion of that plenty sufficient for his needs, through his own work." He explained his theory at some length, including a significant sentence: "A glance at the situation today only too clearly indicates that equality of opportunity as we have known it no longer exists." Later in the campaign he made the same point more forcefully, using rhetorical shock treatment: "I believe that the individual should have full liberty of action to make the most of himself," he started off, again conventionally, and then continued, "but I do not believe that in the name of that sacred word, individualism, a few powerful interests should be permitted to make industrial cannon fodder of the lives of half the population of the United States."

"Industrial cannon fodder"—one of his most felicitous phrases—boomed across the country like a bombshell which cleared the air for the suffering millions who were gasping for breath. And there were literally millions of them by this time. According to the latest figures from the Department of Labor, no less than fourteen million unemployed were struggling to keep alive. Whole families huddled in "Hoovervilles," the ragged edges of towns where the unemployed were shunted away like lepers; fathers and mothers standing in breadlines; the pathetic army of apple-sellers on city streets—all of these and many others less drastically affected but suffering, too, living in fear that the disease would nab them next—took heart at Roosevelt's ringing call to action for recovery through reform, through faith. He was a man who knew what "recovery" meant and how to fight for it as no other leader could. He was their man.

On he went, seeming to gather energy as he traveled. When he made a swing through the South, he sent word to Warm Springs that he would make it one of his campaign stops, delivering a speech especially for the patients. The news caused quite a flurry, and it was only through the lightning action of Fred Botts that they were able to gather the props for a small but impressive parade of three cars, which met Roosevelt's motorcade at Greenville, the halfway point on the highway from Atlanta. First in the Warm Springs line-up came Franklin's old Model-T Ford, packed with patients in uniforms and period costumes, depicting his years as Secretary of the Navy; next followed his blue Model-A, polished up for the occasion, decorated with signs marking the high spots in his career as Governor of New York; and last, in the latest model of "heavy-make" car, Fred sat behind the wheel in a high silk topper and formal cutaway, borrowed finery; a pince-nez, perched on the bridge of his nose, left little doubt as to the future era his outfit foretold. With much honking and tooting of horns, they roared into the resort road and pulled up before Meriwether Inn.

A makeshift platform had been set up in front of it, and from this Franklin spoke to his friends in the evening. He included some of the issues he had been dealing with everywhere, but his remarks were in a framework of anecdotes about the early days at Warm Springs and the struggle to establish the center, a battle which was by no means ended. He closed with a promise to return as soon as the campaign fight was finished; just now he had two or three other engagements in Georgia.

It was on one of these that he experienced a mishap, an incident that was to be duplicated only five or six times in all the years of his public life. He was speaking in a little hall which had no lectern but a table at the front of the platform; the place was jammed to the doors and, as he spoke, he looked out on a sea of friendly faces, addressing them with much the same informality he had used in Warm Springs, because by now he felt at home anywhere in Georgia. Suddenly the table, none too sturdy in the first place, on which he had to lean heavily, slipped under his weight and sent him toppling to the floor! Gus and Earl Miller were beside him in a moment, helping him up inside of seconds. On his feet again, he did not even pause to catch his breath, but kept on talking, taking up his sentence at the very word where he had left off. He made no mention of the fall. The audience went wild with admiration; their cheers almost burst the hall.

He toured the rest of the southern states; he saw the misery of the "deep South," the backwater hamlets of Mississippi, where the depression hardly made a difference except that the breadlines were longer, the soup kitchens more crowded. He never made an issue of the race question, but he implied equality by his attitude toward Negroes, one in which color was no consideration. He saw the soil erosion in certain parts of the country, the depletion of forests in others; he made a mental note to include conservation in the New Deal. In cities he saw the idle factories, the towns where the street lights were out at night because there was no municipal money to take care of the power costs. And everywhere he presented his plan, everywhere he gave out hope.

When November came, he was elected by a tremendous majority—22,813,786 people went to the polls and voted for him, as against 15,759,266 for Hoover; fifty-seven per cent of the popular vote went to Roosevelt, the first Democrat in eighty years to win a clear majority. The electoral college figures were 472 to 59. As in his second-term run for governor, Franklin was himself surprised at the margin by which he won. It was the reflection of the grave needs of a people crying for help, and his joy in triumph was tempered with full knowledge of the responsibility he was shouldering.

His strength temporarily exhausted, he went to Warm Springs for a complete rest, but this of course was impossible. Conferences had to be held with top Democratic leaders, politicians, statesmen, and advisers. (Louis Howe was like a father whose son has fulfilled his dream, now that Franklin had been elected.) Most of the cabinet members were appointed while Franklin was at Warm Springs, and both the Inn and the "Little White House," as his home was already called by newsmen, were overflowing with important guests. Any vacant cottages were snapped up. Besides his bodyguards, a squad of secret service men accompanied Franklin, following close behind him even when he went for a short drive. His gang seldom saw him at the pool, and, if he did come to bathe, he had no time for water sports or the old-time workouts in the pool.

He stayed for Thanksgiving dinner and was in high spirits, refreshed by those few weeks, in spite of the constant activity. As usual, there were songs and impromptu acts of entertainment,

and he joined in the fun as he had on the first "Founder's Day";
no one felt any restraint because he was now the President-elect.
The children laughed at the way he asked for a "count of noses,"
and when it proved to be two hundred and seventy-five, he commented with fatherly pride, "The family is certainly growing!"

Fred presented him with a check for $722 in *Polio Crusader*
memberships, a national group which had been formed at the
time the magazine was started. Franklin expressed much pleasure
in the check, which he said was a sign that Warm Springs was
gaining national recognition. He urged them to continue the
"crusade" for a nationwide attack against the disease on all
fronts, and said he hoped that in seven years the $700 would be
$7,000. (By that date, in the miraculous way the things he
visualized took life and form, a national organization was sky-
rocketing across the country to bring in nearly a million and
a half in "dollars and dimes.")

He went to New York for the Christmas holidays, but returned
to Warm Springs with Basil O'Connor late in January for a
last visit before he took office. Never had the little resort seemed
so tranquil. The southern skies were soft, a warm breeze brushed
the tops of the pine trees. Usually in January it was still rather
chilly, but for a few days the sun smiled on them as a draft of
tropical air blew over from the Gulf Stream. It was like a
promise of a springtime to come to a nation that sorely needed
a new awakening.

Franklin made the most of the interlude. He bathed in the
pool and watched the sunsets from the porch of his home over
Pine Mountain valley. In the little time he had, he pondered
the complicated problems he would have to reckon with as soon
as he was in office; the country was so severely stricken by
economic paralysis at this point that it seemed to have less power
to move than he had had in the beginning of his illness. (It
could not even "wiggle a large toe." In the weeks since election
night, conditions had worsened until the whole land was apparently succumbing—state by state—becoming more paralyzed.)

He made one or two further appointments to his Cabinet, sent to Washington for Cordell Hull, and, when the "elder statesman" appeared, it did not take long until the question of his Secretariat was decided. Some of the "privy council" came down to work on the inaugural address—five men in particular were to act as his counselors: Raymond Moley, Sam Rosenman, A. A. Berle, Jr., Rexford Tugwell and Hugh Johnson, who had been brought into the cabala by Bernard Baruch. Two others, Joseph D. McGoldrick and Lindsay Rogers, both professors at Columbia, along with Tugwell and Berle, had played important roles in the 1932 campaign, but were not so active now. O'Connor, who had made the train trip with Franklin, was part of the group, but spent much of his time going over the various projects at Warm Springs.

Two or three of the Trustees of the Foundation were visiting or in residence for the winter, so they had a meeting of the Board, which was called to order on the twenty-sixth of January in the Little White House. Dr. Hoke and Keith Morgan were elected to the body as new Trustees, and Dr. Hubbard's resignation was accepted. Other business was taken up. At the close of the meeting, Franklin consulted Arthur Carpenter on a matter that was on his mind toward the end of his stay, as the first of March drew closer. He told "Carp" that all the Warm Springs patients were to be invited to Washington for the Inauguration, and wondered whether the manager thought travel arrangements could be made for those who were able to take the trip. "Carp" was quite sure this could be accomplished and set about consulting executives of the Southern Railroad to see if a Warm Springs Special could pick up the patients at the village siding. Franklin wanted as many of his gang to come as possible, and it looked as though there might be at least sixty of them at the ceremonies.

He went up to New York in February to look after last-minute details before leaving for the Capitol. Eleanor was packing, and the first floor in the house on Sixty-fifth Street was a shambles.

Boxes and barrels stood in the hall, some of them filled with papers Franklin had sent down from Albany, material that would have to be sorted and filed before it was shipped on to Washington. Several trunks occupied a good deal of space, and there was scarcely enough left for him to get to the stairs. In the living room, rugs were rolled up and paintings rested against the wall. (They were going to rent the house, and Eleanor was ready to leave the pictures, but Franklin felt they should take the portrait of Eleanor's Grandfather Roosevelt, the first Theodore. "You can't rent your grandfather; take him along with us," he said.) The press had moved in temporarily downstairs: typewriter tables were set up and the keys were clicking and the telephones were ringing. Some of the furniture was broken. When Frances Perkins came for an interview regarding her appointment as Secretary of Labor the following week, she had to step over a pile of muddy overshoes near the door and wade through a sea of littered newspapers all over the floor. (In the room above, which was Franklin's study, she met the one-time fighting "Bull-Mooser," Harold Ickes, still belligerent in political beliefs and loyalties. Franklin had just appointed him Secretary of the Interior, and these two members of his Cabinet, the last to be appointed, were the only two who remained at their posts from his first to his last days in the White House.)

Several days before the inauguration, Franklin went to Washington with his family. Ramps had to be put down leading to the platform in front of the Capitol, where the swearing-in was to take place. Others were placed over the steps to the office of the Sergeant-at-Arms of the Senate, where Garner was sworn in beforehand as vice-president. Franklin would have to walk about thirty-five feet. James was to accompany him that day, and they rehearsed a few times to be sure their appearance before the crowds would be smooth and unmarred by unnecessary halting.

He was not too busy with these arrangements to forget the plans that had to be made for the Warm Springs "family." Their train was switched around to stop at an area where there were no steps—and no curious crowds to stare. Cars were provided to drive them to their stopping-places and to take them wherever they wished to go on individual tours—not herded together in a sight-seeing group for the handicapped. A representative from an agency was to meet them and see to it that they were well cared for all during their stay; they were to come to tea at the White House in the afternoon on Inauguration Day . . .

Dark days preceded that March 4, 1932. Unemployment had reached the stark figure of fifteen million; banks were failing everywhere. Business seemed to have turned to stone. Though his confidence had always been high, Franklin felt deeply that he wanted, and needed, special spiritual guidance before he took on the burden of averting a complete national collapse. He sent for his old mentor, Dr. Endicott Peabody, who arrived just a day or two before the ceremonies. Together they selected a simple but significant service from the *Book of Common Prayer;* Franklin chose the hymns and psalms. Late on the evening of March 3, the members of his Cabinet received word that Roosevelt would like to have them and their families meet him at St. John's Church at ten o'clock the next morning for divine worship before the inauguration ceremonies. The service was to be private and kept secret; such a thing had never before been part of the program. It was a mystic sort of precedence-breaking, in keeping with his intuitive knowledge of things to come, and his profound feeling for humanity.

He came to the church that morning with Eleanor and his mother, his Uncle Frederic and several of the children. He took Jimmy's arm going into the chapel. With him, the handful of people gathered together for private prayer sensed the solemnity of the hour; it was a time in history when men needed to pray. As Dr. Peabody read out the service, everybody in the little congregation, regardless of their individual faiths, prayed for divine guidance for "Thy servant, Franklin, about to become President of these United States."

He himself felt his confidence reinforced by the words of spiritual strength sounded forth in the resonant tones of the Rector's voice. If he said a silent prayer for physical strength to carry out his gigantic task, it was forever his secret. But when he left the church, he seemed to "walk" straighter, and the pressure of his fingers on Jimmy's arm was not so intense.

And there was no faltering in his gait as he moved up the long ramp later on, and down the short one leading to the speaker's platform outside the Capitol portico. His movements were slow but steady, and made with ease, and he smiled confidently at the multitude of faces that craned upward to get a look at him. His legs were rigid in the braces, but his manner was much more relaxed than the grim, unbending figure of Hoover standing stiffly beside him. (The ride to the Capitol had been, he was sure, the most difficult and uncomfortable part of the whole Inauguration Day. Hoover sat next to him in stony silence on the back seat of the limousine, looking to neither side as they passed the thousands lined along the parade route leading to the Capitol. Franklin, who was bowing, smiling, and lifting his tall silk hat from time to time, was suddenly aware of the gloomy ex-President, who was staring straight ahead, his taciturn countenance a study in pessimism. Realizing that Hoover had little reason to be cheerful, Franklin tried to lift him out of his funk with small talk as they rode along, but he got no response whatever. Finally his eye caught the glint from the steel girders of a new government building under construction and, in a last attempt, he murmured something about the "nice steel." It must have sounded inane, but he was desperate— and it was in vain, anyway. After that, they had both remained in embarrassed silence till the limousine pulled up before the entrance that led to the Sergeant-at-Arms' office.)

Now they both stood facing Chief Justice Hughes, who held out to Franklin the Dutch family Bible which had been used in Albany and was brought to this ceremony, also, at his request. He put his hand on the cover without a perceptible shift in balance and, when the Chief Justice asked the usual question: "Do you solemnly swear to support the Constitution of the United States of America?" he answered in clear, ringing tones, "I DO." Then he turned to face the throng of citizens waiting to hear his inaugural address.

It was characteristically simple and direct. He recognized the blackness of the situation, but his heart was full of high hope, and he was not afraid. He knew, as no other President could know, that fear could be a symptom of despair, a deadly weapon of self-destruction. His words were a reflection of his feelings, of the wisdom that had come to him through his illness.

"This is pre-eminently the time to speak the truth," he told them, "the whole truth, frankly and boldly. Nor need we shirk from facing honestly conditions in our country today. This great nation will endure as it has endured, will revive, and will prosper. So, first of all, let me assert my firm belief that the only thing we have to fear is fear itself."

Across the country there was an almost audible sigh of relief and a great resurgence of hope: the people had found a leader.

CHAPTER XVII

The Last Specter Vanquished

HE WAS PRESIDENT. The immediate pressure of a thousand therapeutic measures to revive the ailing economy kept him from dwelling on the fact for long, but when he did, it was with a kind of joyous exuberance. He had made it—just as he had made the governorship. And because he had in some way divined that he would be President some day (perhaps as long ago as that morning in 1916, when he and Josephus Daniels stood on the balcony of the Navy Building and looked over at the official residence), Franklin settled into the White House as if he had come home at last.

He pitched into action with the zeal of a young medical reformer putting his theories into practice. "Dr. New Deal" was a phrase he often used in referring to the methods he employed to rehabilitate the nation, just as he had called himself "Dr. Roosevelt" in the early days at Warm Springs. Five days after inauguration, Roosevelt called a special session of Congress to deal with the national emergency, and one of its first acts was to declare a "Bank Holiday" while all the banks were closed and investigated; those that were sound would reopen right away; the others would be reorganized. The panic of runs on the banks stopped as suddenly as they had begun, and the people, oddly enough, relaxed. Nobody had any money, nobody could write checks; but the Government—the President—was *doing* something about the situation! Within twenty-four hours, and without debate or consideration in committee, Congress passed the necessary legislation to reorganize the banking system. From then on, for the next three months and more—exactly one hundred days—the President, his Cabinet, and the Congress worked closely together, administering hypodermics to a prostrate country.

The Banking Act was followed by a bill to economize on government expenses, and on March 13, less than ten days after he had taken office, Franklin asked for the repeal of Prohibition. Two days later a program to save farmers from ruin was authorized; part of this bill concerned farm relief and part contained the groundwork for a system of subsidies on farm prices, which had fallen to such low levels that farmers could hardly afford to take their produce to market.

In a few days banks began to open and the Stock Exchange resumed trading. To keep the people informed, Franklin hit upon the idea of giving a weekly "Fireside Chat" over the radio and, when he addressed them as "My Friends," a million John Does listened and felt they had indeed found a friend.

Out of his imagination and his love of trees grew a project which would preserve the forests, turn the wilds into state parks, build roads and shelters, and give jobs to thousands of young men. He set the plan for this conservation program before Congress on March 21, less than three weeks after he became President.

The "bonus marchers" chose this time to descend on Washington again, a ragged remnant of the veterans' army that had encamped on the Anacostia flats in 1931 and was burned out by the regular soldiers, with General MacArthur and his aide, Dwight Eisenhower at their head, acting under orders from President Hoover. Franklin had been shocked at the ruthless method of disbanding the marchers, men who had risked their lives for the country in time of war; he wanted to show them now that he was sympathetic, not afraid of them. He and Louis conferred, and the next day he took time out from the endless cabinet meetings to show himself to the veterans, riding in the presidential car; he waved his battered fedora and called words of good cheer to the seedy-looking groups standing around in the chilly March wind. At Louis' suggestion, a canteen was set up for the men; lunches were served and the coffee flowed continuously. One day Eleanor drove out with Louis, unaccompanied even by a police escort, and had lunch with the veterans. Their surliness began to disappear. A veterans' committee came to see Louis, funds were found to help them return to their homes, and they began to disband peacefully.

The cabinet meetings and the emergency Congressional session went on. To protect investors from being fleeced in the stock market, as many were before the crash, legislation dealing with the issuance of securities was passed. Less than a week later, the plan to set up the vast Tennessee Valley Authority was pushed through the Congressional mill in less time than it ordinarily took to call a committee meeting. From the chart to reclaim an eroded valley in Tennessee came the tremendous power, soil conservation, and settlement program that meant a new life for thousands of poverty-stricken families. To save countless homes, an act providing for loans at rates that an average-income man could pay, went through Congress on April 13, and a week later the country went off the gold standard.

Some form of emergency relief had to be provided as soon as possible, but this took a little more time. Frances Perkins sent for Harry Hopkins, who had been in charge of relief administration in New York State, and by cutting red tape all the way down the line, the Federal Relief Agency was set up early in May; Congress had to hold hearings on appropriations, and the Agency opened on May 22 with a working capital of $500,000,-000 with which to start the "economic pump priming," as Roosevelt called it in one of his fireside chats.

He could not, of course, take much exercise with a schedule like his. From early morning until late at night, he saw people, one after another; he held conferences at every available moment, and more than one meeting of his Cabinet went on until the small hours of the morning. He had to leave the household arrangements and social engagements, even family visits, up to Eleanor, but these, too, took time and energy. Yet he seemed to thrive on the intensity of action, the excitement of marshaling a nation's forces to cope with the emergency. He worked at high pitch day and night and was exhilarated by his labors. He seemed to draw strength from the very fact that he had to show supreme strength and decisiveness. In spite of the multitudinous events of each day, he could relax at night, when he was able to get to bed at a reasonably early hour, by sorting stamps for a little while. Sometimes he would watch a movie short, preferably a Mickey Mouse cartoon, in a room on the second floor near his bedroom. He slept soundly, once he was helped into bed, and rarely woke up until morning. (His first bed was a narrow brass "single," a size too short for him and not roomy enough. Eleanor had a wide four-poster made for him at the Val-Kill furniture factory soon after they moved in, and this he used all during the White House years.) He continued his practice of having breakfast in bed, and then he always read the newspapers. He could get around the White House in his wheel chair, which fit easily into the elevator, but he did not like to receive people until he was seated behind his desk or the long conference table where he held Cabinet meetings, and the same procedure held for formal or state dinners.

In the opening months there were a number of such occasions, because he thought it was of the greatest importance to be on friendly terms with as many countries as possible, and, more particularly, England and South America, as well as Latin America, "our good neighbors to the South." He would be carried into the dining room, and was seated at the head of the table when the guests arrived. If the visitors were people Franklin wanted to talk to privately, he would meet them afterward in the Oval Room, where they could have undisturbed conversation. Usually there was a quiet "family" dinner on the night of a guest's arrival; at the close of it, Eleanor would lead the way into another room for coffee, and shortly afterwards Franklin would come in holding someone's arm. Often during the first few months it was Jimmy's, since Franklin had asked his son to be one of his secretarial aides for a time. Sometimes they would listen to music, or they would watch a movie before retiring. If the guests were heads of countries, there would be a formal dinner and a reception later on. At receptions, Franklin worked out a formula for receiving hundreds of people by taking ten- or fifteen-minute breaks when the line would be stopped and he would sit down, relieving the strain on his legs. Then he would stand up again, rested and relaxed, and the signal would be given to start the line once more.

Among those who came to stay at the White House during those early weeks in 1933 were Prime Minister Ramsay Mac-Donald and his daughter, Ishbel, to whom Louis Howe took an immediate liking, a rarity for the sardonic little man. They were followed by the Prime Minister of Canada and then Edouard Herriot of France. An Italian mission, a German, and a Chinese mission were received; a Japanese envoy came to lunch. The Governor-General of the Philippines came a little later in the year, and the Prime Minister of New Zealand, who came with his wife for lunch. All of the official entertaining, as well as the personal, had to be fitted in with the heavy schedule of work, which went on day and night.

Luckily, Franklin was one of those people who are able to relax when they stop to rest; and he could work harder than any man in his whole entourage. Because of this, he woke up every morning ready to take up the load of proceedings no matter how complicated they were, nor how snarled the threads had seemed the night before. Admiral Ross T. McIntire was his doctor and kept a close and careful watch on his health during all the years in the White House; he was assisted by Lieutenant Commander George Fox, who was equally careful; both doctors agreed that Franklin showed more physical fortitude than men whose bodies were in no way damaged by illness. Except for his incapacity to walk, Franklin's paralysis was hardly a handicap. He was capable of accomplishing more than any ten men of "normal" physical ability.

Shortly after the inauguration, the *New York Daily News* started a subscription drive among its readers for a swimming pool to be installed in the White House, and construction began almost immediately. After it was finished, and the affairs of state had settled into some sort of routine, he tried to find time to "get in a swim every day in the late afternoons"; it was not like being in the water at Warm Springs, with its wonderfully revitalizing minerals, but he could exercise his legs with the motion of swimming, which did a great deal to relax him generally. Usually he went to his room right afterward, where George Fox gave him a rubdown, and then he would rest, during which time he would go through the evening papers, just as he read the morning papers before he got up. (He always looked to see what the opposition had to say before he read the friendly reports on his administration. In these first few months there was little the press could print by way of unfavorable criticism, because the country was in such dire distress that anything was better than Hoover's inaction. The one move which occasioned real antagonism was his taking the United States off the gold standard, which brought more of a gasp than a protest; no less a person than Lewis Douglas said, "This means the end of western civilization," a comment which only caused his target to chuckle with delight. One of Franklin's greatest assets was that he could always maintain a blithe attitude toward his enemies; if he had felt bitter toward his critics, it would have been fatal to carrying out his policies. Nevertheless, he considered it of the utmost importance to know what the press was printing—pro and con—and perusal of the newspapers was part of the routine he never omitted.)

When he was dressed again after his swim, he met the family in his study for a cocktail before dinner, and they enjoyed a little informal visit together. Missy and Louis, who both lived in the White House, were usually present, as well as close friends or relatives who came to see the Roosevelts. Occasionally Uncle Frederic Delano, who moved to Washington at this time and devoted the rest of his life to public service, would pay a family call and was always welcome. No one, except possibly his sister Sara (who was the only mother in American history that lived to see her son become President) was prouder of Franklin's triumph than Uncle Frederic, who had been so concerned all during his nephew's illness, not only for his physical, but his mental and emotional state. Now the same loyalty and concern led him to throw his interests in with Franklin's, putting as much energy into unpaid civic jobs as he had formerly poured into his business.

The extraordinary session of Congress continued. The first measure for relief was merely a temporary stopgap between the people and the tidal wave of destitution; it took care of the necessities of life—food, clothing, fuel, shelter, and medicine— but it did little more than keep people alive and give them hope. (Harry Hopkins once analyzed the value of Federal relief in simple terms: "We can only say that out of every dollar entrusted to us for lessening of distress, the maximum amount humanly possible was put into the people's hands. The money, spent honestly and with constant remembrance of its purpose, bought more of courage than it ever bought of goods.") When Hopkins explained that most families found it degrading to accept relief and, in a conference with Roosevelt, proposed a Civic Works Program, Franklin was quick to act on the idea. First Congress passed legislation to reorganize the railroads, and then authorized an appropriation of over $3,000.000,000 for a public works program—in those days a staggering sum, but granted by both Houses almost without a murmur.

Something had to be done, however, to bring about complete recovery and that required careful planning, as detailed as it could be made in the short space of time they had to work. To devise a system which would stimulate business once more without damaging the sacred "free enterprise" called for a trick little short of magic; and there was more than one night when the lights in the conference room in the White House never went out. Franklin and the members of his Cabinet discussed and argued and scribbled and tore up papers and began all over again. The quill cigarette holder—sometimes empty—hardly left Franklin's mouth as he bit down on it in a fury of concentration. (Like his old-fashioned pince-nez clamped on the bridge of his nose, the angle at which he clenched his cigarette holder was fast becoming the butt of cartoon jokes and caricatures, yet he showed no signs of moderating his smoking habits any more than he would abandon the type of glasses he had worn since his schooldays.) Once or twice, when he knew in advance that they would be in for an all-night session, he asked William Woodin, who was an accomplished musician, to bring his violin to the White House; and around two in the morning, when they were all bleary-eyed with strain and fatigue, he rapped for a recess, sent down for sandwiches and coffee, and told "Bill" to play them a tune on his fiddle. And after the strains of "Clair de Lune" had echoed faintly through the quiet corridors, they all felt more like continuing their labors.

By the beginning of June they had hammered into shape the plan which created the machinery for the business recovery so sorely needed; it was passed on the fifteenth of the month. On the sixteenth the bill to set up the Federal Deposit Insurance Fund and guarantee bank deposits went through the Legislature and marked the hundredth day of the history-making session. Then Congress adjourned.

Franklin was confident that the country was out of immediate danger and on its way toward recuperation, and its leaders were in need of a brief vacation. As usual, Washington temperatures had begun to soar about the time the magnolias along the avenues faded and dropped their waxy petals in the middle of May; by the middle of June the days were sweltering and the sidewalks sent up a blast of heat at night. Franklin recalled the terrifically hot summer when he had sat in the offices of the Navy and pounded out the refutation of the charges brought against him, sweating when he might have been swimming, enjoying the cool climate of Campobello. And quite suddenly he made up his mind to return to the island.

It had been twelve years now since he was stricken with poliomyelitis, and he was on top; he had beaten the disease, not only from the standpoint of his health, but from the achievements he had begun, and would continue, to make. Even he could not know how far he would go, but he had reached a vantage point and was going to make the best possible use of his position. The wine of victory did not go to his head, but stimulated him to extend all his efforts toward bringing the country back to health. With such an attitude, it was easy to face a return to Campobello.

Jimmy had made arrangements to rent a boat for the summer— a schooner called *Amberjack II*—and was planning to sail up the coast to the resort in any case. Franklin would go along: a cruise was just what he needed. Elliott was out west, but the other two boys joined them, and each brought a guest. Eleanor was going on ahead with a friend on a motor trip through the Gaspé Peninsula and would meet them at Campobello. Their house was rented to some friends. Of course, the *Amberjack* had to be accompanied by an official fleet of two Navy destroyers, the *Bernadou* and the *Ellis,* in addition to other boats. Secret service men and reporters were on board; since he had become President, Franklin could not travel anywhere without protection, whether he felt the need of it or not.

Nevertheless, he enjoyed being out on the open sea again,

and once he had decided to make the cruise, he was the skipper; none of the boys disputed his place at the wheel. Jimmy was, in fact, delighted that his father wanted to take over. It was a rough trip; they ran into stormy weather, just as Franklin had run into choppy seas when he had sailed up a dozen summers before. The radio messages were running thick and fast between the schooner and the destroyers; the boys were afraid their father might slip and tear the ligaments in his leg again, as he had on the *Larooco*. But Franklin himself was unperturbed and kept the schooner straight on her course. The storms passed, but it was still foggy when they reached the Narrows; the weather was certainly repeating itself; if he had not run into fogs here many times in the past, he would have felt eerie. As it was, he kept navigating, his hands firmly on the wheel, hoping the fleet would follow his lead . . . Now the fog was lifting a little . . . Cool and green, the island of Campobello rose out of the mists like a mirage; but it was not a mirage . . . There were the rocky coves, crowned by wooded heights . . .

"Land ahead!" called the boy in the bow, but Franklin knew they were still in the Narrows and kept going at top speed.

Presently the shore came into view, and then the docks, where a crowd seemed to be gathered—quite a large crowd, they saw as they came closer. The people Campobello—native islanders, as well as summer residents—had turned out to welcome him.

Franklin was surprised and touched; although he might have expected such a gesture, since he was President of the United States, he was moved by the demonstration of pride and affection from this island community that had been more or less disinterested about the comings and goings of the summer colony. He spoke to them informally, standing at the rail of the schooner, holding onto the stays for support.

"I think I can only address you as my old friends of Campobello—old and new," he added, for he realized that there were many faces in the crowd he did not know. "I was figuring this morning on the passage of time, and I remembered that I was

brought here because I was teething, forty-nine years ago. I
have been coming for many months almost every year until
twelve years ago, when there . . . was . . . a gap . . ." He hesitated,
and then continued with a smile, "It seems to me that memory is
a very wonderful thing, because this morning, when we were
beginning to come out of the fog off Quoddy Head, the boy from
the Lookout in the bow called out 'Land Ahead.' Nevertheless,
memory kept me going full speed because I knew the place was
the Lubec Narrows . . ." The crowd cheered, and he smiled more
broadly. He thanked them for coming to welcome him back,
and a short time afterward was riding up to the house with
Eleanor and his mother, his two bodyguards, Gus Gennerich and
Mike Reilly (Earl Miller had not gone on to the White House
with him), and with secret service men preceding and following
their car. It seemed strange to be riding up to the cottage instead of running up along the cliff way.

And in the days that followed, he found that all the "kick"
was gone; the flavor of a rugged outdoor life of sports that he
had loved so well was missing now. The water, even in the
lagoon, was much too cold for swimming, and the ground too
rough for the kind of walking he could do; nor could he
manipulate a wheel chair very far (and he disliked being in
one, anyway, except around the house). Even the fishing had
little lure for him, except the deep-sea fishing from the solid
deck of the destroyer. It was true, the scenery was beautiful,
and the air was cool and bracing after the heat of Washington.
But at night it was chilly, and he did not like to feel in the least
chilly. . . .

He had stayed away all these years because he was aware that
it would be like this—and yet he had not expected it would be
quite like this . . . He was not so much experiencing or suffering
regret, when he remembered all the things he had once been
able to enjoy here, as he was impatient with the quiet and the
lack of mental stimulation, after a day or two of rest. The plain
fact was that even if he had been able to partake of all those

athletic delights, he would not have been particularly interested any more. He was a great deal more absorbed by the details of Eleanor's trip—and asked a hundred questions about conditions in Canada and Maine. It was amazing, but he found himself wondering how things were going in Washington, wishing he were there—never mind the heat! His sense of values had changed vastly since the days when he had come to Campobello for summer vacations, even as late as that last summer in 1921. He was glad, however, that he had come back; because now he realized that he was not missing out on much—that there were many activities more fascinating, more satisfying than the pleasures of an island in the sea. Down in Washington a whole new world of ideas awaited him, a new order was in the making, and he had given it impetus—his place was there.

CHAPTER XVIII

Conquest of New Worlds

HE DID NOT STAY long at Campobello, not only because the state of the union was still so unstable that he felt he could not be away any length of time, but because he had no strong desire to remain on the island. Jimmy had chartered the *Amberjack* for the summer and was going to stay at the resort for a time, so Franklin and Eleanor made the return trip aboard the *Bernadou* and immediately became embroiled in the details of launching the NRA.

In the same month, a project was begun at Warm Springs which was destined to serve as the pilot for the gigantic promotion that led to the establishment of the National Foundation. A prominent Georgia businessman appeared at the Meriwether Inn one day and offered, in the name of the people of Georgia, to raise money for the new hall that was next in line for construction on the campus; Basil O'Connor had come down for the express purpose of seeing what could be done to get the building program under way. The offer to finance the new hall seemed nothing short of providential.

The estimated cost was $100,000, and the aim was to have the structure, which was to be the central "administration building" of the campus, including offices, recreation rooms, and a dining hall, as well as bedrooms, completed before the end of November, so the Thanksgiving dinner could be held there. The year that marked Roosevelt's first term in the White House was to mark a new era for Warm Springs. The Georgia businessman seemed undismayed by the ambitious plan or by the fact of the depression. The people of Georgia wanted to do something for the President; they would contribute the money in nickels and dimes. Cason Calloway, a mill operator with whom Franklin had become friends and a man of no little influence, accepted the chairmanship of the drive, and soon the nickels and dimes and dollars began to flow into the fund for "Georgia Hall" at Warm Springs. The response was proof that the center had caught the public sympathy; it had "appeal," a valuable asset in the eyes of Keith Morgan, the official fund-raiser. As the ground was broken and the walls of Georgia Hall began to rise, he decided to try the fame of Warm Springs outside its own state. A benefit concert, one of the first of its kind, was presented at Carnegie Hall in New York City, and $25,000 was raised in a single night. If one state could raise $100,000, and one concert in a city almost a thousand miles away could bring in $25,000 in one night, what could not be done in forty-eight states and hundreds of cities and towns? The possibilities were staggering.

Keith Morgan cast around for some likely "angel" who would subsidize the rest of the building program for Warm Springs— the hospital, which Franklin insisted should be as *unlike* a hospital as possible, additional dormitories, and other improvements—someone whose donation would spearhead a nationwide drive. Morgan remembered that Carl Byoir was public relations man for Henry L. Doherty, who had acquired horns from some of his financial practices, but could afford to sponsor a charitable institution and might welcome the idea. Doherty had suffered from crippling arthritis, and the only relief he had found was in the mineral waters at Battle Creek, Michigan, similar to those at Warm Springs. . . . Morgan got in touch with his friend Byoir and learned that Doherty was in Washington. . . . He took the first train.

At the White House, Missy LeHand received a rather peculiar request—could the President meet with Henry L. Doherty in the latter's trailer one afternoon to discuss a plan for Warm Springs? Missy, knowing well "the boss's" love of the bizarre, said she did not see why not; he had so many things scheduled anyway, one more could not possibly make a difference, especially since it concerned Warm Springs.

Franklin was tickled with the notion of anything so unofficial as meeting in a trailer, and took time off from the endless conferences to attend this private conclave in the eccentric Mr. Doherty's hideaway while the secret service men fumed and paced outside. Keith Morgan and Carl Byoir were both present at the informal get-together, the upshot of which was an invitation to Doherty to come down and see Warm Springs for himself; Thanksgiving Day might be a good time, when Georgia Hall would be finished.

All during the rest of the hot summer of 1933, Franklin stayed in Washington, leaving only for a few weekends at *Hyde Park,* where Eleanor was spending most of the time. Already the country was beginning to stir out of its coma. At first, the mere fact that "the poorer people," as Garner called them, were eating regularly again lessened the sense of fear throughout the country. The Relief Administration had only the sparsest cupboard to work from. Franklin's optimism regarding the outcome of the measures passed in the hundred days led him to turn to the next project as soon as one was set up; it was up to the individual administrators to find ways and means. Harry Hopkins, as relief administrator, had an enormous job on his hands. Few cities had staffs anywhere near large enough in the social service department to handle all the cases. A whole crop of June graduates from municipal and state universities and colleges became relief investigators, after taking a qualification examination. Old buildings were turned into warehouses filled with surplus staples; every week a family that had been found needy received a supply of flour, beans, a slab of bacon, and other foods that would not spoil.

For perishable items like milk and a limited supply of fresh meat, they were given scrip or a small cash amount to use at the stores. The people felt cared-for, reassured. The grocery stores, butcher shops, and dairies were doing some kind of business again. Although they were loath to plead destitution, most needy families had no choice in the matter during the first few months; and at least their government was looking after them. President Roosevelt was like a newly-found father to thousands of people who had felt hopelessly lost.

The NRA, particularly Title I, dealing with private enterprise and the forces of production, Franklin regarded as a shot in the arm for business and a boon to labor—both of which it proved to be almost as soon as it was launched. The fact that the various boards and agencies connected with it were to become quarrelsome and jealous, or that management and labor were both guilty of infringements on its basic principle of mutual endeavor—opportunists, both after their own gains—made little difference to Franklin so long as the results were favorable; and for some months the NRA seemed to be an unmixed blessing.

He had known something of the operations of industry, but the workings of labor were more or less of an unknown quantity to him, although he had had some contact with New York labor leaders when he instituted unemployment insurance as Governor. Now he was learning enormously from his conferences with men like William Green of the AFL and Sidney Hillman, president of the Amalgamated Clothing Workers, and the browbeating John L. Lewis, all of whom represented labor on the Advisory Board of the NRA. (He was especially interested in the long-range planning for social and economic welfare presented by Hillman, a practical visionary who sought to do the utmost without damaging the democratic process. Franklin had to translate the theory of mass welfare into that of the individual, as usual. He understood the facts and figures of academic "economic planning" much better when he heard of the fourteen-year-old boys who went to work bearing sewing machines on their backs in the old days, of the cutters who still plied their scissors in dimly-lit factories, and the "baby strikers" in Pennsylvania cotton garment plants. (In Allentown, the plight of teen-age girls was so deplorable that the Governor's wife, Mrs. Gifford Pinchot, entered the fight and joined the picket lines with the girls, who were earning nineteen cents an hour, some only a dollar a week.) He asked Eleanor to go where he could not go in order to give him a picture of the situation in various parts of the country, and he was able to see, through her descriptions (evoked often by his searching, penetrating questions on her return from trips), the way it was with the people, and he could act accordingly.

Eleanor became his most valued envoy. She was in a very real sense his legs. No other wife of a President before or since was called upon to do the traveling she did, because it was not necessary. This was a time of emergency (as, later, World War II was to be, when he traveled a great deal) and even if Franklin had not been paralyzed from the waist down, he could not have left the Capitol as frequently as necessary for thorough appraisal of the situation in all parts of the country. Eleanor, whose social consciousness went back to the days of the Rivington Street Settlement House, accepted her husband's assignments with an alacrity that sometimes surprised even Franklin. When he suggested that she visit the miners in the strike region of West Virginia, she not only went, but was lowered into one of the mines to see the working conditions with her own eyes. She learned to see as she had never seen before; she had had some practice when Franklin was Governor and they had driven through New York State visiting various institutions—hospitals, orphanages, prisons. Franklin would drive around the grounds in the car while she went inside and was conducted through the corridors to the wards, kitchens, and basements. Now she began to notice details more minute than any she had discovered in those tours. She was able to give accurate reports, and Franklin could say in Cabinet meetings, "My Missus says those mines are death-traps," or "My Missus says they have typhoid fever in that district," or, "My Missus says that people are working for wages way below the minimum set by NRA in the town she visited last week," and his advisers realized that he was fully aware of the situation in all parts of the country.

Title I of the NRA, dealing with industry and labor, under the dynamic eye of its explosive Administrator, General Hugh Johnson, began its operations almost immediately. The codes of fair practices set up in each industry, and passed on by the Labor Advisory Board, improved working conditions and provided for fair competition and honorable practices. Trade unions hailed its Section 7-A as "labor's Magna Charta" because they found in it the right to organize and to bargain collectively. As conditions in factories were improved and prices stabilized, work hours were shortened and wages increased. Among the majority of the people, the cause was not understood, but its effect was electric. The symbol of the NRA, the Blue Eagle, with its motto, "We Do Our Part," shone from store windows, gleamed from all kinds of products from clothing to kitchen utensils, and was paraded through the streets on blue-and-white banners. Franklin was happy over the initial success of NRA's Title I and never doubted that its spirit of co-operation would not last.

Title II, the Public Works program, was much slower in getting under way. It required appropriations, long-range city planning, and allotment or allocations of funds for construction work. Uncle Frederic was one of the key figures on the National Planning Board, and he and Franklin often conferred together, finding another common interest outside of the family relationship. Harold Ickes, whom Franklin appointed Administrator of Title II, did not employ the war-horse methods of General Johnson in getting projects started, and Congress, with academic Budget Director Lewis Douglas pointing out the pitfalls of public works, took its time about voting appropriations. So it was that when Harry Hopkins came back from a field trip to Chicago around the middle of October and had lunch at the White House, Franklin suggested that funds for the Civic Works plan Harry proposed in place of relief might come out of the general allotment for public works.

He was more and more impressed with the young Relief Administrator. Of all the "New Dealers" that arose out of the crisis in which the country found itself in 1933, Harry Hopkins was perhaps the closest match for Roosevelt in energy, drive, and imagination. Although their backgrounds were entirely different, both men had a deep feeling for humanity, coupled with an apparently inexhaustible capacity for work (though Hopkins, lean, lanky, and taut, was much less robust in appearance than Roosevelt). Hopkins probably smoked more cigarettes and drank more coffee during long-drawn-out sessions than anyone but Louis Howe; sometimes he kept going for days on nervous energy; he did not take as good care of himself as Roosevelt because it had not been necessary. One of the sources of Franklin's power came from the fact that he could not rush around, and so wear himself down. He had to stay in one place, more or less; people came to him, not he to them. He attended almost no affairs outside of those in the White House, and he kept early bed hours whenever it was possible. If he could have taken the time to do the muscle exercises regularly, his legs would have continued to gain power instead of slowly losing strength; but a daily workout was not possible, and for it he substituted dexterity in pulling himself up and catching his balance quickly each time he took a "step." Psychologically, he felt the need to keep himself physically fit because of his handicap in the face of his tremendous task. If Hopkins had been through an ordeal like Roosevelt's, it is likely that he would not have worn himself down to such a nub from time to time that Franklin had to insist he go away on vacation. But Hopkins felt no need to watch his health, and his social consciousness was far stronger than any personal concern; so he drove himself as no one since Louis in his early days had driven himself to get the job done, whatever it might be.

Franklin took to the idea of civic works in exchange for relief, particularly for the "white collar" people who were out of work—the professionals: actors, musicians, painters, teachers—and there were many in each of those groups. It was Harry Hopkins who first pointed out the plight of the actors and entertainers, the dancers and musicians.

"Hell, they have to eat, too!" he said in his usual hard-boiled way, out of the corner of his mouth. Few people had money for theater tickets or concerts, or the extra income to give their children dancing or singing lessons. Public school boards had their payrolls drastically cut, and in some places the teachers who were retained had to be paid in scrip. The Agency lent money to rural schools and put some of the teachers back to work. It set up road building and construction projects for new or repaired backroads and schools in rural communities. It built new playgrounds and parks. It found ways to employ writers, musicians, painters, and entertainers in community shows or gatherings. The history of many a state was set down on paper for the first time. Though it lasted only four or five months, the Civic Works Administration, in addition to tiding four million people over a difficult, severe winter, accomplished a great deal in a short time and laid the groundwork for the greater Public Works and Works Progress Administrations which followed.

The Conservation camps were in full swing by the end of summer. Here the combined forces of three departments worked swiftly and, in the main, harmoniously to produce some of the most effective results of the "New Deal" program. The Forestry Service was delighted to find at long last a President who was truly interested in conservation; the Army, though at first truculent about using its supplies for civilian camps, soon became reconciled to the project; and the Department of Labor, or, rather, the leaders it summoned, at first leery of the idea of combining the labor force with the military, became mollified when Franklin suggested that labor should be in charge of selecting recruits. The young men of the country, who had been aimlessly wandering the streets, hanging around in front of the corner drugstores without a dime in their pockets; a large percentage of the bonus marchers; and Reserve officers, now unemployed or starving at their professions, were called into action and welcomed the outdoor living, the sense of accomplishment brought by the CCC.

Probably no other agency gave its creator as much satisfaction, unless it was the great Tennessee Valley Authority, and there Franklin was more the catalytic agent for George Norris' long-cherished dream. The wasteland of that valley was already humming with the activity that was to make it a rich and fertile land, and Franklin, as well as the fighting liberal Senator, viewed its progress with a pride that bordered on the emotional.

All this was under way when he went down to Warm Springs in November for the first Thanksgiving dinner in the newly-completed Georgia Hall (which had been finished just in time). On the wall of the building was a bronze plaque, inscribed: "Built by Georgians as their contribution to a great humanitarian work." It was a gala occasion. Dinner was preceded by the "Polio-Physio Follies of 1933." Fred Botts was master of ceremonies, introducing the acts staged by both staff members and patients. The new dining room, spacious, well-lighted, and airy, shone with freshness and the radiant faces of nearly three hundred patients. Franklin sat at the head table surrounded by children, some of them in wheel chairs, who were served the first portions of the turkeys he carved. Eleanor was there, and Missy, Grace Tully, and Toi Batchelder, who was now on the White House secretarial staff, an "alumna" of Warm Springs to whom they could all point with pride. Henry L. Doherty was there, also, and was much impressed with the proceedings. He listened to Franklin's speech after dinner with more than ordinary interest;

he had bathed in the pool in the morning and had conceded its beneficial effects.

The next day he was ready to talk business at the Board meeting held in the offices of Georgia Hall. He would not give one penny to the Warm Springs Foundation—but he would put up $50,000 for a national campaign for funds; they would have to decide how the drive was to be conducted, what sort of promotion scheme they would provide. . . . Out of this conference came the idea for the birthday balls.

Franklin had to leave for Washington immediately after the dinner, and when he received a telegram requesting permission to use the date of his birth, January 30, for the nationwide dances, he wired back: "If my birthday will be of any help, go ahead and take it." The committee consulted Basil O'Connor, headquarters were set up in New York, and a whirlwind campaign began to publicize Warm Springs and its work from Maine to California. They had only two months to accomplish the job, but it was done. On January 30, 1934, the initial "President's Birthday Balls" were staged in every city and town of any size across the country. There was hardly a village that had not experienced the effects of poliomyelitis on its population. The story of Warm Springs struck a universal note of sympathy, and the bands played for people to dance so that those stricken by the dread disease could walk again or could be brought back to an active life once more.

In Warm Springs the patients clustered around the radio and listened to the reports of the gatherings that came over the air between the jazz numbers and the entertainment that was broadcast—speeches by theater and movie celebrities, songs and skits. From the grand ballroom of the Waldorf to the lowliest country schoolhouse, people were celebrating the President's birthday in the patients' behalf; it was unbelievable and very exciting.

Franklin was listening in Washington and, when the evening was at its peak, he broadcast a few words over a nationwide hookup. His Warm Springs companions heard his voice, clear and resonant: "This is the happiest birthday I have ever known," he said simply, and the words came from his heart. He went on to explain the purposes and aims of the Warm Springs Center, the hopes they had of spreading the knowledge they had acquired to other centers throughout the country; at this time he did little more than to try to impress on the people the importance of combating polio, and he succeeded. A flood of 175,000 letters came pouring in to the White House. Although the staff had developed a system for handling mail, it had a difficult time taking care of the thousands of letters that arrived every day. At Warm Springs Meriwether Inn was torn down and its rotting lumber burned; the Foundation had $1,000,000 in the bank.

When Basil O'Connor handed Franklin a check for that amount, he beamed with pleasure and wanted to know how the money was going to be distributed. He would not take back one cent of the money the Foundation owed him, and it was no use for O'Connor to try to persuade him. His law partner muttered, "Damn stubborn Dutchman!" and told him that seventy per cent of the fund would be used for treatment centers all over the country; the rest would go to Warm Springs. Franklin was satisfied that the all-out attack on polio had begun. A commission was established to work on research for an effective vaccine against the disease and on new therapeutic techniques to overcome paralysis.

While Franklin was at the center, Dr. Hoke gave him a muscle test and found that the power was slipping, but it was hardly noticeable and he would allow no word of it to get to the other patients. He came to Warm Springs mostly to relax—at least as much as he could, with the ever-present scores of attendants that had to be there. The secret service men came down first to check every detail for his safety. One thing he refused to allow was the construction of a barbed wire fence around the Little White House. "Absolutely not!" was his edict.

Workmen installed special switchboard and telegraph facilities so the lines of communication between Washington and Warm

Springs would be rapid and efficient. The President's company of Marines marched in to make its camp beside the golf course and set up patrols along the roads leading to the resort. When the Presidential train rolled into the little station, there was always a crowd to greet him as he stood on the platform with his wide-legged stance, grinning and waving his hat. The ramp would be attached and he would come down, slowly, more slowly as the years passed, but the people did not notice the difference, since his manner was more hearty than ever.

He swam in the pool, but not at treatment time. He liked to hold press conferences from his car, out in the open, before he took off for a spin through the hills. He had a "bump gate" built into the white paddock fence which surrounded the grounds near the house, so that he could drive out or in by himself. The gate was designed to open by pressure from an automobile bumper; as soon as his car touched one side or the other, the "bump gate" would swing open on a central pivot, allowing him to pass through; then the gate would swing shut after him by the force of gravity. He enjoyed nothing more than giving the secret service men the slip by taking back roads that were too narrow for their heavy cars. A CCC camp had been set up nearby and boys were building a scenic highway and preparing to make Pine Mountain into a state park; Franklin made a point of inspecting their work every time he went down: it gave him the same deep feeling of satisfaction he felt at the Foundation's success, or when he gazed down from his porch on the "Knob" and saw in the undulating green fields of the valley the country's first farm resettlement project. It was one thing for a man to dream—and quite another for him to see those dreams materializing in front of his eyes, to know that this was taking place not only in the limited area of Warm Springs, but over a whole teeming land . . .

And the spirit of a reawakening America extended to other shores. One British commentator observed: "The courage, the power and the scale of Roosevelt's effort must enlist the ardent sympathy of every country, and his success could not fail to lift the whole world forward into the sunlight of an easier and more genial age." Winston Churchill, with his sonorous prose, writing in a magazine article in the fall of 1934, put it even more strongly: "Roosevelt is an explorer who has embarked on a voyage as uncertain as that of Columbus and upon a quest which might conceivably be as important as the discovery of the new world."

Certainly his conquest of new worlds had only begun. And while at times the turn of events was enough to cause another man deep discouragement—as, for example, when the NRA became snarled up with intrigue, bickering on the boards, and malpractices, and the Supreme Court declared it unconstitutional—Franklin, with the spirit of a modern Don Quixote (but with far less frustration) tried another line of attack. If one method did not work, another might; they could only try. It was this spirit of experimentation that led to many lasting improvements in the social system without eradicating free enterprise—a prospect feared by big business as soon as it started to recover. The worst "Roosevelt-haters" were men who should have been the most grateful to him for preserving the existing system while initiating tremendous reforms. It was ironic, and Franklin was sometimes rather bitterly amused—but almost always amused, nevertheless.

However persistently his enemies might abuse him, he knew that much legislation of lasting worth was evolving out of the "New Deal": The Fair Labor Standards Act, which cauterized the long-festering sores in labor-management relations and did away with some of the evil conditions in factories; a revision of the Pure Food and Drug Act; the Public Utility Holding Company Act; the Farm Security Administration and the Rural Electrification Administration, for which the nation's farmers praised him (albeit he was severely criticized for his policy of doing away with surplus hogs to raise the price of pork, a mistake he acknowledged later). At the head of all of his first-term achievements he put the sweeping Social Security Act in 1935. Explaining its premises to the people during one of his fireside chats, he used the phrase he had coined while they were drafting the speech, a phrase that was later picked up by British economist, Lord Beveridge: security for everyone "from the cradle to the grave." (Franklin was offended and irritated when Beveridge used the same words to describe his plan in 1942. "How can Beveridge take credit for this?" he demanded of Frances Perkins. "It's the Roosevelt plan!" He was not jealous, but annoyed that Beveridge had not given him credit for the "cradle to the grave" concept he had created nearly ten years before.)

He had no doubt that the great majority of the people were with him, because he had been given sufficient evidence of their support in letters and telegrams and hundreds of gifts sent as an expression of gratitude, most of which eventually had to be relegated to the White House basement. By 1935, the state of the union had so far progressed from the low point of 1933 that he could say extemporaneously at a press conference: "The social objective, I should say, remains just what it was, which is to do what any honest government of any country would do: to try to increase the security and happiness of a larger number of people in all occupations of life and in all parts of the country; to give them more of the good things of life, to give them a greater distribution not only of wealth in the narrow terms, but of wealth in the wider terms; to give them places to go in the summer-time—recreation; to give them assurance that they are not going to starve in their old age; to give honest business a chance to go ahead and make a reasonable profit, and to give everyone a chance to earn a living." He considered the objective no more than reasonable and was determined to push ahead toward his goal no matter how much the opposition might blast him. The doggedness that had propelled him toward his own recovery from polio helped him to propel the country toward recovery from economic paralysis. What was more, he enjoyed the good fight for a prosperous nation to a far greater degree than he had the titanic struggle against chronic invalidism. And physically he felt fine. One of the physicians who had examined him in Albany in 1931, Dr. Foster Kennedy, who stopped in at the White House one morning in 1935, looked him over at Franklin's own request and pronounced him in better all-around condition than before he left the Governor's Mansion. Clapping him on the back, Kennedy said with a laugh, "Nothing seems able to kill you; we'll have to take you out in the yard and shoot you like an old horse."

Franklin was used to the rugged humor of the medical profession. "Oh, you can't do that," he smiled, jerking his thumb toward the ever-present guards. "Too many of those fellows out there watching!" Yet he wanted a more definite statement from the doctor, who had seen him before he became embroiled in the "New Deal" and the intensive schedule the presidency required. It was true that he felt, in the main, fit for any amount of work and strain, but there were times when he had serious doubts about the length of time he could keep going at such a pitch.

"Really, Doctor," he asked, "do you think this carcass of mine will stand the racket a while longer?"

Kennedy's answer was unequivocal: "Yes, it will—but I have a lot of high-flown Wall Street friends who are quite sure that the country cannot." At that Franklin threw his head back and let out a roar of laughter; he asked no more questions.

He was planning then (and earlier) to run for a second term, and wanted to be sure he could "stand the racket" at least another five years. When the convention met in Philadelphia in 1936, he was nominated "by acclamation," which was better than he had expected in the face of a group of Democratic conservatives, including his erstwhile backers, Al Smith and Raskob, who had formed a so-called "Liberty League" to fight the very reforms Smith had once promoted. They were so obvious in their motives (Smith now had a top position with the DuPont interests) and so outrageous in their "smear" campaign that Franklin had not been too worried as to the amount of harm they could do, yet he hardly counted on being renominated by general acclaim. His old friend, Judge John E. Mack, put his name up again (as he had in 1932) and felt that the "kidnaping" he had done in 1910, when he persuaded his young neighbor to run for State senator, was more than justified. (Louis Howe, who had begun to fail some time before, had died on April 18, and Franklin could not help thinking of the way he would have relished this acclamation in the teeth of the perfidious Liberty Leaguers.)

Duplicating his action in 1932, Franklin went to the scene of the convention—this time at Franklin Field in Philadelphia—to make his acceptance speech. Jimmy was with him, along with Gus and Mike Reilly and several others, as he started his customary slow walk to the platform, stopping now and then to greet people so that the pace at which he moved seemed simply unhurried, even nonchalant. He was holding Jimmy's arm and carrying a few notes for his speech in the same hand. Among the line of faces that pressed forward as he passed he recognized the aging and white-bearded poet, Edwin Markham.

He halted his slow march to shake the hand of the distinguished man of letters, whom he had known for a number of years, when, without warning, his left brace came unlocked and he pitched forward! The lurch threw James off his balance, too, for a moment; but luckily Gus and Mike were close enough to move in and keep the President from sprawling. Gus snapped the lock in a lightning gesture, and Franklin, exasperated with his untrustworthy braces but in full control of himself, said tersely to Mike, "Clean me up!" One of his trouser legs had mopped up the dust of the convention field, and Mike brushed him off, while Jimmy picked up the papers which had scattered. It was a momentary mishap, and the group of men had closed around him so quickly that few realized what had happened. Poor Markham was thoroughly unnerved, but Franklin, once he was confident that the brace was securely locked, took a second longer to grasp the old poet's shaking hand and whisper a word or two of good cheer before he continued making his way to the platform. There he stood calm and smiling before the cheering mass of faces and ad-libbed a few remarks while he reorganized the pages of his speech, which he delivered as if the incident had never occurred. (In this address, he attacked the "economic royalists," and spoke of the "rendezvous with destiny" the people had.)

He made a strenuous campaign, but it was beneficial to his leg muscles to have the forced exercise of walking and standing again, and by the end of it he was moving with real dexterity. He followed much the same procedure on this campaign as on that of 1932, except that the string of cars was longer and the equipment more complicated. There was a direct telephone line between his car and the engineer, and a radio setup kept him in close contact with the White House. His train carried an automatic brake, so that under no circumstances would there be a risk of its slipping back and running into somebody in the crowd waiting to see him at campaign stops. The multitudes that turned out from whistle-stop to big-city stations this time were a revelation and a barometer of the climate of approval brought by the achievements of the "New Deal." He still used the ramp to get off the platform, and most of the time the train was spotted for a stop where the incline was gradual; but, in a few places where it was steep, Franklin insisted on having the ramp attached and put down anyway, so he would not have to be carried. (By 1940 the danger of identification was too great, and Navy engineers substituted an elevator contrivance instead of the ramp to get him on and off the train.) In 1932 he had been only a candidate; now he was the President, a candidate for re-election, and his popularity was enormous. He liked to travel slowly during the day—the speed limit was thirty-five miles an hour—so that he could see the countryside, how the crops were doing, the results of the agricultural and conservation programs; he was also more comfortable at a slow rate of travel, since he could not brace himself with his feet the way most people did. He gave instructions to the engineer to make up the time at night, and he usually slept so soundly that he had no idea how fast they went.

He had a world of fun on this tour. His own physical condition was at its peak, and his spirits soared to a new high as he saw how far the nation had recovered in spite of the hitches and occasional failures of the "New Deal." Toward the end of the campaign, he and Eleanor made an automobile tour through New York and some of the New England states. Eleanor's heart was in her mouth half the time when mobs of people crowded against the car as it moved slowly through the streets of some town or city—particularly in Boston, where masses of admirers ran the risk of being run down in order to touch the President or throw a handful of flowers into the back seat, where she and Franklin were riding. She was afraid only for the people—not for the safety of those in the car, but of the milling, pushing throngs outside it.

Franklin, however, remained serene and smiling through all the commotion. He loved the crowds and they loved him; that was all. And he was re-elected by the most stupendous majority vote ever awarded to any President in the history of the country. On election night, the Roosevelts listened to the returns from the house in Hyde Park (as they did also in 1940 and 1944) instead of Democratic headquarters in New York. Franklin and his intimate advisers sat around the dining-room table, and in the little alcove off to the side the machines were clicking with the latest returns. As the figures came in, everybody made out averages. The newspaper people and various guests were in the library, where Franklin's mother and Eleanor kept them supplied with drinks and refreshments and saw to it that nobody except a favored few got into the dining room. Before the evening was half over, it was clear that Franklin would carry every state except Maine and Vermont. Eleanor came into the dining room

for a few minutes to listen to the returns, and Franklin said
to her, with a wicked gleam in his eye, "I knew I should have
gone to Maine and Vermont, but Jim wouldn't let me." She
nodded, laughing, and went back to the library. Later the villagers from Hyde Park came marching up the road in a torch-
light parade, which was to be repeated on future election nights.
Franklin, leaning on Jimmy's arm, followed by Eleanor, his
mother, Anna, any of the others who were at *Hyde Park,* and
a few close associates (like "Henry the Morgue," who was one
of those around the dining-room table) went out onto the porch,
where the people were gathered beyond the pillars, their torches
glowing in the darkness. Franklin returned their warm greeting
with a few informal words, though the night air was chilly and
they all stood shivering in the November cold.

When the final returns were in, Franklin had won by the
most tremendous landslide in the history of the country;
the electoral count was 523 to 8, an unheard-of majority; the
Landonites were sheepish, the Liberty Leaguers appalled, if not
ashamed. The Senate and House were overwhelmingly Democratic—the President had swept in a Congress of his own party:
75 Democrats against 21 Republicans in the Senate; 334 to 89
in the House. The figures were enough to make any man gloat.

Yet he did not take time to savor his victory or bother to
point out the errors of his enemies—the election returns were
answer enough. Before the printer's ink was dry on the headlines, he was off to Latin and South America on a tour planned
in conjunction with the State Department—more particularly
the able Undersecretary, Sumner Welles, who offered a fund of
information about South American affairs and had been promoting the "Good Neighbor" policy in his own quiet way. Since
there was to be an "Inter-American Conference for the Main-
tenance of Peace" held in Buenos Aires, Welles wisely decided
it would provide an ideal occasion for a good-will tour of South
American countries by the President, in addition to attending

the peace conference. Franklin had been in full agreement with Welles's plan.

He asked Jimmy to come along on the trip, not only because his son, like Gus, had a reliable arm, but because he liked to have some member of the family with him when he went on a voyage. They sailed aboard the cruiser *Indianapolis* and, as always, Franklin found his vigor renewed by the bracing air of the sea. They had Thanksgiving dinner aboard—one of the few times he was not at Warm Springs on that traditional day— docked at Rio de Janeiro on November 27 to call on President Getulio Vargas, and then went on to Buenos Aires. (Franklin's open manner created friends for himself and the United States from the beginning. The Brazilian President and his wife, to show their gratitude, sent Eleanor, who could not accompany Franklin because she had previously arranged a lecture tour, a number of gifts, among them a huge aquamarine. Franklin accepted the stone graciously; but, knowing her modest tastes, bought his wife a small aquamarine pendant as a souvenir, realizing full well she would never make use of the enormous jewel.)

From Rio they proceeded to Buenos Aires, where, on the first night, a sad and totally unexpected misfortune befell the cruise: Gus Gennerich died. Franklin, who knew nothing about it till the next morning—he had gone to bed exhausted after a state dinner and his physician, Dr. Ross McIntire, did not think it would be wise to waken him with such news—wrote to Eleanor as soon as he had recovered somewhat from the shock:

Dearest Babs,
 The tragedy of poor Gus hangs over all of us. On Monday he was happy and well all day, though it was a jumpy sort of day—a vast, surging throng all the way, 4 miles, from the ship to the Embassy—then another equally long trip to the Presidential Palace and back again—crowds, tossed flowers, cheers, people running out, balconies filled.
 When we finally got in at 7 P.M. Gus lay down while I had a

bath and dressed for a 9 P.M. Delegation Dinner and immediately after the dinner Gus & Fox & Clauch went in to a cafe . . . He danced once or twice, & Capt. Bastedo & Pa Watson saw him looking apparently cheerful and well. At about 1:30 he came back to the table after a short dance, making a joking remark . . . & suddenly fell forward. Fox got his pulse, but inside of a minute and a half it had stopped. They did everything to revive him but he had died without ever knowing he was ill . . . There was of course no question that it was a straight heart attack—I knew nothing of it till I woke at 8 & Ross & Jimmy came in to tell me—and of course it has been a real shock & a real loss for as you know good old Gus was the kind of a loyal friend who simply cannot be replaced.

He requested a simple service for Gus at the United States Embassy in Buenos Aires; and later, when they returned to Washington, another service was held in the East Room of the White House, a tribute Franklin had paid to Louis Howe the April before. Both men had been close to him in vastly different ways, and both had shown staunch friendship, and he wanted to give them a suitable farewell.

His second inaugural address was delivered on January 20, 1937, and there again, he broke a precedent: he had seen to it that a reform bill, also sponsored by the progressive Senator Norris, was passed, doing away with the cumbersome "Lame Duck" Congress, which heretofore had always been in session until the new administration took over on March 4. To Roosevelt the Lame Duck Session, in which the defeated legislators sat around unable to accomplish much in the three months following the November election, was definitely a handicap, and certainly he was one to overcome a handicap wherever possible.

Ten days later, the third "Birthday Ball" celebration was held across the country. It had been preceded by a "March of Dimes" campaign—a phrase coined by the actor, Eddie Cantor. Theater people had been more than helpful in promoting the fight against infantile paralysis, and Franklin appreciated their co-operation. During the campaign, one of the Broadway shows had been brought to the National Theater in Washington for a benefit, and Franklin had attended the performance, though he rarely went to the theater. (He loved to see a good play, but it was difficult for him to sit with his long braced legs confined in the narrow space between the seats, even in a box. If he stood up and moved around during intermission, it was an effort, and, he felt, drew unnecessary attention to his own handicap. In later years, he was too busy, too preoccupied with world events to attend the theater.) Afterwards, Eleanor had invited the cast to come back to the White House for supper and the kind of informal gathering Franklin always enjoyed.

His birthday proper was a full day for all of them. The stage and movie stars who were appearing at the balls came to the White House for lunch, afterwards being conducted on a tour of the place by Eleanor (Anna and Jimmy helping her to show the actors around). In the evening, Eleanor made the rounds of the hotels where birthday balls were being held, while Franklin stayed at the White House and visited with the stars who came there to take part in the broadcast, which went on most of the evening. Eleanor came back in time to hear his speech, which went out over the air when the celebrations were at their peak. He enjoyed the company of actors and their animated conversation, sprinkled with anecdotes of the theater. And he was touched by their sympathetic help and interest, which was doing so much to spread the spirit of an all-out attack against crippling diseases by great numbers of people.

Throughout the latter half of 1936, an investigation was conducted by Arthur Carpenter to discover whether the birthday balls were the best means of fund-raising, how the proceeds should be used, and what sort of national organization was to be formed. He went from one state to another, visiting hospitals and clinics; he consulted with orthopedists, chairmen of birthday balls. For some time a Research Commission, headed by Dr. Paul De Kruif, had been performing experiments and gathering data on the disease, and Carpenter correlated his report with the laboratory findings. He presented a plan for a new organization, to fight on four fronts: scientific research, epidemic first aid, proper patient care, and funds for treatment centers. And on September 23, 1937, Franklin announced from the White House the formation of the National Foundation for Infantile Paralysis.

Now he went into greater detail than he had in earlier broadcasts. "The general purpose of the new Foundation," he told the millions who were listening, "will be to lead, direct, and unify the fight on every phase of this sickness. It will make every effort to ensure that every responsible research agency in this country is adequately financed to carry on investigations into the cause of infantile paralysis and the methods by which it may be prevented. It will endeavor to eliminate much of the needless after-effect of this disease—wreckage caused by the failure to make early and accurate diagnosis of its presence." He paused to let this point sink in, remembering what he had endured because of a faulty diagnosis.

"And then there is also the tremendous problem as to what is to be done with those hundreds of thousands already ruined by the after-effects of this affliction," he continued forcefully. "To investigate, to study, to develop every medical possibility of enabling those so afflicted to become economically independent in their local communities will be one of the chief aims of the new Foundation.

"Those who today are fortunate in being in full possession of their muscular power naturally do not understand what it means to a human being paralyzed by this disease to have that powerlessness lifted even to a small degree. . . ." He thought of the unforgettable moment when he had managed to haul himself to a sitting position by means of the trapeze fastened above his bed. And of the day "Dan" Draper first helped him to walk. . . . "It means the difference between a human being dependent on others, and an individual who can be wholly independent." In his mind's eye he saw himself struggling to the platform at Madison Square Garden in 1924; he saw Convention Hall in Chicago, and the 1932 campaign; he looked around the walls of his office in the White House, and smiled to himself. "The public has little conception of the patience and the time and expense necessary to accomplish such results. But the results are of the utmost importance to the individual."

Franklin insisted that Basil O'Connor run the new organization and that the Foundation, besides conducting a full research program, continue the policy of giving free care and treatment to those who could not afford to pay. Research was important, but no more important than aiding those who needed help immediately to ease their suffering. The birthday balls continued, and the "March of Dimes" moved ahead. New structures rose in Warm Springs—a new school and occupational therapy building, where children could study and receive vocational training; and a new medical building—the finest, most *un*-hospital-like polio hospital in the country—would soon stand across one end of the campus: a full-length porch, along which patients could be moved in any kind of weather, was one of its main features. New doctors came to staff the hospital, and the number of physiotherapists was increased. Muscle-testing became a real science, and the brace shop developed further techniques, new appliances. The campus became a landscape achievment. Builders Hall, for the male patients who were fairly independent, and Kress Hall, for female patients, were surrounded by sloping green lawns shaded by pine trees.

Franklin no longer had to worry about Warm Springs. For him it became a haven of rest as the stresses of the presidency, and the threats to freedom and peace in the world, grew greater.

By the end of 1937 the country had developed the "itchiness" of the convalescent. Labor broke out in a red rash of sit-down strikes, Congress grew restive, and the Supreme Court hampered progressive legislation by its ultraconservatism. And, across both seas, dictators in the east and west were gobbling up small countries. In October, Franklin delivered his "Quarantine" speech against the aggressors, principally Germany and Italy; he was deeply concerned about the ultimate effect of the sick behavior of those countries on the entire world. He stated flatly that the people had to decide "whether our civilization is to be dragged into the tragic vortex of unending militarism punctuated by periodic wars, or whether we shall be able to maintain the ideal of peace, individuality, and civilization as the fabric of our lives." Before we became infected with the same militaristic fever, he pointed out, we should "quarantine" the aggressive countries. His speech did not have the impact he had expected; people were still too taken up with domestic problems, and he realized that there were many yet to be solved.

In his own impatience to get things done, he tried to push through Congress a bill to "pack" the Supreme Court with more than nine members, so that he could appoint a few Justices who would be more sympathetic to reforms; but his scheme failed. So did his efforts to "purge" the Congress of reactionary elements the following year. In both instances, although he was disappointed, he said philosophically to Eleanor, "Well, it's water over the dam, now. I may have made a mistake, but I'm not sorry I tried to do what I thought would help." In the case of the Supreme Court, time accomplished his aim; vacancies opened up through the natural process of old-age resignations or death; but the Congress voted in by the people in 1938 contained a considerable loss of Democratic seats in both Houses. Again his philosophy was, "Now we'll try to have my past actions do as little harm as possible to the program we must consider for the next two years." His serenity amazed his supporters and irritated his enemies; even Eleanor commented on his hopefulness and confidence in the face of defeat. However, he had been conditioned to setbacks in the hospital more than fifteen years before, and during his early convalescence, when he had a relapse after what seemed to be a steady gain in his health. He knew from experience that if he kept his eye on the objective, the goal ahead, he would get through the setback and start gaining once more.

The goal, moreover, was farther reaching than it had been in 1933 or even in 1936: now it bid fair to encompass the world, which was rapidly growing more feverish. In 1938 Hitler had just accomplished the "anschluss" in Austria; Poland would soon be invaded, and then Britain bombed. During the next two years Franklin did what he could to see that the country's defenses were maintained, if not increased (in vain he urged the preparedness of Naval bases like Pearl Harbor), and sought to bring peace through diplomatic moves. He and Eleanor entertained a series of royal visitors at the White House and *Hyde Park,* concluding with the King and Queen of England in 1939. His strong feeling that Great Britain and her people were our first line of defense carried over to the reception their majesties received in Washington and wherever they went. People thronged to see them and were charmed by their ease and simplicity. (Franklin took the attitude that they were two "very nice young people staying at the White House," which gave their whole visit an air of informality.) After the first dinner, the lines were so long that Franklin was not the only one for whom they had to be interrupted: the Queen began to feel faint with the heat after an exhausting day, and asked to have them slowed up.

At *Hyde Park* the Roosevelts had a picnic, complete with hot dogs, for the royal couple on the grounds at "Top Cottage," a little house Franklin had built for himself on the crest of a hill. During this visit, Franklin and the King swam in the pool, but Eleanor had to sit outside of it with the Queen, whose sense of propriety kept her from getting into a bathing suit or having her hair disheveled by a swim.

Before the year was out Britain began to feel the scorching blast of the blitzkrieg coming closer and, in October, Franklin listened to a refugee scientist, Dr. Alexander Sachs, explain the facts of nuclear fission, so far as they were known. It was enough to stimulate Franklin's curiously clairvoyant mind; his instincts prompted him to tell the scientist to continue his experiments, to set up a commission, headed by Sachs and Dr. Vannevar Bush, for the study of uranium. . . . That same year, he persuaded his mother to deed part of the land at *Hyde Park* to the Federal Government, and he proudly laid the cornerstone for a library— a place to store documents for safekeeping, if necessary. . . .

Every fiber in his being sensed what was coming, yet he tried to avert a global catastrophe. He used all his powers, and there were times, as 1940 appeared and progressed, when he suddenly felt tired. His legs, from lack of regular use and exercises, became more wasted than they had been; his "haunches froze," as Basil O'Connor put it, and moving around was more difficult. Yet, as the country became more deeply involved in defense, and convention time drew near, Franklin had to make up his mind whether he would add to his record of breaking precedents— whether he would run for a third term. On one hand, he would have liked to return to private life, to settle down at *Hyde Park*, to do writing at "Top Cottage" and farming on the land below; he had recently set out a whole tract of Christmas trees, in which he intended to specialize. The unexpected spells of fatigue he had been experiencing, though they did not last long, were disturbing; and after eight action-packed years he was somewhat tired generally. He had gone so far as to sign a three-year contract with William L. Chenery of *Collier's* to serve in an editorial capacity and do a number of articles a year; as an avocation, he could think of nothing more delightful than raising Christmas trees. He was indeed one of those rare people who know how to live life to the fullest, and he would have had no difficulty in occupying his hours. Before anything else, he would spend time at Warm Springs, regaining his muscle power, and after that he would keep in condition; he would divide his time between the center and *Hyde Park*. And he would travel on his own, unofficially; he and Eleanor would circle the globe for the sheer joy of it, seeing other lands, learning to know their people . . .

On the other hand, the time was too critical: he was too involved in averting a catastrophe to give up the course he had prescribed to anyone else; for a while he had considered grooming Harry Hopkins for the candidacy, but Hopkins' health failed completely and he had to go away on vacation to avoid collapse. The Democratic Party offered no one else, except Henry Wallace, and Franklin felt he was too inclined to vacillate; he would probably be the best running mate, outside of Cordell Hull, who was Franklin's first choice when he considered a third term. This was in many ways similar to the decision Franklin had to make in 1928, but the situation was more serious, of greater moment, and the conflict went on for a matter of months instead of days. It was, moreover, a public as well as a private controversy, and may have served an unsung purpose as an antidote to public panic at the approaching holocaust of war. The third-term issue was a diversion from the dread of war, and everyone made the most of it, including Franklin himself, by keeping his own counsel, letting world events shape his decision in the meantime. (One of his prize possessions from this period was the huge papier-mâché caricature of the President's head as a Sphinx, complete with tilted-up cigarette holder, given to him at the Gridiron dinner that year.)

In the end, he decided to run if he were nominated—and of course he was. Again he altered his pattern by *not* going to the convention to accept the nomination. He had made it clear that if he ran, he wished to have Henry Wallace as his running mate, and on this point the real controversy of the convention raged. Eleanor, who had gone to the convention reluctantly when she was called there at the insistence of Harry Hopkins, Frances Perkins and others, spoke for her husband; and in her brief address, with quiet dignity, was able to unify the delegates in backing Roosevelt's choice for vice-president.

The campaign trips were short this time; Franklin admired his opponent, Wendell Wilkie, and took his strength into account more than he had his other political adversaries. On election night, as he sat with his little group around the dining-room table at *Hyde Park,* he was not so sure of the margin by which he would win; he was in fact less sure of winning this election than any. The popular vote was close; it took more concentration to "figure the averages." In the electoral vote, Wilkie carried ten states, more of a showing than any of F.D.R.'s other rivals for the presidency.

Yet, as before, Franklin was exhilarated by the contest and strengthened by it, spiritually perhaps more than physically, because the third-term election meant that he had the confidence of the people, which he felt had been shaken by the 1938 Congressional elections. He was aware that the "New Deal" had lost its appeal, and now he set out to win fresh approval by acting quickly to prevent the ills of war from spreading. He gave out, through a newspaper column, that " 'Dr. New Deal,' the good old family physican and internist, had had to call in his partner and consultant, 'Dr. Win the War.' " The analogy would probably not have occurred to him if he had not learned the value of specialization in his own battle for health, but it proved to be most effective. The country responded to the renewed zeal with which he set about establishing war agencies, lining up defenses, and working generally toward "preparedness."

The old energy returned; the glow sent out its radiations and revitalized others. He sat behind the White House desk and summoned the interviewers, the administrators, ministers from other countries, and his Cabinet secretaries and other co-workers. He would hail them with the sweeping gesture of welcome, the friendly nod, and they would capture energy from him, strength to go about the gigantic task ahead. The War Production Board was established earlier, and went to work to see that the country produced "50,000 planes a year." Overage destroyers were sent to England in return for bases in the Atlantic; British aviators were trained in the United States; British warships came here for repairs. All this was accomplished in the face of isolationists,

America Firsters, Bundists, and defeatists. But the majority of the people were behind him, and that was all that counted.

On January 6, 1941, Franklin delivered his "Four Freedoms" speech and in it set the keynote of his future course. On January 10 the Lend-Lease Bill was introduced, and two months later went into effect. One measure after another was taken to aid the war effort against dictatorship and destruction in Europe; in the Far East the forces of evil were not so carefully checked, but Franklin did what he could. As in the "hundred days" after he took office, he seemed to gather strength because he had to be strong; he made decisions quickly and gave orders firmly. He seldom took time to swim in the White House pool, and more often than not had his lunch and dinner served at his desk, sometimes eating by himself, though frequently Harry Hopkins was with him. Eleanor learned not to count on his presence at meals; she did not expect him, even when there were guests he would be sorry to miss seeing—relatives or close friends he especially enjoyed.

During the first week in August, Franklin told Eleanor that he was going on a "fishing trip" in the Cape Cod Canal, but his mysterious smile also told her he was going to do considerably more. She had learned not to ask questions. He did go fishing with a party of friends aboard the *Potomac,* but under cover of darkness he was transferred to the *U. S. S. Augusta* and, escorted by five other warships, proceeded up to Argentia Harbor for the momentous meeting with Winston Churchill which culminated in the drafting of the Atlantic Charter. Aside from the solemn purpose of agreement between two great democratic powers, the venture was a lark for him. He chuckled over the fact that the "fishing party" remained on the *Potomac* in the form of five stand-ins, dressed to look like the President and his friends, while he and the top government and military officials "stood out to sea." He enjoyed hugely the surprise he gave Elliott and Franklin, Jr., both of whom were stationed in the area at the time, by commandeering their services as aides, but keeping it a secret until they "reported for duty to the Commander-in-Chief." He enjoyed his talks with Churchill and his inspection of the British ship, *The Prince of Wales,* covering as much of it as he could in his wheel chair, which, for the sake of convenience, was part of the equipment on all of his wartime trips. To get him up the side of the British battleship required careful planning beforehand. It was a laborious task, but in speaking of the Argentia meeting at a press conference on his return, Franklin told reporters casually that most of the conferences with Churchill were held on the *Augusta* because "it was a little bit difficult for me in getting over on *The Prince of Wales.*"

After his return from Argentia Harbor, he felt more hopeful of finding an end to all war, and a way to disarmament and lasting peace through "a permanent system of general security" after the Axis was defeated. But *how* to defeat the dictators without getting into the war! He had promised the American people in a speech delivered shortly after election that their boys were "not going to be sent into any foreign wars," and he meant to keep that promise. As much as anyone else, he wanted peace, but it became increasingly hard to remain "neutral" when he—and most of the country—was not neutral. (The crimes of the Nazis against the Jews and the Poles were unspeakable to him; he could not bear to discuss them as many people did.) He became increasingly worried and tense as the weeks went by. For one thing, it was a strain not to mention any of the innumerable state secrets he kept in his head.

He went to Warm Springs for Thanksgiving and found some diversion in the new physiotherapy program and the amazing development that had come about in muscle treatment; he approved of the methods of the new specialist in physical medicine, Dr. Robert Bennett, a graduate of the Mayo Clinic, who had recently joined the staff.

The Thanksgiving dinner had been held on Saturday, November 29, instead of the traditional Thursday, because Franklin had been too involved with foreign affairs to leave Washington.

He planned to stay only over the weekend, perhaps not that long; he did not know when he would be called back. After the dinner, he sat in the lounge in Georgia Hall, talking to some of the staff. "I'm sorry I won't be able to have a swim while I'm here," he said to Duncan Cannon, who was in charge of the pool.

There was no hydrotherapy on Sunday, as most of the staff was off duty. The water was drained out Saturday night and the pool was not used until Monday.

"I wish I could stay over," Franklin said.

He seemed so regretful at not being able to enjoy a swim that Duncan offered to fill the pool especially for him on Sunday. It was a spontaneous gesture of devotion, and Franklin was touched. "I'll let you know tomorrow morning," he said.

At ten o'clock the next day, Duncan received a message from the Little White House: the President would be there around eleven o'clock. When he arrived, as he rolled toward the bathhouse in his wheel chair, he called out, "Come on in and talk to me while I change, Dunc." Inside, he thanked young Cannon for going to the trouble of filling the pool for him. "I never would have had a swim otherwise," he said. "I've just had an urgent message to return to Washington, so I'm taking the 1:30 train." He hesitated, and then explained briefly, "The talks with the Japs aren't going so well."

A week later, on December 7, he had just finished having lunch with Harry Hopkins in his study. Two of his favorite cousins and their children were spending the weekend in the White House, but he had to tell Eleanor he "couldn't make it for lunch"—a message to which she had become accustomed. (If the guests had been limited to his cousins, he might have joined them, but there were to be thirty-one people at table and he did not feel up to that much of a gathering. His sinus had been bothering him for some time; "Ross" was giving him nose drops two or three times a day.)

He planned to relax a little if he could; it was Sunday, and he had no definite meetings scheduled. He was wearing an old gray sweater, a hand-me-down from one of the boys (one he often put on at night instead of a bathrobe because it was easier to get into), and he thought he might work on his stamp collection in the afternoon. At one forty-seven the phone rang, and the switchboard operator apologetically told him that the Secretary of the Navy, Frank Knox, insisted on speaking to him.

"Put him on, Hacky," Franklin said.

Then he heard the shocking news that Pearl Harbor had been bombed.

It took him eighteen minutes to recover, to figure out what must by done first, and to go into action. He was perfectly calm; in a way, as Eleanor saw and the members of the Cabinet noted when he called them together that evening, he felt more serene than he had in months. The long uncertainty was over: the country had been attacked and there was nothing to do but fight back; there was no other course but war.

By January 1943 the entire world had been plunged into the holocaust, and there was probably no place that was not considered a danger spot; yet Franklin began arrangements for a series of unprecedented trips to consult with the country's allies on matters of strategy. He went by plane to Casablanca, his first air trip since 1932. The preparations were secret, intricate, and so numerous that a whole staff was required to plan it. Franklin left Washington by train for Miami with such secrecy that no one knew where he was going. The names of the cars had been painted over, and the train headed north, as if he were going to Hyde Park; but, at a siding near Baltimore, it turned around and went south. The regular porters were replaced by Filipino mess boys, who were forbidden to send so much as a post card from Miami. The train was broken up and kept at a siding near Jacksonville for several days before it was sent north again. The President's party crossed the Atlantic in a C-54. Mike Reilly went ahead to make arrangements for safe headquarters in Casablanca, but among the bodyguards on the plane a new agent by

the name of Hipsley kept an eye on Franklin. He was a powerful swimmer, who had been brought along for the express purpose of helping the President stay afloat in case the plane, by
some unforeseen accident, crashed into the sea. When they had
crossed the Atlantic, the Atlas Mountains presented a problem
in altitude. Dr. McIntire felt they would have to fly much
higher than he thought was wise for medical reasons; he was
afraid the height would be too much of a strain on the President's
heart. The military advisers said they must avoid Spanish territory because if the plane were forced down there, Franklin
could be interned. Eventually they arrived safely in Casablanca,
where Franklin greeted his son Elliott and Mike Reilly in fine
spirits. He was not tired from the trip, and the height over the
mountains had not bothered his heart in the least. He showed
off the C-54 to Churchill proudly.

Late in the autumn of the same year, November 13, 1943, when
he went to Teheran from Oran, Algeria (after crossing the Atlantic aboard the battleship *Iowa*), he flew in his own C-54. It
had been fitted up for his special use with a galley, two berths,
a space in the center wide enough to hold a small table, and
leg rests against which he could brace himself. Franklin, who
had not been told of the remodeling until he saw it, did not
approve of converting a plane to his needs, because he thought
it was too expensive, especially in wartime; but since the changes
had been made, he admitted that the trip was more comfortable.
A special "knock-down" ramp had also been built for this
journey. (The agents worried over the big thirty-foot ramps
that were usually put down when he was expected, because they
made his arrival so obvious.) The plane flew from Tunis to
Cairo to Teheran and back without a hitch. Franklin had visited
American troops in North Africa by car and jeep—and had had
lunch out of a mess kit in the field at Rabat, making off with
the mess kit as a souvenir afterwards—and on this trip he wanted
to visit Naples, but the secret service men would not allow it;

they would not even permit the plane to circle over a battlefield in Italy. In Cairo the question of altitude arose again, and this time Dr. McIntire said the plane must not travel above seven thousand feet. Major Otis Bryan, "the little fellow who flew us to Casablanca" and had been requested by Franklin to make the Teheran flight, now took the plane up over the mountains on a trial flight, accompanied by Mike Reilly.

"If the weather isn't soup, we can make it easily without ever going much over seven thousand feet," he reported. And they did. In Teheran, Franklin met Stalin for the first time and listened to the "massive rumble" of his speech. Here OVER-LORD was agreed upon by the "Big Three" and a possible end to the war glowed like a distant beacon ahead.

Yet there was much work and strain and heartbreak for a great many people before that day was to come. All during the winter of 1944 Franklin had run a low fever at intervals, but he kept on with his plans for the end of the war—and more, as the months went on, for the peace that was to follow. D-Day came in June; in mid-July he went out to the Pacific and then to Alaska. (It was at that time that the ridiculous story was circulated that Fala had been forgotten on one of the Aleutian Islands and that a destroyer had been sent all the way back just to fetch him.) In August, Missy LeHand died and, although she had been ill and unable to work for a long time, her death was a blow to Franklin and Eleanor, and to everyone in the White House who had known her for so many years.

In late October he had to begin campaigning, although he scarcely felt up to it. He had been nominated for a fourth term at the July convention after a medical checkup by several doctors besides McIntire; they all agreed that he could run again if he did not "overdo," and their decision settled the matter. There was some opposition to the fourth term, but, in the main, people felt it would be wiser not to change presidents at the turning point in the war. He had been at a military conference in San Diego at the time, and had made a brief acceptance speech, but he was tired and preoccupied with the drafting of a plan for peace. The news cameras caught him in a poor pose for the only time in twelve years, and the Republicans made capital of the haggard look on the President's face, as compared with the round ruddy face of their candidate. Franklin seldom wore his braces after he returned from Teheran because the upper part of his body was too tired to pull the weight of his legs with seven and a half pounds of metal on them. However, when he returned from the Aleutians, he had them strapped on for a speech at the Bremerton Navy Yard near Seattle.

He made the walk up the ramp to the platform with Mike Reilly, but the footing was on a slant and his balance was uneasy. A breeze from across the Bay was blowing the pages of his speech and, when he raised his hand to straighten them, he almost fell. He managed to regain his hold and steady himself, but the weakness in his hips and the pressure of the braces against his back made him feel shaky, and for the first time his voice over the radio wavered, and the people wondered . . .

Now, close to election day, he suddenly took an interest in the campaign. He made an after-dinner speech before the Teamsters' Union—the text of which he dictated to Grace Tully at the last moment, laying aside the pages prepared by his staff. "The Republican leaders have not been content to make personal attacks upon me—or my wife—or my sons," he began with mock seriousness; "—they now include my little dog, Fala. Unlike members of my family, Fala resents this. . . ." Most of his address was one vast joke and fierce jab at his opponent, and it proved to be a knockout blow. A roar of laughter rose from those who were with him and from millions of radio listeners, and the old confidence came back. He made four major speeches —sitting down—and from the response, the increased registration, he drew satisfaction and cheer. He said to Eleanor with a chuckle, "I think the people prefer the big man with the little dog to the little man with the big dog."

Toward the end of the campaign, a fifty-five-mile tour of New York City had been planned, and he insisted on making the drive in an open car according to schedule, although a terrific rainstorm and howling winds greeted them at Bush Terminal in Brooklyn, where the tour started. Franklin, wearing the braces for the first time in several weeks, sat in the back seat with Eleanor and Mike Reilly. Mike placed a blanket over his knees, and they were off in the cold, driving rain. People who had been standing for hours, huddled under umbrellas, were rewarded with his broad smile and warm wave of his arm, and the cheers drowned out the rain and the wind. At Ebbets Field the car drove up a wide ramp to the platform, and Franklin got out of the car and spoke, standing in the rain, his braced legs holding him upright with a sudden return of strength that seemed miraculous to those who had watched him in the weeks before. Directly after the speech, they drove into a dry garage, where a complete change of clothing was made for him. He was in high spirits then and, also, at the end of the tour, when, his clothes drenched again, he went to Eleanor's apartment in Washington Square to change and rest. She had been worried about the effect of the tour, but he was exhilarated, as always, by his contact with the people, the warm reception he had been given everywhere; and that evening he spoke brilliantly before the Foreign Policy Association.

He won the election by a comfortable margin.

He was at Warm Springs for Thanksgiving once more, and at dinner he carved a big turkey, but his face was drawn and thin and he coughed frequently. He remained sitting when he gave his little talk after dinner and when he said good night to each of them at the door. He stayed three weeks, and while he was there some of the arrangements for the trip to Yalta were made. In those weeks, he did manage to rest, however, and to swim in the pool. Duncan Cannon, who weighed him when he came and again just before he left, found that he had gained twelve pounds.

Shortly before his last inauguration—and he knew it would be his last—he told Eleanor that he wanted all the grandchildren at the White House for the ceremony. He was so insistent that she realized it was very important to him; and though the White House bulged, all the grandchildren, ranging in age from three to sixteen, were present. The services that year were held in the East Room of the White House, since wartime precautions did not permit the President to go to a "public building," even a church. Afterwards, instead of leaving first, he sat at the door and shook hands with everyone. He was leaving for Yalta the following day and he wanted to say good-by personally to most of those in the room. To Frances Perkins he murmured, half under his breath, "You'd better pray for me, Frances."

The next morning he and Anna (who, with her children, had been living at the White House for several months, and in large measure had taken over Missy's job) left on "Mission Number Seventeen," the most complicated of all the wartime trips made by the President. They crossed the Atlantic by ship to Malta from which point they flew to the Crimea. This time there were fourteen C-54s carrying his party of 135 "Very Important Personages"; his own plane was fitted with an elevator device, similar to the one on his private train, hidden in the belly of the plane. There were times when it stuck, and the pilot on the trip, the famous Hank Myers, worried a good deal about it, but when they landed at Yalta, it worked smoothly and they had no further trouble. Besides Dr. McIntire, a heart specialist, Dr. Howard G. Bruenn, was on this trip. Franklin boarded the plane at Malta at 10 P.M. and went right to sleep. He did not even wake up when they took off.

The conference was wearing and not entirely satisfactory, although Franklin felt that it was a beginning. There would have to be more negotiations with Russia. . . . Before sailing home, he made stops for conferences with Ibn Saud of Saudi Arabia, Haile Selassie of Ethiopia, and King Farouk of Egypt. When Ibn Saud, who suffered from rheumatism, admired the wheel chair, Franklin promised to send it to him as soon as he returned, and he did so promptly, much to the delight of the old Arab ruler.

On the voyage home, Pa Watson, who had been perfectly well, suffered a sudden stroke and died before they were out of the Mediterranean. Franklin had come to rely on the General more and more; his death was the same sort of blow as Gus Gennerich's, and almost as swift. In this case, the shock was even more severe, harder for Franklin to overcome, because he himself was so far from well. Not even the sea air and sun restored his old ruddiness.

When he made his report on the conference to the Congress, he did so sitting down, for the only time in all the years that he appeared before them. He said quietly, almost casually, "I hope that you will pardon me for this unusual posture of sitting down during the presentation of what I want to say, but I know you will realize that it makes it a lot easier for me not to have to carry about ten pounds of steel around on the bottom of my legs; and . . . I have just completed a fourteen-thousand-mile trip. . . ." With his old flair for color and detail, he made his report, and by the end of it the Congressmen forgot that he was sitting down because his legs would not hold him up.

He did not come back the way he should have, and toward the end of March he decided to go down to Warm Springs, where he thought he would have a better chance of getting the rest he needed. (Before he left, he told Frances Perkins that he and Eleanor were planning a trip to England in May, after the San Francisco conference. When she protested that it might be dangerous, he whispered, "The war in Europe will be over by the end of May.")

He took two of his cousins, Laura Delano and Margaret Suckley, to Warm Springs with him; they were good company and would not discuss affairs of state. (It was Margaret who had given him Fala, and she had always been among his favorite relatives.)

He was very tired the day they arrived. When the little

elevator let him down to the platform of the station, his figure
slumped in the wheel chair and those who were there to greet
him were stunned by his appearance. But after a week or so of
lounging about the Little White House, he seemed to feel
stronger, and on Easter morning went to services in the little
chapel and sang with the others. He began to think about the
Jefferson Day speech he had to prepare . . .

In the weeks before he left Washington, he had been increasingly occupied with the plans for a United Nations that
would go far beyond the old League in maintaining peace in
the world, and he wanted to emphasize his hopes at every opportunity. He would do so again in the Jefferson Day address,
on April 13. Some of the correspondents got the idea for an
old-time barbecue, and the patients and staff were putting on
a minstrel show for the President the day before. A well-known
painter, Madame Elizabeth Shoumatoff, who had done his portrait some time before, was making some further studies for a
current portrait, and he was posing for her. He had written
in longhand an ending for his speech which had come to him
as he thought of the doubting Thomases who were already raising objections to his peace plans. He wrote shakily, "The only
limit to our realization of tomorrow will be our doubts of today.
Let us move forward with strong and active faith." He smiled
to himself. At least he had the ending of his speech—that was
a beginning. It was nearly time for lunch, and he could look
over some papers while he posed. "Now we have about fifteen
minutes," he said pleasantly but firmly to the painter. She
nodded and kept on with her brush strokes. It was very quiet
in the Little White House, though occasionally one heard giggles
from the kitchen, where Daisy Bonner was preparing lunch with
the help of Lizzie McDuffie—their choice of menu was not in
the President's official diet. . . .

Suddenly Franklin let out a low moan and pressed his hand
to his temples. "I have a terrible headache," he said. Then he
fell backward in the chair in a faint . . . The painter screamed;

the President's valet, Prettyman, and a houseboy came running; they picked him up and took him into the bedroom. His cousins, momentarily frozen with dread, called down at the pool, where Grace Tully, Dr. Bruenn, Toi Batchelder, and his other assistants were taking a dip. Dr. Bruenn had just made a routine call to Washington to let Dr. McIntire know that all was well—he had been calling every day. Both doctors had been concerned about Franklin's heart for some time, although they were pleased at the way he had withstood the trip to Yalta. Dr. Bruenn had found no murmurs and a normal pulse that morning, no more than two hours earlier. Now he rushed up to the cottage, followed by the others. He immediately called Washington again, and Dr. McIntire got in touch with an Atlanta specialist who had examined Roosevelt in the past, an internist by the name of Paullin. He was at Warm Springs in an hour. The President, he said, had been seized by a massive cerebral hemorrhage, without warning. The hypodermic he injected was of little use—death came a few minutes later, at three thirty-five P.M.

Everyone had to be told—Washington, Eleanor, his children, the people down at the playhouse ready to go onstage, those preparing the barbecue, Basil O'Connor—but for the moment everyone in the Little White House was completely stunned. His cousins sat on the sofa, weeping quietly. Grace Tully walked into the bedroom and kissed the cool, white brow, now smooth and calm. In the kitchen, Daisy Bonner, weeping, wrote above the drainboard, "In this room for the President, Daisy Bonner cook the first meal and the last."

And Fala, who had been sitting quietly in a corner of the living room, suddenly shook himself all over as if he were trembling, crashed through the screen door with frantic barking, and never stopped running till he reached the top of the next hill. Then his yelping ceased, and he stood stock still as if in vigil.

Franklin had gone from life in the place he had brought to life—and to immortality, because the work at Warm Springs would always continue. The Foundation was only one of the aims he achieved in his lifetime, but it was a symbol of his whole being. Shortly before he made his last journey there, he summarized his outlook in one of his speeches: "I am everlastingly angry at those who assert vociferously that the Four Freedoms and the Atlantic Charter are nonsense because they are unattainable. If those people had lived a century and a half ago they would have sneered and said that the Declaration of Independence was utter piffle. If they had lived nearly a thousand years ago they would have laughed uproariously at the ideals of Magna Carta. And if they lived several thousand years ago, they would have derided Moses when he came down from the mountain with the Ten Commandments. We concede that these great teachings are not perfectly lived up to today. *But I would rather be a builder than a wrecker, hoping always that the structure of life is growing, not dying.*"

He was a fighter, a valiant one, but more significantly a builder, whose works stand among the monuments of history.

CHAPTER XIX

Fulfillment

THIS BOOK HAS endeavored to tell the story of Franklin D. Roosevelt's personal triumph over poliomyelitis and to suggest the effect it may have had on his character. The effect on his life was an important one, even though after he had conquered his handicap it seemed in later years to have been almost lost in many other conquests much more important to him and to the nation and the world at large.

Since this was, however, a strong thread of his life that was woven into the pattern of achievement throughout his days, it may be of interest to present a brief summary of the present-day consequences of a struggle that was first "a good fight" for himself, and later expanded into "a good fight" for thousands, perhaps millions, of others.

After Franklin was gone, the work at Warm Springs went on, and the National Foundation kept alive the search for a scientific means of ending the destruction wrought by infantile paralysis. The quest, which began officially on September 23, 1937, with the President's speech creating the Foundation, continued from that moment to the end of his days and onward.

The saga of the Salk vaccine, fraught with early frustrations in the struggle to establish the cause of poliomyelitis, had its beginning not quite a year later, when, on July 6, 1938, the National Foundation made its first research grant to the polio unit of Yale University. In those days, the fact that the disease was caused by a virus was as yet unproven, and Dr. John R. Paul, Yale virologist, was the grantee.

Increasing concern over the war against dictatorship kept Franklin from following the war against the disease as closely as he wished, but he insisted that the Foundation give fellowships to medical students as well as research grants to medical laboratories. Jonas E. Salk was one of those students, and eventually he became a virologist.

From 1938 until 1958, the twentieth anniversary of the Foundation, when the scientists who contributed to the discovery of a successful vaccine were honored at the ceremonies dedicating Founders Hall in Warm Springs, the history of the achievement was one of trial and error, of wild hope and disappointment, of baffling mysteries that seemed unsolvable; but always there was the faith, imbued by the spirit of the initial "Founder," that the riddle would be solved.

The men who pursued the study and experimental research with the help of the National Foundation had only the findings of four major scientists in the field before 1910: Dr. Jacob von Heine, the first to describe poliomyelitis accurately in a book published in Stuttgart, Germany, in 1840; Dr. Oscar Medin, a Swedish scientist, who first recognized polio as an acute infection; Dr. Iver Wickman, Swedish pioneer in the study of polio epidemics, who, in 1907, first pointed out the wide prevalence of nonparalytic polio; and Dr. Karl Landsteiner, a Viennese physician, who demonstrated that polio can be transmitted to an experimental animal—the monkey—and published a paper on this work in 1909.

From that date until 1938, experiments were performed and knowledge of the disease grew, but it was still diffuse; the mystery of the virus clouded the horizon. In 1939 Dr. Charles Armstrong, a physician in public health service, discovered that certain strains of polio virus could be transmitted to cotton rats, greatly simplifying vital polio studies. Grants were given to scientists at Johns Hopkins, Yale, the University of Michigan, and other qualified laboratories, so that the study could be carried forward "on all fronts," as Franklin had said in his address. He was confident that if enough effort was put into the attack, the disease could finally be "licked"—if it took fifty or a hundred years. He never dreamed it would be done in twenty. So the scientists, and the students who became scientists, went to work.

For twelve long years they labored more or less in the dark, because, when they began, none knew there was more than one type of virus which produces polio. Until that was discovered, the knowledge could not grow. Then came the first big break-through: in September 1951 scientists on National Foundation grants identified three major types of polio virus, and light suddenly burst on the whole polio problem. From this point on, the work progressed rapidly.

From the late fall of the same year until the summer of the next, the Foundation spent $15,000,000 on "gamma globulin" field trials, held to determine the effectiveness of circulating antibodies in the bloodstream in the prevention of polio paralysis. Before these tests were completed, in April 1952, the scientists—particularly Dr. David Bodian of Johns Hopkins, who demonstrated the theory—obtained the first evidence that polio virus circulates in the bloodstream before reaching the vital nerve cells of the central nervous system; therefore, it could be blocked by antibodies in the blood, and a preventive vaccine, if one could be found, was entirely feasible!

The next development was made by Dr. Isabel Morgan, another Johns Hopkins scientist, now at Columbia University, who prepared an experimental vaccine from virus inactivated with formaldehyde and with it succeeded in protecting monkeys against paralytic polio. A fellow-scientist of hers, Dr. Howard Howe of Johns Hopkins, was the first to demonstrate that chimpanzees can acquire polio infection by mouth; and he carried out small-scale experiments in human beings with a vaccine consisting of formalin-treated polio viruses.

All this time Jonas Salk, now a graduate virologist at the University of Pittsburgh, was working toward a successful solution to the problem, and on March 28, 1953, less than a year after the discovery that the virus circulated in the bloodstream, he published the first medical report on an anti-polio vaccine which could be safely used. He tested his vaccine on himself and his three children and conducted tests on thousands of children in the Pittsburgh area. A year later, on April 26, 1954, nationwide field trials of the Salk vaccine were begun, with 1,830,000 school children receiving shots. Dr. Thomas M. Rivers, often called the "Dean of American virologists" (now medical director of the National Foundation's Vaccine Advisory Commission), supervised the field trials; and Dr. Thomas Francis, Jr., epidemiologist at the University of Michigan, directed the vaccine-evaluation program of the trials, which demonstrated the safety and effectiveness of the Salk vaccine against all three types of virus.

The major difficulty of the mass experiment was the production of the vaccine in quantity. The Foundation used $9,000,000 to keep it coming out of the laboratory so the tests could continue.

Then Dr. John F. Enders, one of the scientists at the Children's Medical Center in Boston, made the second big move forward when he discovered a method for growing polio virus in cultures of nonnervous tissue, a vital step toward the production of a safe and effective vaccine in quantity. His discovery was hailed, not only by the Foundation, which could now continue the nationwide tests easily, but by the world. For their work in this field, Dr. Enders and his colleagues won the 1955 Nobel prize in medicine.

On April 12, 1955, ten years to the day after Roosevelt's death, the Salk vaccine was pronounced safe and effective by the Polio Vaccine Evaluation Center at the University of Michigan and was licensed by the Government for general use. In the same month, the National Foundation launched a program of free vaccination for children in the first and second grades throughout the nation. By December 31, 1956, over forty-five million Americans had had at least one injection of the vaccine, and reported polio cases dropped forty-seven per cent. In the spring of 1957, the Foundation's 3,100 chapters, located in nearly every state, launched a widespread promotion of vaccination for all under the age of forty. (In the autumn of 1957, the chapters started a nationwide census of those who had had polio, for "Operation Comeback," a gigantic rehabilitation program.) On December 1, the United States Public Health Service estimated that sixty-four million people had received one or more of the required three injections of Salk vaccine in the two years since it had been issued on a wide scale; and paralytic cases were down by eighty per cent.

Excellent as the results were, the search for a vaccine which would be one hundred per cent effective went on (and is still continuing). Dr. Albert Sabin, a Cincinnati University scientist and a leader in the search for a live virus vaccine against polio (one that would be one hundred per cent effective and yet safe), conducted his experiments, with Foundation grants, at the same time the Salk vaccination program was being carried out. Sabin's work also helped to demonstrate the means by which the virus reaches the central nervous system, an important contribution to the whole knowledge.

With an eye on the world aspect of preventive vaccine against polio, the Foundation sponsored a study by Dr. Joseph L. Melnick, a Yale University scientist, now at the National Institute of Public Health, who carried out field trials of Sabin's vaccine in many parts of the world (including Russia) and did extensive research on polio incidence in other parts of the world, gaining vital knowledge of the development of immunity in populations exposed to the virus.

Late in December 1957, the National Foundation mapped a campaign to rehabilitate as many as possible of the estimated

300,000 who survived paralytic polio. And on January 3, 1958, on its twentieth anniversary, the Foundation honored the fifteen scientists "whose work spanned two continents over a period of more than a century," and the two famous laymen who organized the polio fight. The "Polio Hall of Fame," a line of seventeen bronze busts riveted to the wall of Founders Hall, was unveiled at anniversary ceremonies. Eleven of the scientists were present, including Dr. Salk; only one of the laymen—Basil O'Connor— stood before the line of bronze casts as it was unveiled. The initiator of the battle against polio, Franklin D. Roosevelt, was gone.

Eleanor, standing there with the rest, knew perhaps better than any of them how much it would have meant to Franklin to be present in this moment of unveiling. (He always loved the "show" of any ceremony, and this one would have been deeply significant.) Yet she and the others knew that he was with them in spirit; and, characteristically, she did not dwell on the fact of his absence when she introduced Dr. Salk, but spoke mostly of the scientist and his achievement. "As a result of his fellow-ship," she ended her brief talk, "—part of the National Foundation's vast professional education program, which has trained almost seven thousand men and women in a variety of medical specialties—Dr. Salk became a virologist. It seems somehow just and right that he whose career in the field of virology began with National Foundation support should also have developed the polio vaccine with National Foundation support."

The work goes on. Centers like Warm Springs flourish in many cities. Handicapped people in New York have their own organization, their own print shop. "Hire the Handicapped" has become a familiar phrase. Perhaps one of the greatest contributions Franklin made to the general welfare of the handicapped was the acceptance of polios and other paralytics as "normal" people, in spite of their physical limitations. At Warm Springs, the Georgia Warm Springs Foundation has become perhaps the most modern and best equipped rehabilitation center in the world. Roosevelt Hall, built in 1954, contains a complete household for the education of housewives who learn to take care of their homes in spite of handicaps. It has a vocational guidance school and shop; a theater, where patients may watch movies or road shows brought to Warm Springs by the Foundation; a traffic light and curbing, which may be set up for practice in crossing streets; an automobile, in which patients practice getting in and out of a car. The finest physical therapy equipment is there for exercising and bringing back muscles damaged by paralysis.

Physiotherapists and doctors in physical medicine receive training and experience during residency at the Foundation. A large indoor pool has been built for patients who are too crippled to use the outdoor pool, and for all patients during the winter; the glass enclosure has been removed because it was not effective during the colder months and cost the patients more in loss of energy getting to it than they gained in strength. In summer the outdoor pool is used by the staff and by patients mobile enough to make the trip down the slope.

The orthopedic hospital is one of the best of its kind, and, in 1958, performed 647 "procedures." Yet, in accordance with the prescription of the first "doctor" at Warm Springs, the atmosphere is as "*un*like a hospital as possible." Soon after an operation, children are receiving instruction from private tutors (and later at the schoolhouse). Radios, phonographs, and television sets are much in evidence. At the brace shops, which make all kinds of appliances—from corsets to crutches and long-leg and short-leg braces and splints, from wheel-chair attachments to cellulose jackets to hand splints and canes—patients go to be fitted or get "alterations"; they joke with the mechanics who design and fit appliances; they visit with other patients. (If a little boy of two and a half is scared when he is first put on his feet to see if the braces will hold, he is soon reassured by the hearty yet comforting manner of the men in the shop.)

As Franklin had envisioned, the Warm Springs Foundation today treats all kinds of paralytic cases which respond to the same
treatment as polio—rheumatoid arthritis, traumatic paraplegia,
amputations, birth defects, and others. Unfortunately, large
areas of the population failed to take advantage of the Salk
vaccine and, in 1959, there were severe epidemics in the Middle
West (particularly in Detroit, where the vaccine had not been
widely used because of reticence on the part of the people), which
increased the number of polio patients again.

Yet, whatever the disease, the paralytic patient who goes to
Warm Springs does not feel he has entered a hospital for treatment. The sight of patients stopping at the coke machine in
the center lounge of Georgia Hall, or lingering over a second cup
of coffee and a cigarette as they sit in wheel chairs in the dining
room; or of two teen-age girls sunning themselves on the main
"campus" the first warm afternoon in February, harmonizing
"Down by the Old Mill Stream" and "Workin' on the Railroad,"
conveys the atmosphere of a college or a country club in a
beautiful setting of pine-covered hills. If Franklin could see
Warm Springs today, he would probably smile—a broad smile
of satisfaction: those rough sketches on scraps of paper came out
even better than he expected!